Music and Politics in Thirties Britain

Music and Politics in Thirties Britain

Raise the Standard High

John Morris

BLOOMSBURY ACADEMIC
LONDON • NEW YORK • OXFORD • NEW DELHI • SYDNEY

BLOOMSBURY ACADEMIC
Bloomsbury Publishing Plc
50 Bedford Square, London, WC1B 3DP, UK
1385 Broadway, New York, NY 10018, USA
29 Earlsfort Terrace, Dublin 2, Ireland

BLOOMSBURY, BLOOMSBURY ACADEMIC and the Diana logo are trademarks of
Bloomsbury Publishing Plc

First published in Great Britain 2023
This paperback edition published 2024

Copyright © John Morris, 2023

John Morris has asserted his right under the Copyright, Designs and Patents Act, 1988,
to be identified as Author of this work.

For legal purposes the Acknowledgements on pp. viii–x constitute an extension
of this copyright page.

Cover design: Terry Woodley
Cover image © English conductor Sir Reginald Goodall (1901–1990), 24 February 1945.
Photo by Erich Auerbach/Hulton Archive/Getty Images.

All rights reserved. No part of this publication may be reproduced or transmitted in
any form or by any means, electronic or mechanical, including photocopying, recording,
or any information storage or retrieval system, without prior permission in
writing from the publishers.

Bloomsbury Publishing Plc does not have any control over, or responsibility for, any third-
party websites referred to or in this book. All internet addresses given in this book were
correct at the time of going to press. The author and publisher regret any inconvenience
caused if addresses have changed or sites have ceased to exist, but can accept no
responsibility for any such changes.

A catalogue record for this book is available from the British Library.

A catalog record for this book is available from the Library of Congress.

ISBN: HB: 978-1-3502-7122-7
PB: 978-1-3502-7123-4
ePDF: 978-1-3502-7124-1
eBook: 978-1-3502-7125-8

Typeset by Deanta Global Publishing Services, Chennai, India

To find out more about our authors and books visit www.bloomsbury.com and
sign up for our newsletters.

In England all the boasting and flag-wagging, the 'Rule Britannia' stuff, is done by small minorities. The patriotism of the common people is not vocal or even conscious.
George Orwell, 'England Your England', 1941

Contents

Acknowledgements	viii
Introduction	1
1 New technologies	31
2 Unfinished symphony	71
3 Musical experiment and fashion	97
4 Responding to Germany	123
5 Domestic concerns	147
6 National music	183
Conclusion	235
Bibliography	245
Index	251

Acknowledgements

The author gratefully acknowledges the permission granted to reproduce the copyright material in this book.

Though this volume concerns domestic politics in the 1930s, Constant Lambert's observations about trends in musical composition at that time are relevant, because they are not detached from what we would now call 'culture wars'. Lambert's 1934 work *Music, Ho! A Study of Music in Decline* was a major inspiration for this book, as was Ralph Vaughan Williams's essay 'National Music', published in the same year. I quote from these works extensively, and I hope that their juxtaposition with primary sources such as *The Times* paints a vivid picture of both musical and political life in 1934 Britain, and it is that particular year on which the focus of this book is largely concentrated.

I am grateful to several members of my family for their enthusiasm for the project, and especially to Lizzie Rose (1939–2016), and others who helped in proposing a working title (*Top Hats and Chamber Pots*, the reference, care of Lambert himself, becoming clearer in the text). I am also grateful to John Hely-Hutchinson for access to *Carol Symphony: The Life and Times of Victor Hely-Hutchinson, His Role in the Explosion of Musical Entertainment in the First Half of the 20th Century*, an unpublished biography of his father.

Viewing British history of the 1930s and 1940s from the perspective of an outsider looking in, so to speak, has been my privilege, first through the auspices of the University of Cape Town's summer school, then through working with Associate Professor Lesley Marx, who invited me to her Honours programme. As a long-time permanent resident in South Africa, I had a unique perspective on my native Britain, and my subsequent doctoral studies with the University of Exeter under the supervision of Professor Steve Neale and discussion with Professor Jeffrey Richards completed the circle.

The staff of the BBC Written Archives in Reading was, as ever, very helpful in allowing me access to documents from the time, and I am also indebted to my new circle of friends in Hermanus. Professor Edwin Heese read an early draft of the manuscript and I am grateful for his tacit endorsement and for his urging to carry the project through. A Mozart aficionado, I am also indebted to him for my discovery of – and subsequent appreciation for – William Walton, whose music he urged me to explore following the completion of my master's thesis on music and British film melodrama of the 1940s, which I completed at the University of Cape Town in 2008. My thanks also to Professor Nancy Odendaal at UCT and to the staff of the Book Cottage, Harriet Scheffers especially, who cheered me on in the final stages of completion. Special thanks also must go to Clare and Marion da Silva, whose relation to Arthur Bliss added an extra layer of insight.

Finally, I am especially grateful to Emily Drewe at Bloomsbury Academic for taking on this project, which has been several years in the making, and to Abigail Lane, who has expertly guided its final production.

Standards of one kind or another – whether signifiers of cultural excellence, or the flags of political movements, unions and countries – are also symbols of the establishment, of the military. Trooping the Colour, the ceremonial highlight of many a marching season, and intermingled with religious significance at the 'church parade' in many a garrison, was the highlight of the military year (which included marching to the cenotaph on Armistice Day) at my own school which was, technically, a regiment of the British army. It was a matter of curiosity for me that the chapel was festooned with military paraphernalia, either side of the nave adorned with the military colours of previous generations. To be fair, the singing of *Jerusalem* was occasional, evidence perhaps of an acknowledgement of the need to downplay the repeated singing of hymns that were, by the time I was there, perceived as too jingoistic. This struck me as a schoolboy; hindsight confirms the perception. Nevertheless, the school hymn at the time begins 'Oh Lord, Thy Banner Floateth O'er us / Beneath its folds we stand and sing'. Not very far from the marching anthems of the British Union of Fascists (Raise the Flag) and the Communist Party (The Red Flag) but which also invokes God's name on the side of the 'Sons of the Brave'. The ambivalence between Christian soldiery and the military kind seems forever blurred, but I suspect that this also explains my personal interest in the question of music and militarism, its relationship to nationalism, patriotism and propaganda. In its time, a song of the same name was hugely popular with the Australian bass-baritone Peter Dawson making a recording for HMV in 1932, and though rarely sung by the 1970s, would have probably been sung with the gusto that one might expect in the old world of an army-establishment education of the 1930s, complete with military band, Church Parade and an annual Trooping the Colour ceremony. *Sons of the Brave* was also the name of an 1898 march by Thomas Bigood (1858–1925), which was dedicated to the boys of the Duke of York's Royal Military School and the hymn of the same name, written by G. H. Andrews in 1901 for the school's centenary, was set to music by J. H. Maunder. My own part in the military band was rather limited. As a diminutive schoolboy, the powers that be in their wisdom assigned me – together with my brothers – to the corps of drums. The side-drum didn't offer much musically (apart from the odd paradiddle) or physically (if that were the aim) and, alas, the powers that be prohibited me from learning the potentially more musically satisfying clarinet.

But that was a different kind of music. Fortunately, I did have the benefit of hearing the late Reginald Adams (1917–2009) playing the organ works of Oliver Messiaen in Chapel to an 'audience' of indifferent schoolboys. It is to him and his wife Anne Adams, both of whom were my piano teachers, that I dedicate this book. It is their kindness and teaching to which I owe much, and to their discreet acknowledgement (against a backdrop of outdated petty militarism) that perhaps I was headed in the more aesthetic direction of musical appreciation. 'Reggie' steered me through 'O' level music and introduced me to the music of Vaughan Williams and especially to the *Serenade to Music*, that sublime 1938 setting of words from Act V of *The Merchant of Venice* which also happened to be one of the set works for English Lit. that year and, aptly enough, was the opening work of the 2021 BBC Proms season.

Introduction

The title of this book references both *Die Fahne Hoch* (or, the Horst Wessel song, the title literally 'the flag on high', but usually translated as Raise the Flag) and a line from *The Red Flag*, 'Raise the Scarlet Standard High'), which is sung, of course, to the tune of *O Tannenbaum*: there were flag-bearers on both sides of the political divide. In his essay on the Arts and the politics of the far right in 1930s Britain, Roger Griffin writes that while he is neither concerned with the biographical profiles of individual artists and intellectuals who devoted their creative or critical skills to the British Union of Fascists (BUF), nor with actual performances of theatrical or musical works put on by BUF members or under the aegis of the BUF, but he hopes 'that a student of fascism is waiting in the wings to fulfil this lacuna'.[1] In this volume, I attempt to contextualize the importance of music to people on *both* political extremes, and explore the organizations that were largely responsible for its dissemination, as well as individuals who contributed to the debate, and in many cases, where musicians have taken a very specific point of view that would align them with one group or another. In the absence of what the general public might have thought about the far right's attempts at performance, therefore, we do at least have the opinions of those for whom music was an important aspect of culture. A 'highbrow' taste until the advent of recordings and the means to hear it, even George Bernard Shaw regarded the performance of a Beethoven symphony as a 'once in blue moon' experience, especially the so-called 'Choral', performances of which 'were extraordinary events separated by years'.[2] Who but the well-heeled could attend a rare performance at the Queen's Hall to hear it? As David Cardiff has explored, recognizing that the 'ordinary listener' had probably never heard a Beethoven symphony, and might need help to appreciate it, in its early years the BBC engaged both music critics and music teachers 'to explain the meaning of music' on air. In his seminal work on broadcasting between the wars, Cardiff has also explored the role of the BBC in shaping musical taste, as well as the true 'democratization' of music, radio providing the final means of achieving it.[3]

In his recent exploration of twentieth-century history, David Edgerton has commented that 'We have barely begun to study not only how the future was imagined, but how the future was actually created' in Britain, where its perceived 'backwardness' could be observed by 'just how much modern creative talent came from abroad'. Not generally known as a country known for gravitating foreign talent, Edgerton recognizes that from the 1930s, Britain 'was by force of circumstance a particular place of refuge'.[4] In this book I explore some of the arguments about foreign talent, and not only the perceived threat to British employment that came with it, but also the beneficial raising of standards that resulted. At the BBC, for example, David Cardiff has noted that throughout the period two distinctive aspects of music policy prevailed: 'the pursuit of standards of excellence in the authentic performance of great music, and a commitment to increasing the new listening public's taste for, and appreciation of, such music'. The BBC's music department 'showed more enthusiasm' for the former, writes Cardiff, with John Reith and senior policymakers favouring the latter. There was also a distinction made from the very beginning between serious and popular music, the latter developing further distinctions throughout the decade. Always keen to play its role as educator, the BBC's long-running *Foundations of Music* programme, which ran for ten years was revamped in 1934 and finally axed in 1936, by which time it had outlived its use as planners began to make way for lighter music.[5] From the late 1930s, efforts to educate listeners declined even further. 'By then,' writes David Cardiff, 'the efforts of programme policymakers and planners were increasingly directed at efforts to lighten and brighten' in favour of entertainment.[6] By late 1939 serious music seemed to have disappeared from the airwaves altogether, with Adrian Boult complaining that during the first two weeks of the War, only fifteen minutes of music that could be appreciated by the serious music lover could be heard, with Beethoven banned and Mozart barely permitted,[7] the BBC seemingly in a quandary about broadcasting German music.

The BBC's role in reflecting views and tastes was a matter of political concern on the left and the right, though Edgerton points out that 'One cannot properly understand British history as a matter of progressives of the left and reactionaries of the right'.[8] 'All wanted change,' he writes. In his discussion of the period, when modernity tried to offer a vision of the future, Edgerton notes that in the case of music, 'Edward Elgar, Ralph Vaughan Williams and William Walton do not have the musicological status of, say, Stravinsky or Schoenberg, though Elgar was perhaps the first British composer to make any mark at all on the continent for centuries'.[9] Musicologist Paul Harper-Scott has commented that in no way could Walton be considered a modernist and had not the slightest 'left-leaning' inclinations at all.[10] At the time, Walton did attract attention at home, and Vaughan Williams was increasingly recognized abroad as the leading light in English music. Elgar, however, was an establishment figure by the time of his death, not at all 'modern', and by the late 1930s, Walton and Vaughan Williams were attracting attention from abroad, instead. By the time the War came, Elgar's brand of patriotic music was regarded as somewhat outdated and was rejected in favour of a less jingoistic and more bucolic vision of England, the kind of composition that stood less for military might than a depiction of what the country was fighting for.[11] This perspective was also apparent to George Orwell who wrote in his 1940 essay *England Your England*, 'No politician could rise to power by promising them conquests or military "glory", no Hymn of Hate has ever made any appeal to them.' In fact, in the First World War, 'the songs which the soldiers made up and sang of their own accord were not vengeful but humorous and mock-defiant.' Orwell adds a footnote to say that lines like 'I'd rather stay at home' were not the spirit in which men fought. 'The only enemy they ever named,' indeed, 'was the sergeant-major.'[12]

This is not a book solely about fascism or Roger Griffin's 'ideal type'. It is about music and musicians and how people with differing political outlooks viewed the place of music in the broader culture. It is puzzling to know that writers in *The Blackshirt* seemingly shared views with figures such as Ralph Vaughan Williams, recognized by them as the nation's pre-eminent composer of the period but who was, in turn, agnostic, Socialist-leaning and a fervent defender of German music while, at the same time, doing his best to nourish the 'tender flower' of its English counterpart. In this volume, I explore some of these apparent contradictions and, where possible, place them in the context of what Roger Griffin has called the 'palingenetic' form of ultra-nationalism. Did Vaughan Williams's 1934 'National Music' constitute a *mild* form of nationalism? Where do we draw the line between different expressions of nationalism? And how was music used to project British interests as an aspect of a rich cultural heritage and as a form of cultural propaganda?

This is only one aspect of a fascinating and compelling era of British cultural history. My own fascination with the period between the Wars was strengthened through researching classical music and British propaganda both in the period leading up to the Second World War, and during the conflict itself. As a student of music in film, I was intrigued by the ubiquitous presence of Beethoven's music in British cinema of the 1940s, and this led me into the exploration of the use of music for the purposes of 'publicity'. After I had completed my work, which covered the creation of the Music Advisory Committee of the British Council in 1935 and ended with that organization's activities in Germany in the immediate post-war period, I was left with several intriguing pointers to the year immediately preceding the period covered in my book. Just before composers, officials and filmmakers began to turn their attention towards issues of national identity and the like, there is an important pre-text to all those activities, and it can be seen in the events, concerns and creative output in music composition in a single year.

The mid-1930s saw the height of the BUF, whose membership reached its peak, the party enjoying its highest level of support until the notorious rally at Olympia in June. The BUF's version of the *Horst Wessel* song was sung on many controversial marches, and it was even to commission an anthem from none other than William Walton. It is still difficult to comprehend – especially in the light of later events as they unfolded – the level of support enjoyed by Oswald Mosley's Blackshirts. Crossing the floor from Conservative to Labour, and then forming his New Party in 1931, Mosley was 'the best Prime Minster we never had'. The second edition of his vision for the country, *The Greater Britain*, appeared in 1934. The Movement, as the party was known to its members, was publishing two newsletters a week, and much space was devoted to matters of arts and culture, not least music. Music was an important part of its organization and, during the year, composers and songwriters were encouraged to contribute to its song book. At the other end of the political spectrum, the communists too sought to encourage the arts, with their characteristic approach to music.

Julian Symons's retrospective on the 1930s, published barely thirty years after that turbulent decade, begins with a discussion of the emergence of Oswald Mosley's New Party in 1931 and its subsequent metamorphosis into the BUF. Few of the intellectuals who had happily joined the New Party followed Mosley into the new organization despite believing, like Mosley, 'that there was no parliamentary solution to the problems of Britain', and that the nation's rebirth could only come through chaos and catastrophe. 'This idea, with sometimes the chaos and catastrophe stressed, sometimes the rebirth,' wrote Symons, 'was the basis of the art of the Thirties.'[13]

The 'low, dishonest decade' (in W. H. Auden's famous words) was a time of political extremism, and yet one of the period's dominating political figures was the homely Stanley Baldwin, who had been Conservative Prime Minster from 1923 to 1929 (with a break in 1924 when Ramsay MacDonald headed the first Labour government) and again from June 1935 until his resignation due to ill health in 1937. Despite his basic decency and down-to-earth approach, however, he was puzzled by the public's response, captured in the lament, 'Why do the people hate me so?' Baldwin envisioned a 'property-owning democracy' and with the first 'green shoots' of economic recovery underway from 1934, much new building was now taking place with William Morris providing the affordable family car, and consumer goods of all kinds available in the shops. The new Piccadilly Line, built to service some of the extensive ribbon development out of London reflected the building boom also seen in the development of new towns in the South, even if the North remained economically hampered.

There is a marked contrast at the beginning of 1934 compared to the end as to the likelihood of international conflict. By the end of the year, Germany, Japan and Italy emerged as what they would be collectively known as the axis powers and which, together, were recognized as a threat to world peace. It serves as a picture of the progress from 'peace' to almost inevitable war at the end of 1934 (and why H. G. Wells could predict the outbreak of another world war by 1940) that saw an important rearmament debate in the House of Commons in November. The debate placed Churchill's views over those of Stanley Baldwin, who was 'viciously attacked by Churchill for allowing Hitler to rearm while Britain did not, so that Germany had obtained parity'.[14] Britain's pacifist mood could not be ignored altogether. Britain wanted peace, but it was not to be, and its pursuit allowed a dangerous escalation of arms to proceed in Europe. In fact, John Simon was telling his cabinet colleagues on 11 December that because of the debate, 'Hitler was now saying the British Government's announcement was tantamount to a legalisation of German rearmament'.[15] Yes, Hitler used the House of Commons debate as his cue, and rearmament in Germany began in earnest from 1935 onwards.

At the beginning of 1934, however, Sir Thomas Beecham was able to reassure the public in an open letter published in several broadsheets: 'Nothing in this letter is intended as criticism of the politics of modern Germany. My plea is solely for the fitting recognition of moral courage and the maintenance of an ideal, things which the English public has always been the first to recognise and honour.' By the end of the year such sweeping generalizations were no longer possible, the realization having dawned of the belligerent nature of the new regime in Germany. Events at the Berlin Philharmonic and Furtwängler's resignation made the nature of the Nazi project clearer. The impact on German life and the scale of the Nazi machine is recorded in that notorious record of the 1934 *Partietag*, Leni Riefenstahl's film *The Triumph of the Will*, a sort of Wagnerian *Gesamtkunstwerk* featuring music by the party-approved composer Herbert Windt. This vast display of the Nazi aesthetic is contrasted with the sombre tone and pageantry of the funeral of Hindenburg and, for the first time, shows what the new Germany had become.

What happened to the Berlin Philharmonic after Hitler's rise to power in 1934 and reaction to those developments forms part of the story of music and politics in Britain. It is a year of reflection, and of attempts to understand and identify the meaning of music in a rapidly changing society. Broadcasting was still in its infancy. In the publications of the BBC such as its yearbook, and in various newspapers, there remains a tone of the experimental, a realization that this was still a very new world that people were trying to understand and even shape. The previous few years had seen a huge growth in audience size with more and more people able to afford a wireless set and to tune into the BBC. In 1934, Walter Benjamin, a displaced German Jew residing in Paris published *The Work of Art in the Age of Mechanics*, in which he explores the juxtaposition between art and mechanical reproduction (including, of course, broadcasting).

Music was present at the very start of British broadcasting. Nellie Melba's broadcast of *Home, Sweet Home* marked the first British concert broadcast in June 1920, and even before the BBC began transmitting in 1922, British amateurs were picking up the Dutch station PCGG from The Hague, from where they could hear musical concerts every Thursday and Sunday.[16] Ten years on, the BBC was able to contribute a concert of British works in a Europe-wide relay that had begun with concerts from Vienna and Brussels. At that stage in February 1932, 'Music still seemed to offer the closest thing to an international language available to wireless internationalists.' These relays were 'linked explicitly with the broader peace movement and with memories of the cataclysm of the Great War,' writes Simon Potter in his recent volume on global radio and propaganda. Indeed, music appears to have been the chief means for achieving this. From *The Merry Wives of Windsor*, in December 1923, to *Prince Igor* from Brussels in 1924, *The Marriage of Figaro* from Cologne in 1928, to broadcasts from Bayreuth in 1931, the Barber of Seville from Salzburg and the International Broadcasting Union's 'National Evenings' of live broadcasts beginning with a live concert from Budapest in 1931, Adrian Boult's concert was the third of these European Concerts.[17]

These efforts seem to have achieved little, however. As Lewis Foreman has noted, 'The generation of composers beginning to emerge in the 1930s was, by and large, profoundly affected by the moral issues posed by the rise of fascism in Europe and especially by the Spanish Civil War. This tended to result, as the decade passed, in vocal rather than purely orchestral or chamber works – and possibly Britten's *A Ballad of Heroes* in 1939, with its contemporary texts ('It's farewell to the drawing-room's civilised cry. . . . For the Devil has broken parole and arisen') by Auden and Swingler.'[18] Indeed, comments Potter, 'No international language was required to understand the broadcast conflict' apparent in Spain during the Civil War. 'Even the music carried by Spanish stations reflected and offered a means of identifying their political agendas,' with opposing stations playing the Internationale, fascists either the *Horst-Wessel-Lied* or *Giovinezza* and Barcelona broadcasting *Els Segadors*, the 'Catalan-Separatist' hymn. 'Music no longer seemed an uncomplicated agent of wireless internationalism,' he writes.[19] Meanwhile, in England, Vaughan Williams was completing *Dona Nobis Pacem* which was a refutation – 'a warning against impending war in Europe in texts from Whitman, John Bright and the Bible'[20] – of the political situation. Though the Fourth Symphony was not entirely written in the same spirit, Wilfrid Mellers points out that its ferocity inevitably encouraged a response in programmatic terms, the Symphony commonly interpreted as a prophecy of the Second World War:

> Vaughan Williams denied any such naïve literalism, though the fact that the Symphony was composed alongside *Dona Nobis Pacem*, the text of which explicitly concerns war, suggests that it was a product of the decade's turbulence. It could not have been otherwise, for Vaughan Williams could not regard the background of his art as separable from the outside world. No less than the Cantata, the Symphony is an appeal, if not for peace (that comes in the Fifth), then at least for the renunciation of war – in a psychological rather than a material sense.[21]

Begun in 1934 and first performed in 1936, *Dona Nobis Pacem* uses two Walt Whitman poems which come from his experiences during the American Civil War.[22] To *Beat, Beat Drums* and *Reconciliation*, Vaughan Williams added words from an 1855 House of Commons speech by John Bright ('The Angel of Death has been abroad throughout the land; you may almost hear the beating of his wings') and verses from the Bible, linked together by a soprano voice repeating Dona Nobis Pacem giving the cantata its name. The first performance under Albert Coates took place in October 1935, the same month of the Italian invasion of Abyssinia. 'The Soprano's cry for peace gave the work a topical overtone that it has never lost,' observed Ursula Vaughan Williams.[23]

'Many commentators continued to argue that broadcasting could encourage international understanding and peace,' writes Potter. 'Broadcasts from Europe and elsewhere meanwhile widened the artistic horizons of British listeners, breaking down their "musical insularity".'[24] This latter point is debatable, however, because if anything, musical artistic horizons of British listeners were, in the 1930s, firmly rooted in the canon of the three Bs – Bach,

Beethoven and Brahms. Nevertheless, not all in officialdom supported the BBC's efforts in encouraging world peace, the Foreign Office regarding its efforts an 'unrealistic attempt' in what amounted to interference in what did not concern them.[25]

This book is about music and it is also about the effect political events and ideologies had on music. The year 1934 was one for portentous events, whose consequences were realized only in the years that followed. In his biography of Stanley Baldwin, Jeremy Dobson writes that 1934 had been a quiet year, one in which the worst of the depression was over and when the international crisis had scarcely begun. 'It was a time of optimism, that at last a better way of life might be provided for the people,' he writes. 'If 1934 has been a year of tranquillity, at least as far as Britain was concerned, by 1935 all could now hear the drumbeats of war echoing through Europe once more, at least if they chose to listen.'[26] The value of cultural propaganda under those circumstances did not go unnoticed by the institutions of Government. Set up to handle all kinds of what was euphemistically known as 'publicity', the British Council was established in November 1934, part of its remit to mobilize the forces of culture in the setting up of a number of committees during the course of the following year, including a Music Advisory Committee. The committee, under the chairmanship of Ernest Makower and supported by the tireless efforts of its formidable secretary Pamela Henn-Collins, first sat on 24 July 1935, with a remit to promote Britain through the means of music.[27] In recognition of the importance of the arts, the establishment of the committee heralded a new age in the use of music as a weapon in the propaganda war, much of which was directed at disseminating the British view against what many considered from 1935 onwards was the inevitability of war.

Nevertheless, there was also a certain optimism and the nascent broadcasting system continued to inspire and excite, and many were keen to experiment with the new technologies that became increasingly available to ordinary people. Television took a great leap forward, and *The Times* published a sizeable supplement on broadcasting in August. Following Max Steiner's success with the score for *King Kong* in 1933 (which can be said to be Hollywood's first major film score), the first real film music appeared in Britain in 1934, care of none other than William Walton. The year 1934 is also the year of Glyndebourne's birth and of the premiere of several major new British orchestral works, not least two large-scale symphonies from Ralph Vaughan Williams and William Walton. The former, thirty years Walton's senior, emerged as the nation's pre-eminent composer, and the *enfant terrible* Walton astounded the world with the first performance of his wild, relentless First Symphony, a work of genius that was so eagerly anticipated that it was first performed without the final movement.

The year 1934 is also an extraordinary year in publishing. Vaughan Williams's important essay 'National Music', on the place of music in British life, appeared and it is also the year in which Constant Lambert presented *Music, Ho!* to an astonished world. This book examines the opinion of the day, from the earnest contribution to *The Blackshirt* on matters of music, through H. C. Colles's criticism in the pages of *The Times*, to what was recognized as the first Marxist analysis of music and the esoteric work of Cyril Scott and John Foulds. In *Music and Politics in Thirties Britain: Raise the Standard High*, I explore the banner-waving of the far right as well as the contributions of Continental artists – some of them migrants – who did so much to enrich British musical life. I also examine the raging arguments about 'cacophony' and 'symphony' how this was part of a wide political debate, as well as the ever-accelerating development of a vast range of new technologies and the expansion of broadcasting, and the effect this had on musical life.

The receding waters of anti-modernism were evident elsewhere in 1934. Eric Blom, for example, complained that South African composer and later head of music at the University of Birmingham Victor Hely-Hutchinson's new Piano Quintet, despite being constructed 'with some originality of plan' in seven sections – *Idyll and Diversions* – 'asks a rather stiff allowance of conventionality from the listener', achieving no 'distinctive style' in the process:

> It does not stand for anything, not even for its own time. That it does not ape a fashion, but would rather express itself in a romantic idiom which may be anything between Schumann and the Cesar Franck school, is in a way to the composer's credit. But new music that does not represent anything that is characteristic of the day can't possibly be expected to have a future. If one welcomes this quintet, it must be on the understanding that there is no reason why chamber music should not have its pleasing ephemera.[28]

By that time Hely-Hutchinson's priority, however, was to communicate with the common man, 'even if this meant simplifying his style'. Hely-Hutchinson had developed the common touch during his role as a broadcaster, a 'prominent agent in the movement which transferred music from an entertainment for the privileged few to a message which could be enjoyed by all'.[29] Though he spoke mainly to the common man, writes John Hely-Hutchinson in an unpublished biography of his father, Victor 'became part of a large circle of friends at his own intellectual level'. There is an amusing anecdote recounted in the biography regarding the emergence of television in 1934. One of those friends was the father of television, John Logie Baird, whose process had been used for the BBC's first broadcasts in January. One evening, the two men and their wives met over dinner and Baird agreed to a demonstration. The BBC was broadcasting at that time for an hour late in the evening using the Baird Process, but the demonstration did not go to plan and no sound emerged from the set:

> When John asked [Hely-Hutchinson's wife] Marjorie what she thought of it, she said it was an interesting experiment without much entertainment value. He looked at her for a moment and said 'Do you know, that's what my wife thinks of me!' In spite of its ground-breaking originality, John's television apparatus, being largely mechanical, and with limited resolution in time or space, was eventually superseded by the all-electronic system devised by EMI.[30]

This book is also a survey of the commentary that appeared at the time, whether in *The Times*, or in the monthly and quarterly music journals, in books and periodicals of the period, as well as on the fringes of journalism. It is a companion to *Culture and Propaganda in World War II: Music, Film and the Battle for National Identity*, in which I explore the years from 1935 to 1945. I intend to demonstrate that even on a purely musicological basis, the influence of cultural politics could not be avoided, with criticism levelled from the left on the neo-romanticism, say, of William Walton's First Symphony and on what some considered on the right to be the 'cacophony' of Stravinsky's music. Much of these broad themes are exemplified within the contrasting ends of one particular year. As a result of the deaths, in quick succession, of three major composers, Edward Elgar, Gustav Holst and Frederick Delius during the first half of the year, 1934 has been called the 'black year' of British music, even an *annus horribilis*. Certainly, their deaths were a blow to many.

The BBC's review of 1934 recognized that 'Memories of 1934 must necessarily be tinged with regret, since in the last year British music – at a moment, too, of increasing prestige at home and abroad – has sustained the loss of our three greatest figures', but took some consolation from the thought that 'during their last years all three composers were represented in the principal music broadcasts by many of their most important works'.[31]

Vaughan Williams – though never close to Elgar – particularly felt the loss of his friend and collaborator Holst, who died at just fifty-nine. Elgar had been working on his Third Symphony, leaving only a few sketches behind. And the loss of Delius, that wholly original creator of highly unusual but appealing music – an English sound despite the composer's long-term residence out of the country – was felt keenly, too. Indeed, a performance of Delius's *Mass of Life* which began the 1934 winter season of symphony concerts was 'a fitting memorial to this great composer'.[32] Given that most major composers contributed in some way to propagandistic efforts in the years that followed, particularly through film, it is tantalizing to imagine the contributions that these three greats might have made. In remarkably different ways, their music can be said to have set the standards for what constituted 'nationalism' in music.

The events – musical and political – of 1934 set the scene for exploring attitudes between the ravages of the depression and the rearmament and appeasement that led to the outbreak of war, and my particular focus is on that year. It is also the year of a new dawn in British music, and I hope that this book will demonstrate its importance. Inheriting by default the mantle of Britain's most important composer, Ralph Vaughan Williams's output that year included his *Suite for Viola and Small Orchestra* (written for Lionel Tertis and unlike anything else by that composer, a work that remains relatively unknown), and the first performance of his *Fantasia on Greensleeves* at the Proms. Perhaps the quintessential English tune, it points to the composer's particular brand of nationalism present in many of his works. He was also working on his menacing Fourth Symphony, begun in 1931, a work that continues to invite speculation as to its meaning, political or otherwise. December 1934 saw the first performance of William Walton's (incomplete) First Symphony, a work of genius that was also composed over several years and which provoked a strong reaction. It seemed also to symbolize what Kenneth Clark called the 'heroic materialism' of the age. Clark used a full five minutes of the opening of the symphony to introduce the final part of his seminal 1969 television series *Civilisation*, an exploration of European culture over the centuries, Clark dispensed with narration and simply let the music reflect the spectacle of a helicopter ride over New York City to the strains of this powerful music – image and sound, presumably, saying enough. In 1934, Walton was regarded as the leading composer of his generation, a position he held up until the later 1940s when Benjamin Britten emerged as his successor. Britten made *his* views known on hearing the symphony at its first performance, as we shall see.

There were other deaths that year. We no longer remember Sir George Henschel (1850–1934), a concert baritone and composer, born in Breslau, who directed the London Symphony Orchestra (LSO) and was the first conductor of the Scottish Orchestra – a reminder of the extremely close ties that existed between nation cousins, Britain and Germany. Although there is much to explore over on the Continent, particularly in Germany, I restrict this survey to music in Britain, though I cover political developments in Europe, where they are pertinent to the British perspective and experience. The year 1934 was the year of Yehudi Menuhin's first performance, for example, and, significantly, of the Glyndebourne Festival too, a collaboration that was made possible in no insignificant measure by the politics of the time. Though the first performance of Licinio Refice's *Cecilia* on 15 February preceded the birth by just a few days of Renata Scotto, whose relatively recent recording of that work makes for a tempting diversion, this, unfortunately, is beyond the scope of this volume. Other significant births that year include those of Alfred Schnittke and, in Britain, of Peter Maxwell Davies and Harrison Birtwhistle as well as that pioneer of music in a future era, the American engineer Robert Moog, whose synthesizer did much to change music half a century later.

The fortieth Proms season provided its founder Sir Henry Wood with a very mischievous opportunity to reveal a certain anti-British bias in the reviews of the music critics of the period, finally revealing the identity of his 1929 discovery Paul Klenovsky. The 1934 season was the most highly attended yet and the year also saw the London premieres of much new music from abroad, including a ground-breaking and much acclaimed (though not universally appreciated) broadcast concert performance of Alban Berg's *Wozzeck*. Broadcast by the BBC, it was 'the outstanding event' of the Queen's Hall spring symphony concert series.[33] The opera also provides a useful marker in the debate about what constituted highbrow, lowbrow and middlebrow tastes, and whether such works could be approved of at all, particularly among the far right.

From this viewpoint Graham Macklin has also analysed jazz in his article on music and the BUF, with jazz regarded as in opposition to the BUF's 'conservative cultural aesthetic', and their belief in its degenerative effects.[34] Further analysis of contemporaneous attitudes towards jazz reveals a wide-ranging and sophisticated response. Opposition to jazz was not an exclusive marker of right-wing conservatism, or fascism, only. For Australian academic Keith Barry, the use of the saxophone as the chief instrument of the jazz orchestra, which gave ears 'little rest these days', as well as the immoderate use of syncopation led to monotony – the 'chief crime' possible in a world where the deadliest sin is dullness:

> Monotony eventually kills everything, and it is steadily killing jazz. The jazz age is going, and the complicated orchestral arrangements of the dance music of the day are an outstanding advance on what we suffered immediately after the war.[35]

But he reserves a special mention for a new kind of symphonic jazz, and it is Constant Lambert whose name he mentions first. Lambert's own views on jazz were particularly nuanced, and he too differentiated between varieties. An early appreciation for its perceived character, its rhythm, can be seen especially in his 1922 poem 'Jazz Blues' written towards the end of his school career and which, given his later references, may not be just an indication of his 'versatility and range of tastes':

Cockatoos!
Cockatoos!
Swinging in chains from the painted roof
Chatter and scream and flap their wings,
Flinging their gaudy bodies in time
To the ragtime tunes,
The ragtime tunes.

The poem was 'to be chanted with uniform rhythm'.[36] *Music, Ho!* writes Lambert's biographer Stephen Lloyd, 'was greeted with considerable acclaim', with Michel-Dimitri (M-D.) Calvocoressi believing that in the book, Lambert had succeeded far better than anyone in seeing music against its social background and, in particular, his commentary on the rise of Hitler ('in relation to the banning of the music of Alban Berg whom he rated highly') proved he was sufficiently up to date.[37] In this groundbreaking and provocative book, Lambert's approach was unorthodox, setting out an alternative to standard music history. Rather than beginning with German music of the nineteenth century, he began with the Russian nationalist school, starting with Glinka. Isaiah Berlin pointed out that Lambert's allegiance to Mussorgsky (not as obscure then as, perhaps, now – a trio was used in a famous scene in David Lean's *Brief Encounter* in 1945) and to Borodin colours all his writing, especially in his attack on Stravinsky and Hindemith. Earlier, Cecil Gray had complained about Stravinsky's obsession with rhythm in his 1924 work 'A Survey of Contemporary Music', and Lambert takes up the comment that in Stravinsky, rhythm 'without melody' is mere 'metre', or 'measure' – a metronome, in other words.

These comments on rhythm, taken with 'Jazz Blues', allow us to contextualize the predisposition towards the typically 'tongue-in-cheek erudition' that characterized him. I am sure that this was a youthful attempt at mocking jazz, which later became explicit in *Music, Ho!* or perhaps which pointed, rather, to his ambivalence towards it. Indeed, on the one hand, he considered jazz to be 'mere aural tickling',[38] and for him, Gershwin's *Rhapsody in Blue* betrayed the composer's 'inability to cope with concerto form'.[39] On the other, he expressed his open admiration for Duke Ellington, whose artistry he admired above all else, and singled out *Mood Indigo* as an equally remarkable piece of writing of a lyrical and harmonic order, Ellington thereby preparing the way for the symphonic jazz of so-called highbrow composers.[40] Ellington's appearance at the London Palladium in June 1933 'stirred him' to write in his regular *Sunday Referee* column how 'the orchestration of nearly all the numbers show an intensely musical instinct'.[41] Roger Wimbush's response, published in the newspaper a couple of weeks later, exemplifies extreme objections to the perceived dangers of jazz. Unable to see how jazz could be taken seriously as an influence on music, he wrote that there could be little doubt that 'to Western minds jazz is definitely unhealthy', a 'Jew-ridden racket and the child of mammon', as opposed to genuine creative music which is, by nature, 'a spiritual experience'.[42]

Written in 1933, this letter bears the same tone as the commentary pieces that were beginning to appear in *The Blackshirt* and *Fascist Week*. But Lambert was able to retort, again with his nuanced approach, distinguishing between 'composed' jazz and 'putting frills round the latest song hit', that if Wimbush felt 'so strongly about the Jewish influence on jazz, why [was] he not more pleased to find that its most distinguished exponent is coloured [sic]?'

Correspondence of this nature was not uncommon in the press. Earlier, a similar exchange of views took place between Lambert and the conductor and pioneer of choral music in Sheffield, Sir Henry Cawood (1849–1944), who disliked jazz, describing it as 'atavistic, lowering, degrading and a racial question' and 'composed of jingly tunes, jerky rhythms, [and] unquestionably grotesque forms'.[43] Sir Henry was 'a classic Victorian, a self-made man from a humble background who rose to the top by his own efforts,' writes Jeffrey Richards. 'Profoundly patriotic and imperialistic', he was the son of a Sheffield-born cutler, and later was regarded as one of the best cutlers himself, following in his father's footsteps in Sheffield at the age of twenty-two. Both his parents were musical, and Cawood made a major career change into music at the age of forty.[44] Cawood's own account of the 1911 tour of his Sheffield Choir was published in 1933. '"The tour of the world," he believed, was "such a unique event, and its worldwide musical, ethical and political repercussions have been so marked," that it required a full account.'[45] His world view, which can refer to his father's lowbrow musicality in such terms, also finds its grandest imperialistic expression in his 1885 cantata Queen Victoria and Her Reign, which contains the lines:

> We go to carry English thought
> And enterprise and skill

> To lands which heav'n has long reserved
> For English hands to till,
> To plant the flag of liberty
> On heights yet unattained;
> To consecrate by truth and right,
> Each peaceful conquest gained.⁴⁶

The cantata was, by the 1930s, a relic of a bygone era. 'Writing from the perspective of 1933 and as a Victorian evidently at odds with the new age, Cawood defended choral singing as the greatest form of music "from a humanist point of view". His reasons for this locate him precisely, culturally and politically. Choral singing, he thought, was possibly the most socialistic – 'using the term in its proper anti-Bolshevist sense' – of all the amenities of life, promoting as it does fellowship and friendship. It is the most democratizing force in 'the true political sense'. This undeniably links him almost measure for measure to Vaughan Williams's own view on the place of the choral society in English music, for whom they formed the bedrock of British musical tradition (building on music at home). For Cawood, all the choral societies in which he was involved, 'the rich and poor, gentle and simple, the lady of high degree and the less exalted worker, mix together in happy companionship to the ousting of class distinctions'. He also regarded choral music as a bulwark against the 'baneful influence of atavistic jazz', which he dismissed as 'sloppy and slithering', its devastating influence on the prestige of the white races its chief indictment, and it was beyond his comprehension that people might prefer this kind of 'singing' to choral music. 'It is horrible and humiliating to think about it,' he wrote.⁴⁷

Earlier, 'arch-conservative' Cawood had aired his views in a response to Constant Lambert's first article for the *Radio Times* in July 1928, 'The Future of Jazz', in which he explored the possibilities of symphonic jazz. Cawood's response, published a few weeks later, was unequivocal:

> For seventy years I have been acquainted with the salient features of the twangy strains and grotesque posturings of negro music and dancing.⁴⁸

While Lambert agreed with some of what Cawood had to say, for him 'the appeal of jazz lay much deeper' than its popularity, and could be found 'in the technical side, in the virtuosity of both its performance and orchestration', despite the tendency in Lambert's words 'to over-emphasise the more grotesque timbres'.⁴⁹ Despite the long-running *Radio Times* correspondence precipitated by Sir Henry's outburst, his views were clearly not to be shifted, as the introduction to his 1933 book attests. Lambert's views were more nuanced, differentiating between the 'exhilarating rhythmic qualities' of jazz on the one hand, and a tendency to use harmonic cliché on the other. 'At the time that this article appeared,' writes Lloyd, Lambert's *The Rio Grande* was 'the most successful English example of symphonic jazz'.[50] For music critic Neville Cardus it 'transfigured jazz into poetry', the score 'perfectly poised'.[51]

Two broadcasters and collaborators on *The Gramophone* perhaps, between them, exemplify the tension between what was 'popular' and the Reithian ideal. The BBC's definition of 'light entertainment' or Variety, included operetta, musical comedy, vaudeville, cabaret and dance music. 'Whatever may be the wider aims of broadcasting,' Variety must set out to *please*, was the official stance.[52] Compton Mackenzie's *Gramophone* magazine employed Christopher Stone as its London editor. The latter was a popular figure, appearing at the London Palladium, and there was even a wax model of him at Madame Tussaud's. At the same time, *The Gramophone* was in decline, and Stone believed that one solution was to attract more readers and adapt to modern taste. The contrast between the highbrow and lowbrow was apparent, where Mackenzie's editorials appeared at the front and Edgar Jackson's expertise on jazz at the back. This was Stone's work.

Moreover, writes D. L. LeMahieu, 'As the simple rhythms of "Yes, We Have No Bananas" evolved into the more complex sounds of Duke Ellington, jazz attracted a number of other influential defenders, including Constant Lambert, who integrated the music into his own compositions and argued that jazz represented an important element of twentieth-century music.'[53] Believing that 'the magazine should adapt itself more aggressively to modern tastes', Stone hired Jackson, a former editor of *Melody Maker*, who revamped *The Gramophone's* layout in 1934:

> Mackenzie greeted these changes with mixed emotions. He hated vapid populism but also knew that a fussy purity could lead to bankruptcy. In an editorial for August 1934, he frankly acknowledged his ambivalence. *The Gramophone*, he wrote, had always experimented with new features and though he sometimes disagreed with them, he did not want an 'insensitive conservatism to stand in the way of serviceable change'. He admitted he disliked the space devoted to popular records and artists but wondered if the magazine could afford to alienate readers and advertisers.[54]

Soon, however, the economic troubles of *The Gramophone* were over, and with EMI returning to profit and Decca providing stiff competition, the magazine emerged from the depression with an upturn in advertising, surviving 'with patience, flexibility and sheer good luck'.[55]

How, then, did Lambert regard what appears to be two kinds of jazz? As we have seen, he certainly embraced 'symphonic jazz', but it needed to be of a very high standard (the other kind was the 'lowbrow' stuff). For Lambert, 'harmonically sophisticated European Jazz was closer to a piece by Grieg than to native African music'.[56] Edvard Grieg's many *Lyric Pieces* for solo piano are no doubt what he had in mind. Meanwhile Lambert's dislike for Hindemith unwittingly gives us the reassurance that his objection to jazz wasn't displaced Hitlerism, or sympathy with the notion of 'Entartete Musik'. For instance, Berthold Brecht's libretto for Hindemith's cantata *Lehrstück* (The Lesson) with its 'pseudo-profundities', were 'of a type which one hoped had found its last home in Hitler's speeches'.[57]

Lambert shares a certain rejection of German music with Ralph Vaughan Williams, whose essay on nationalism in music we will explore in detail. Vaughan Williams's rejection was not for the music *per se* but was an expression of his desire to nurture the 'little flower' of English music which had been dominated so long by the German giants. Similarly, Stephen Lloyd writes that in rejecting Hindemith and Stravinsky in particular, 'and German music in general', one would expect Lambert 'to adopt a more sympathetic approach to English music which was itself going through a period of change'.[58] Despite his admiration for the young William Walton, Lambert considered that most English composers were prepared 'to sacrifice or overlook' dramatic intensity and formal coherence in their obsession with mood, and that this had produced 'a movement of rather exaggerated nationalism', in which the pursuit of an 'English atmosphere' was achieved at the expense of 'solidly constructed' music.

Undoubtedly, *Music, Ho!* was received well, despite reservations about English music and objections to Lambert's 'attacks' on Stravinsky and Hindemith. The latter he regarded as 'the supreme middle brow of our times'.[59] It is useful to first establish what we mean by the 'middlebrow' in music. The term first appeared in the 1920s in a debate about high and low culture, responses to growing mass media, and was famously described by Virginia Woolf in a 1932 letter to the *New Statesman*, in which she described the middlebrow as those of 'middlebred intelligence' whose sauntering along in pursuit of neither art nor life, was mixed up 'rather nastily' with money, fame, power or prestige.[60] Aspects of the middlebrow, including music appreciation societies often shared prejudices and championed 'a Eurocentric canon in response to the growing popularity of jazz'.[61] Can middlebrow music be characterized by its popularity? Certainly. Tchaikovsky's *1812 Overture* must be the ultimate example (complete with cannons, bells, fireworks etc.)

of popular appeal. Lambert regarded Sibelius's *Finlandia* and *Valse Triste* 'excellent examples of their genre' unlike Cecil Gray who found such works 'banal'.[62] David Cardiff cites the listener who in 1925 defined his 'lower middlebrow' tastes, 'with perfect accuracy', his choice of 'six great melodies', including *The Blue Danube*, and Elgar's *Salut d'Amour* to the *Radio Times*. Today, one might consider *La bohème* somewhat 'suspect' (*Your Tiny Hand is Frozen*), and Franz Lehar's *The Merry Widow* 'easy'. The latter, strictly operetta, sparked a global craze after its first performance in 1907, and in 1934 enjoyed a film outing with Jeanette MacDonald in the starring role, premiering in London that autumn. Another Hollywood production, *Bolero*, with Carol Lombard and George Raft, was also released in 1934.[63] It was a year for film music of a different kind, too. Just a year after the groundbreaking Hollywood score for *King Kong* was written by Max Steiner, newcomer William Walton was recruited to write for a British production *Escape Me Never*, beginning a significant association with the cinema that was to last well over thirty-five years.

Angus Morrison later commented that the widening gap between serious and popular music at the time was the one thing that Constant Lambert deplored above all else, and that nowhere else in *Music, Ho!* does Lambert write 'with greater sincerity than when he is describing what he referred to as "the disappearing middlebrow", a statement probably even more true today with the average man-in-the-street ignorant of serious music: As far as we can concern any general social trend in the music of today it would appear that the middlebrow composer is disappearing'.[64] Despite the BBC's efforts in 1934, the highbrow *Wozzeck* had virtually no popular appeal. And though Compton Mackenzie 'particularly deplored the ascendancy of jazz', he could also attack opera 'with the same ferocity'.[65] He believed that certain composers could enhance different occasions, citing Brahms and Schubert. His attitude could descend, however, into what LeMahieu has described as prefiguring *Muzak*, agreeing to write an introduction to a record catalogue that included sections on 'Music for the Stars', 'Music for a Bird Sanctuary' and even 'Music for a Power Station'![66] This recalls the disparaging comments made by Lambert on Artur Honegger's *Pacific 231*, which he dismissed at a stroke. These, then, were examples of the 'middlebrow' in music – all failing to satisfy anyone.

David Cardiff's work on aspects of musical taste shows how radio brought into debate the whole question of low-, middle- and highbrow taste in music. Whereas music, until the BBC began broadcasting, existed in an array of economic and social networks, the advent of a universal audience introduced an element of competition for 'airtime', and the unintended consequence was the emerging of a hierarchy of tastes. 'The terms highbrow, middlebrow and lowbrow, widely current in discussions of music and radio in the twenties and thirties, only became meaningful systems of classification when different kinds of music were brought into close proximity with each other,' he writes. Indeed, both lowbrow and highbrow listeners defined themselves by what they hated as well as what they loved. 'But it was not simply a matter of antagonisms between different fields of music, the serious and the popular, highbrow and lowbrow. Within each field there was a hierarchy of tastes that fragmented the unity of the categories.'[67]

The issue is one that also concerns the technical limitations of broadcasting where, on short wave, 'serious' orchestral music did not come across well. The mechanical age had also begun to reach every corner of society with the growing appetite for recorded music and broadcasting, which had entrenched the high regard for music of the German canon in the institutions of musical life. That year the Three Choirs Festival was at Gloucester, and over on the other side of the Atlantic, the first performance took place of Rachmaninov's *Rhapsody on a Theme of Paganini*, with the composer as soloist and the Philadelphia Orchestra conducted by Leopold Stokowski. Florence Foster Jenkins was at the height of her influence in New York musical circles, though she was conspicuous for not 'deploring' Mussolini's attitude, finding herself in the considerable minority of one of her many society memberships:

> When the National Fascist Band arrived from Rome for a long tour in 1934, touting themselves as 'ambassadors of goodwill uniting the musical hearts of America and Italy', she was one of the sixteen honorary patrons for their Carnegie Hall concert in August.[68]

Many exiles appeared in London, some contributing enormously to the landscape of musical Britain. Just as the Glyndebourne Festival owes much to the work of several émigrés, the BBC also benefited from the wisdom of exiled music scholars and critics. Britain attracted much talent from Germany – increasingly so as the year went on – because of the Nazi party's persecution of Jewish musicians and other 'undesirables'. But what was Germany's loss was Britain's gain, though in the face of the influx of music-making from 'Mittel Europa', several figures sought to lay out what was important about British music. Most famous is Vaughan Williams's essay 'National Music', which was adapted from a series of lectures he gave in 1932. Lambert's *Music, Ho!*, his study of 'music in decline', still has the power to surprise with all its wit and insight, even if, like his contemporary readers, we do not always agree with him. In the introduction to the third edition of the work, Arthur Hutchings writes that the 'belated' ascendancy of the taste for Hindemith and Stravinsky in 1934 London, followed by a more rapid – and sooner exhausted – one for Sibelius thus prevented most British listeners from commenting on non-British music made by a British musician, especially one who 'had minimized in himself the proverbial time-lag between continental and insular connoisseurship':

> Lambert's first readers included many who were annoyed by his unmaliciously limited admiration for the English 'nationalist' school, then at the zenith of popularity. Most of them know so little about it from writers who know only a little more than they.[69]

Although 'plainly influenced and fascinated' by Hindemith, Stravinsky, Schoenberg and the French composers, Lambert wrote more harshly of them than he did of British composers, believing that like most twentieth-century composers, they perpetrated 'artistic falsehoods' because 'they could not represent their potential twentieth-century listeners without reflecting the false values of twentieth-century society'. Indeed, it was only 'falseness' that Lambert was really condemning. But it is also useful to understand, as Hutchings points out, 'that few of his contemporaries took the subtitle "A Study of Music in Decline" as expressing more than dissatisfaction with a *temporary* artistic depression, impatience with an insular provision of music'. Surely it was only temporary, because by the end of 1934, and into the following year, several great British works emerged, and an increasingly broader dissemination of music in general, possible not least by the efforts of the BBC, belied the so-called 'decline' in British music. So, what of the 'nationalist' school, and of Vaughan Williams's views? In *his* foreword to the composer's famous essay, Michael Kennedy writes:

> If a book with the title *National Music* had been published in 1934 under, say, a Munich imprint, it would have been looked on askance, just as the word 'nationalist' today has taken on a pejorative meaning for which politicians are wholly responsible. Yet had it been called *The People's Music* it would have been equally suspect and misunderstood.[70]

The book represents the published version of the lectures the composer gave at Bryn Mawr College, Pennsylvania, in autumn 1932. In it, writes Kennedy, 'one hears the voice of Vaughan Williams himself in his writing as clearly and unmistakably as in his music. The style is the man. It was hard-won, and it has a personal integrity that transcends nationality'. Hutchings, meanwhile, equates another 1932 work with that of Constant Lambert, and finds transcendence in both:

> There was a striking similarity of temperament between Constant Lambert and Aldous Huxley, including a taste for Latin rather than Teutonic art. Both were compassionate towards the individual within the herd but both felt towards herd-brutality and philistinism that aristocratic contempt which is nowadays miscalled snobbery . . . in *Brave New World* and *Music, Ho!* we can enjoy the illusory fears and hopes of the 1920s and 1930s while we also marvel that so much prophecy within their covers is true – not 'has some truth'. The best things in *Music, Ho!* apply to the whole history of artistic endeavour and thus transcend a study of Music in Decline.

Published in April 1934, *Music, Ho!* was completed in December 1933. 'Written with the minimum of technical language, without any music examples and without discussing in detail any individual work, *Music, Ho!* was greeted with considerable acclaim,' writes Stephen Lloyd in his definitive biography of Lambert. It was one of several books written about music and published that year, but Lambert's is significant because he was able to bring into the discussion both literature and the visual arts, as well as comment on the political situation, especially in Germany:

> Yet he was sufficiently up-to-date to comment on the rise of Hitler (in relation to the banning of the music of Alban Berg whom he rated highly), and sufficiently avant-garde to mention more than once Joyce's banned novel *Ulysses* and J. W. Dunne, whose theories on time and dreams were then being much discussed among intellectuals.[71]

Lambert found the appearance of the *Horst Wessel* song to be a particularly bad omen, the political feeling expressed in songs of its type the 'least desirable' form of nationalism. He was even doubtful whether the Great War would have lasted barely six months 'without the aid of that purest of the arts, music, whose latest gift to civilisation is the notorious Horst Wessel Song'.[72] Lambert was no doubt aware of its English-language version as an anthem of the BUF. Nicholas Mosley's biography of his father notes:

> The songs that the Blackshirts sang and which, together with their salute and their badge and so on, seemed to many members of the public to justify their seeing the BUF as in alliance with German Nazis and Italian Fascists were, chiefly, their 'Marching Song' which was sung to the tune of the *Horst Wessel Lied* . . . and the song 'Onward Blackshirts', which was sung to the tune of the Italian anthem *Giovinezza* . . .

> The *Horst Wessel Lied* was sung to one of the best and saddest tunes that a revolutionary movement has ever produced: *Giovinezza* was a fine rousing marching song. What is striking is that the words of each are concerned with the image of the revolutionary spirit arising only over the martyred bodies of the dead.[73]

By this time, Oswald Mosley had already begun his relationship with Diana Guinness who took the controversial and bold step of moving into 'The Eatonry' in January 1933. This was a different kind of relationship for Mosley from those that had gone before, one that appeared to have finally broken his wife Cimmie's spirit. During her illness in the spring, she was said to have lost the will to live, both physically and mentally.

And so we are presented with many similarities and contrasts: Huxley and Lambert, Vaughan Williams and Walton, and Lambert and Vaughan Williams, the latter recognized as the elder statesman of British music, and Lambert and Walton, two young men in a hurry, like the year itself. But 1934 wasn't simply a 'black year' for British music, or a year in which politics was the only preoccupation, as we shall discover. Among several Elgar memorial concerts that took place in the spring, on the first Saturday in March, Sir Thomas Beecham conducted a concert of Ethel Smyth's music. Her *Mass in D* for four solo voices, choir and orchestra received a vivid performance at the Albert Hall. 'The most remarkable qualities of the Dame Ethel Smyth's *Mass* is the handling and maintenance of a style,' wrote *The Times*' reviewer, was 'the handling and maintenance of a style which had been fully developed in the Viennese *Masses* of 100 years ago, and on which Beethoven had set his seal.'[74] Ethel Smyth later explained this quality herself only a few days later in a speech she gave at the annual dinner of the Critic's Circle at the Savoy Hotel. Speaking on behalf of 'music', she said that her task was difficult, 'because she contrived to hear little or nothing of modern music, and, what made matters worse, she did not enjoy the wireless with overwhelming passion'. Smyth fancied that music was 'supposed to express certain emotions' but this was 'no longer obligatory':

> What was really happening in music to-day was an expression of the massed vigour, drive, ingenuity, and speed which had brought forth racing cars, aeroplanes, and the stratoscope, or whatever the thing was called, in which people went up 10 miles in the air and then dropped down into a crevasse.[75]

If modern composers demanded emotionalism of a kind that did not fit in with young people instead of 'expressing their ideas,' she warned, 'they might be left high and dry.' One of the signs of the speed at which this brave new world was moving was the ever-growing reach of music courtesy of the wireless. At the same event, the BBC's Gladstone Murray spoke in defence of British broadcasting. The period in which it was regarded as a plaything – a miracle – was short-lived, he said. But it was still in what he called a second stage, 'in which broadcasting had not adjusted its relations with other things', despite the growing sense that it had begun to count, and receive 'serious' attention:

> It needed statesmanship and the guidance of experienced and independent critics to come to the third stage when conflicting interests would be adjusted.

Acting as a kind of musical barometer, *The Times*' interest in and coverage of the arts provides an invaluable insight into music as it was heard or witnessed. H. C. Colles was music editor in the 1930s – he was later to become a member of the British Council's Music Advisory Committee – and he ensured that issues of music in British life were extensively reported, from reviews of new music, the music profession, as well as a regular survey, usually published at the end of every year.[76] The December 1933 survey provided a useful summary of the status of British music at the beginning of 1934. Taking the seasonal sales as its cue 'British Music: A Stocktaking' eagerly anticipates a January fortnight organized by the BBC in which 'the British-made goods of our musical renaissance' were to be exhibited at the Queen's Hall. 'Only living composers will be represented, so that no work of Stanford, for instance, or of the composers who, like George Butterworth, were killed in the War will be exhibited . . . But within the limits deliberately adopted there will be ample variety, ranging from the doyen of our composers, Sir Alexander Mackenzie, through Elgar, Delius, and Smyth next in seniority, to the men who, like Lambert and Walton, are only just beginning to hear the footsteps of the following generation.'[77] The epithet afforded Mackenzie by Henry Colles as the elder statesman of British music, recognizes him as the composer of orchestral music, several operas and the author of books on Verdi and Liszt, and who premiered several major works in Britain, including symphonies by Tchaikovsky. He died in April 1935, a much respected and towering figure in British musical life.

Meanwhile, two 'riddles' – propounded at 'musical parties' – on the nature of a national British music and the difference between 'modern' and 'contemporary' music are imagined. *The Times* thus sets the scene for the mood in 1934 British musical life: a keenness for all things new; a pride in the musical renaissance which had begun thirty years before; and the first stirrings of the debate on national music which was to become an increasingly important subject as the year – and, indeed, the decade – progressed. Those riddles were posed in the form of two questions: (1) Which is the older, modern or contemporary music, and when did it begin? (2) Is there a national British music, and, if so, what composers write it?

Answers to these questions were to be presented by a host of writers during the year, Arthur Bliss tackling the subject in an early edition of *The Musical Times*, Constant Lambert in his celebrated *Music, Ho!* and Vaughan Williams in his contribution to the debate in 'National Music'. Colles takes up the subject of a British national music with a discussion of Ralph Vaughan Williams, whose 'challenging' thought was once again to ask whether 'the British composer has something to say that no one of any other age or other country can say', or, further, whether the message 'may not express itself in the same way as in other nations, it may produce a kind of art which other nations cannot appreciate and which will not be reducible to their standards'. Quoting Vaughan Williams from a recent speech, *The Times* then asks whether his fellow countrymen will 'now listen to the British Composer?' 'We hope so,' was the resounding reply, 'for there is something surely wrong with the view . . . that music to be of any value must be something apart from our real life and therefore either old or exotic.'

Acknowledging that though musicians sometimes angrily asserted that the public treated them worse than it treated artists who work in other mediums, this was not necessarily so. 'Possibly in a worse case than the other arts,' music 'is by no means alone in its divorce from vitalizing contact with contemporary appreciation and understanding,' wrote Colles. After all, there was 'more public excitement about an old master than about the most challenging modern painting, while the challenges of modern sculpture are met with abuse and a reinforced determination to hold to the mediocre so long as it speaks the language of a past generation'. As for the theatre, most modern experiments met 'with a dubious response' although it was true that there was less conservatism about literature, 'and both modern architecture and modern decoration have found a warm welcome from their contemporary public'. The simple reason for the backward gaze in music was merely that 'we are all busy and we are all indolent by nature, we know what we like and we like what we know'. However, if Vaughan Williams was right in saying that 'artistic nationalism goes hand in hand with international unity; the great artists are only international and universal in so far as they are also intensely national,' we may, 'if we will attend to it', find 'something lasting and universal in the music of our own day and country'.

Taking up these themes, Arthur Bliss's 'Aspects of Contemporary Music', a series of Royal Institution lectures given during March 1934, was reprinted in *The Musical Times* in May:

> In speaking about contemporary music I am using the word 'contemporary' in a very wide sense. I do not profess to know, nor do I very much care, what is the latest thing in the world of music, or what the best people, for instance, should listen to in 1934.[78]

Rather than a fashion or 'the plaything of a small and possibly vanishing social order', music is 'a great and permanent enrichment of mankind'. According to Bliss, every fifty years or so music receives an additional impetus that shifts the centre of gravity in music. Fifty years before, it was Wagner who was the single dominating figure in the world of music. But in 1934 there existed 'no single personality whom every musician would acknowledge, whether his music were personally sympathetic to him or not'. Bliss intended 'to show up the false alloy and reveal the gold' in music. Whether that gold was to come from a new Russia, a new America or even a 'slowly evolving new England' remained to be seen but, Bliss maintains, the new musical expression over the period under review were not yet 'summed up' in any one composer, though may well be partially expressed by Claude Debussy, Igor Stravinsky and Arnold Schoenberg. But there were others who were shaping the generation of new music, Bliss naming Richard Strauss, Frederick Delius, Edward Elgar and Jean Sibelius, though their influence was 'hardly making itself felt'.

The problem was that the public (in which he modestly included himself) had only 'enough vitality' to enjoy what had been new thirty years before, with music and the other arts leaving ordinary people 'completely uninterested'. The ability to concentrate on a new work requires an attention that a tired brain or a restricted sensibility will not give,' he said. This is not to say that music of the past could no longer be the adventure that music of the present was likely to be, however:

> Music of the past which continues still to move us is full of this quality of adventure, of an unexpected slant from the recognised convention, of a strangeness – call it what you will. It is *that* which gives it life today.

But the pervasiveness of all the new technologies of the time presented a new concern, that 'the present flowing of the world with music', tended to relegate music to becoming 'a mere commodity', which could be turned on 'like water from a tap', with the inevitable result of 'losing the sense of it as a strange and precious experience' in the process. Unthinkable now, Bliss felt that a month of silence every year would soon be necessary, if music was not, through sheer staleness, to lose its beauty and youth:

> It must always be remembered that the mass of music written in any age is deploringly bad, written either by neurasthenics with feelings but no talent, or by conceited pigmies who intend to be heard, though they have nothing to say; or by that large mass of innocuous and laborious mediocrities who believe

that unless they have something to show at the end of each day, they have not justified their short existence.[79]

If the dream of every artist was 'to be set free to accomplish one's own work', then Bliss's concern, too, was the role that music might play in a political system:

> Art at the mercy of a soulless mechanical materialism ceases to exist just as surely as when it is basely used as propaganda for political or social causes . . . One day, perhaps, a Government will use the names of Byrd, Purcell, Delius, Vaughan Williams, as ambassadors, coupled with our dramatists from Shakespeare and Shaw, to form effective ties of friendship with foreign countries, after more outworn methods fail.

It would not be long before an official body did, indeed, use the names of those composers in its efforts at publicizing Britain. Arthur Bliss sat on the British Council's Music Advisory Committee, set up just a few short months after this article was first published and which did precisely that which Bliss imagines in this lecture. By 1939, the Cabinet Office recognized that the most important 'educational work' formed only a part of the British Council's activities, and that since the creation of the music committee, 'British music has been made known more widely by sending British musicians or choirs to perform abroad, by supplying full scores of works by British composers, and by sending gramophone records of English music, which are often used by foreign broadcasting companies'.[80]

Arthur Bliss's lectures helpfully spell out his ideas on nationalism in music and constitute a useful parallel to Vaughan Williams's views. For him, the only 'international music' was jazz, which was 'a subject of the pathologist rather than the musician'. For him, the best of modern music lay largely in those works expressing most vividly the national genius of the composer's country:

> As in the political world, we in England tend violently neither to the right nor to the left, but extract what is needful to us from opposing principles, welding them together; so do English composers adopt a novel kind of equipoise. They have not the academic thoroughness of the German to pursue a train of thought to its logical and often tedious conclusion, nor have they the volatile spirit of the Latin which makes their best music run on so swift and vivacious a course. They are not dramatic like the Italians, nor dancers like the Spanish. What have they then which gives so distinctive a flavour to their music?

Essentially poetic in nature, Bliss was one of the first to recognize that English music is mirrored in the landscape and springs 'from an immense satisfaction in the aesthetic beauty of the land'. This was to become a truism that underpinned many efforts to corral music for political purposes in the years that followed. Summing up, Bliss compared British music with that of the totalitarian states:

> While new ideals have arisen in other countries, and in other arts, English music in bulk has retained an earlier ideal of beauty, not one envisaged in the formal perfection of the machine, nor one based on a purely intellectual integrity, nor on the exciting dynamic possibilities of contemporary life, but an entirely different ideal – a lyric beauty springing from the inspiration of nature.

Though William Walton was, for most of his life, a true European (you can hear the shimmering Mediterranean in the 1939 Violin Concerto), the fact of his domicile was a factor in the cooling reception at home, where he was regarded by some as 'unpatriotic'. But in the 1930s, going abroad for many of the educated English meant time in Italy (under Mussolini), and Germany was still the preferred destination for educating young people of a certain class. That Vaughan Williams, whose 1945 work *The New Commonwealth* was a kind of post-war anthem for a regenerated Europe, shared a pan-Europeanism with Sir Oswald Mosley is fascinating in this post-Brexit world. What connects these viewpoints from across the political divide? Why in 'National Music' does Vaughan Williams make the case for English music, and why did contributors to the *Blackshirt* apparently agree with this Socialist-leaning giant of music?

Notes

1. Griffin, 2004: 210.
2. Lawrence (ed.), 1981: 758.
3. Cardiff, 1991: 195.
4. Edgerton, 2019: 176.
5. Cardiff, 1991: 203.
6. Ibid., 223.
7. Ibid., 203. Ralph Vaughan Williams later intervened to resolve the matter, explaining to listeners the importance of Beethoven's music to the free world.
8. Edgerton, 2019: 174.
9. Ibid., 176–7.
10. 'Quilting Points: An Interview with J. P. E. Harper-Scott', *The Oxford Culture Review*, 10 December 2012 (accessed online 29 July 2020).
11. I have explored this aspect of Wartime composition in *Culture and Propaganda in World War II*.

12 Orwell, 2021: 56.
13 Symons, 1960: 8.
14 Lamb, 1989: 108.
15 Ibid., 110.
16 Potter, 2020: 21–2.
17 Ibid., 61–2.
18 Foreman, 1987: 153.
19 Potter, 2020: 109.
20 Foreman, 1987: 153.
21 Mellers, 1991: 163.
22 Vaughan Williams, 1964: 210.
23 Ibid., 212.
24 Potter, 2020: 72.
25 Ibid., 71.
26 Dobson, 2009: 243–4.
27 See my volume *Culture and Propaganda in World War II* for a full account of the Music Advisory Committee's activities between 1935 and 1945.
28 Hely-Hutchinson, 2002: 114. The manuscript of the Quintet remains unpublished and resides in the Jagger Library of the University of Cape Town.
29 Ibid., 100.
30 Ibid., 101, quoted from Geddes & Bussey, 1991.
31 *BBC Annual* 1935: 53.
32 Ibid.
33 Ibid., 53.
34 Macklin, 2013: 430.
35 Barry, 1934: 94–5.
36 Lloyd, 2014: 25.
37 Ibid., 180.
38 Ibid., 187.
39 Ibid., 109.
40 Ibid., 192.
41 Ibid., 172.
42 Ibid.
43 Powell, 1997: 39.
44 Richards, 2001a: 450–1.
45 Ibid., 454.
46 Quoted in Richards, 2001a: 453.
47 Richards, 2001a: 459.
48 'Jazz Has No Future!', *Radio Times*, 7 September 1928.
49 Lloyd, 2014: 110.

50 Ibid., 111.
51 Ibid., 114.
52 *BBC Annual* 1935: 57.
53 LeMahieu, 1988: 282–3.
54 Quoted in LeMahieu, 1988: 283.
55 LeMahieu, 1982: 391.
56 Lloyd, 2014: 191.
57 *Sunday Referee*, 2 April 1933in a review of the first performance of the work which had taken place on 24 March under Adrian Boult at Broadcasting House, and quoted in Lloyd, 2014: 188. The piece was entitled 'A Lesson to Us All', a pun on the work under review.
58 Lloyd, 2014: 190.
59 Ibid., 189.
60 Woolf, 1942: 115.
61 'Music and the Middlebrow', *Journal of the American Musicological Society*, Volume 73, Issue 2, p. 328.
62 Lloyd, 2014: 193.
63 Typical of the belligerent commentary of the time, *Bolero* was 'A tepid sort of film. Badly acted, poorly directed and badly danced. Only the music of Ravel is impressive' ('Film Notes', by Dave Bennett in the *Daily Worker*, 4 September 1934, p. 4).
64 Lloyd, 2014: 192.
65 LeMahieu, 1982: 376–7.
66 Ibid
67 Cardiff, 1991: 207.
68 Martin, 2016: 169.
69 Lambert, 1966: 9.
70 Vaughan Williams, 1996: v.
71 Lloyd, 2014: 179–80.
72 Lambert, 1966: 133.
73 Mosley, 1998: 292–3.
74 'Dame Ethel Smyth's Music: The Queen at Festival Concert', *The Times*, 5 March 1934, p. 10.
75 'Dame Ethel Smyth on Modern Music: Massed Vigour and Speed', *The Times*, 19 March 1934, p. 12.
76 H. C. Colles was chief music critic of *The Times* from 1911 until his death in 1943.
77 'British Music; A Stocktaking', *The Times*, 30 December 1933, p. 8.
78 'Aspects of Contemporary Music', *The Musical Times*, May 1934, pp. 401–5.
79 Echoing this view in *Music, Ho!*, Constant Lambert also considered 1934 a 'bad' year for British music.
80 National Archives: CAB 24/288/3/0003 – 'Foreign Publicity' – 10 July 1939.

1

New technologies

No commentary on the role of the BBC in 1934 can ignore the work of Jennifer Doctor, whose book on the Corporation and music between 1922 and 1936 sums up the general tone of the period and the effect that the rapidly changing political landscape had on the State broadcaster, and how such forces inevitably led to a reassessment of both the parameters and goals of this 'large, complex and extremely influential organisation':

> By the mid-1930s, many political, economic and sociological characteristics of the decade were already established, although the full consequences of these trends were not to be realised for some time to come. The rapid rise to power of political extremists, and the reactions to this phenomenon, led to tensions and pressures of shifting populations, as well as ideological stances emphasizing national interests, in place of the international cosmopolitanism of the previous decade.[1]

The ever-changing political climate also influenced reassessments of the nature of the new music, performance and the discourse surrounding politics and music. In her extensive treatment of the BBC and ultra-modern music, Doctor points out that, by the mid-1930s, the BBC had become the most important music impresario operating in Britain. 'As transmission capabilities improved and the number of listeners increased, the Corporation's programmes reached the widest audience of any music-disseminating organization in British history', she writes.[2] In his assessment of her work, Jeffrey Richards has also pointed out how, between the Wars, mechanized forms of dissemination such as the gramophone, wireless and cinema superseded live performance as the principal means by which music was consumed by the public. So not only was the BBC the country's biggest impresario, it was also 'the most important disseminator of music and the foremost employer of musicians in Britain'.[3]

In this chapter I explore the widening reach of the new technologies and the increasingly influential place the BBC took in public life, as well as reactions to the new responsibilities it inherited as a result. Because of its growing status, the BBC was highly influential and its Reithian outlook tended to proscribe the kind of music it felt was appropriate for mass audiences. The broadcast of jazz music was always problematic for the Corporation, and listeners could turn to alternatives. As Julie Gardiner has noted in her book on the 1930s, the BBC had no competition for classical music, and if dance and light music were considered unsuitable fare, it could be found on Radio Luxembourg and Radio Normandie to those with the best wireless sets. The BBC was a 'musical juggernaut', the country's largest single employer of musicians, and a powerful patron. Filling in the slots in the Sunday schedule that were not taken up by religious broadcast or serious talks, classical music also pervaded the rest of the week's output. Invited by John Reith in 1931, Adrian Boult took the post of conductor of the BBC Symphony Orchestra, the formation of which 'hugely raised the low bar of orchestral music in Britain,' writes Gardiner, 'and it was soon recognised as one of the finest orchestras in the world'. Boult also oversaw the Corporation's Music Department, its largest, with a staff of fifty-four by 1937. Considered to be somewhat patriarchal by today's standards, John Reith took his role as chairman of the BBC seriously. He took a personal interest, for example, in the establishment of an Empire Orchestra, meeting representatives of musical life in South Africa on a visit to Cape Town in the autumn of 1934. Reith was in this respect a visionary, who could see the potential for music broadcast. Others were not so sure. Sir Thomas Beecham, in rather typical mode, thought that the performance of music through the wireless could be nothing other than 'a ludicrous caricature'. Beecham went on to form the London Philharmonic Orchestra (LPO) the following year. 'The BBC's remit,' writes Gardiner,

> was to broadcast opera, symphonies, chamber and 'modern' music so 'the shepherd on the downs, or the lonely crofter in the furthest Hebrides and, what is equally important the labourer in his squalid tenement in our all too familiar slums, or the lonely invalid on her monotonous couch, may all, in spirit, sit side by side with the patron of the stalls and hear some of the best performance in the world'.[4]

Testimony to the growing influence of broadcasting and timed to coincide with a major Radio exhibition at Olympia, *The Times* carried a twenty-page supplement about the 'living force' of broadcasting in mid-August. Still a 'new medium', broadcasting supplied a 'social need'. The latter aspect was the view of Sir John Reith, whose principle that the BBC was bound to set its course towards 'British mentality at its best' was accepted as the basis of its role in the political life of the country, in which its 'innate tendency to respect opinions on the one hand and in the main to reject *ex parte* statements on the other', was an ideal which the BBC 'is bound to set its course, in artistic as well as in political and social relations'.[5]

But what did this mean in practice in matters of music as well as those of politics? The kind of minutiae that the BBC had to deal with is illustrated in the case of the British Empire Union's complaint about the National Anthem. Having seen a tiny article in the *Daily Mail* which pointed out that the sheet music of the BBC's arrangement of *God Save the King* was 'Made in Germany' (that is, printed and published in Leipzig). Adrian Boult, in his reply to the General Secretary of the British Empire Union (*'Founded April 1915 for British Influence, Labour, Industries – Britain for the British!'*), had to diplomatically, but firmly, point out that the use of Breitkopf & Härtel's publication of the National Anthem was perfectly normal:

> We are probably already aware of all the existing arrangements. On this occasion it was musically desirable to give the arrangement by Sir Granville Bantock, which happens to have been published abroad. We regret that we cannot undertake to confine our programme in any particular to works published in this country. Several very fine works of British composers are published abroad, notably most, if not all, of the works of Delius, and a number by Ethel Smyth and many others.[6]

The decision to use the Bantock arrangement arises from July 1934 when the use of a 'studio nonet' was considered highly unsuitable for broadcasting the National Anthem. Boult thought Bantock's large-scale setting for chorus and orchestra was the best available and suggested to Beecham that it should be used to open the BBC's season. Boult's correspondence with the British Empire Union, which had objected to the use of the Leipzig-published arrangement, highlights the educational role the BBC was also obliged to play when dealing with the rather fanatical types whose views were typical of the well-meaning but ultimately reactionary attitudes prevalent at the time. A leading article in *The Times*' broadcasting number took up the theme:

> The contemporary world is full of fanatics who 'have changed their coats so often that only their shirts are left.' If they can seize the microphone they will, as recent happenings in Vienna have proved, and if they cannot take Broadcasting House by storm they will to their utmost to 'penetrate' it.

The obvious references to the murder of Chancellor Dolfuss in Austria, and to Sir Oswald Mosley (one-time Conservative, Labour and New Party MP, and now the Leader of the British Union of Fascists, or Blackshirts) constituted a warning of what could happen to broadcasting and cultural life and, by extension, to Britain itself:

> Since the original ban on controversial topics was lifted, the BBC has, with evident honesty of purpose, done its best to distribute controversial opportunity with an even hand, the principle being, where politics are concerned, that all considerable parties are given a chance and the Government of the day has the last word. This is just, and can be continued where propaganda is openly avowed.

Does this approach endure? When the BBC is today accused of bias, it is because it has temporarily forgotten this principle, one laid down ninety years or more ago. The broadcasting number is a wide-ranging review of the progress made in twelve years. In nearly forty separate articles, it provides a comprehensive statement on the BBC's current activities as well as what could be expected in the future. Television, still in its nascent phase, was just beginning, and the effects of other new technologies were being felt everywhere. Henry Walford Davies contributed an article on music education, careful to set a limit on the scope of his subject:

> The opportunities to gain a listening understanding of music have been immeasurably increased for all alike by the invention of broadcasting. And though this has momentous reactions upon music-making, both professional and amateur throughout the world... it seems right in this article to confine the term 'musical education' to an education in the understanding of music itself, not in the performance of it.

Adding a further philosophical caveat, he reminds his readers that 'Music only exists when it is heard; it is only heard as it passes, a note or chord at a time; it is only perfectly heard when perfectly performed', deducing 'three obvious morals' from the observation: 'Let all the best possible music be broadcast, let it be broadcast repeatedly, and let the broadcast performance be the best possible.' These 'morals' have underpinned the BBC's entire policy regarding broadcast music. They were evident in the War, when the argument about the broadcast of German music raged, and they continue to form the basis of music broadcasting right up to the present day. Back in 1934 Walford Davies was excited about the potential good the BBC could do: 'if music can be defined with approximate accuracy as beauty made audible, it is thrilling to think what unheard-of good a wise broadcasting policy may now do,' he wrote. An excited response to all the new possibilities afforded by the ever-advancing march of technology, he also added to the BBC's role two further obligations: 'systematically to bring repeated hearings of masterpieces to every willing ear, and to give new music of note and worth its best possible concurrent hearing.' Perhaps conscious of his recent appointment as Master of the King's Musick, he concluded that, to his mind, 'the greatest gift of the discovery of broadcasting so far as music is concerned is the power it brings to all men to select, hear, and rehear the most perfect beauty ever imagined and made audible by men, in which power, enjoyment and education are happily indistinguishable'.[7]

As is to be expected, there were, however, many dissenting views. For some, the wide reach of broadcast music was not entirely to be welcomed. A chapter on technology entitled The Mechanical Stimulus in Constant Lambert's provocative book *Music, Ho!* begins with the sub-heading, The Appalling Popularity of Music. 'What people do in their own homes is fortunately still their own concern, but what takes place in public streets and public-houses concerns us all,' he writes. The loudspeaker was 'little short of a public menace', with one placed in his own neighbourhood 'every hundred yards or so'. Rarely tuned in to different stations, he had no way of avoiding a 'detestable' foxtrot from one end of the street to the other. But it was not the quality of the music that bothered Lambert so much:

> It would not matter so much were the music bad music, but, as the BBC can boast with some satisfaction, most of it is good. We board buses to the strains of Beethoven and drink our beer to the accompaniment of Bach.[8]

It is a 'psalmist's nightmare,' complained Lambert, because since the advent of the gramophone, and especially radio, music of one sort or another was everywhere, all the time, 'in the heavens, the lower parts of the earth, the mountains, the forest and every tree therein'.[9] The all-pervasive reach of music was also having another effect. No less a person than Igor Stravinsky himself recognized that the very fact there was never a time when music was more widely distributed turned 'the great majority into lazy listeners who want to hear only what they already know or can recognize as familiar in type and form; who are afraid of originality and of new experiences in music'. Stravinsky's views were revealed in an interview he gave to the August 1934 edition of *The Gramophone* magazine. For him, that it was now possible to hear music at any time 'by merely turning on a switch or putting on a record' encouraged 'a superficial attitude towards music that threatens to undermine its foundations'. Accustomed to melody and emotion in music, listeners were too ready to condemn the 'new' music because it was not overflowing with ideas that could be recognized at a first hearing:

> The ordinary music-lover has always found it difficult to understand the new music of his own time – to participate in the emotions and appreciate the melodic ideas of any composer who has something original to say and an original way of saying it . . .
>
> Those who have made music themselves understand better, and those who understand hear better. And we shall never have a world in which music is genuinely understood, appreciated, reverenced and loved until listeners become active again – active not only in performance, but in making definite efforts to participate intelligently and receptively in all they hear.[10]

Writing in anticipation of the first British performance – and live broadcast – of Stravinsky's melodrama *Perséphone*, which received its first performance in Paris in April, and was to be conducted by the composer himself with the BBC Symphony Orchestra at the Queen's Hall, on 28 November, M-D. Calvocoressi warned that the work 'was written in the same spirit as his previous works of the austere order'. Calvocoressi advised potential listeners that they should not 'expect the music to aim at illustrating and emphasising the contents of the dialogue'. Rather, Stravinsky was asking us 'not to try to determine the meaning of the music by thinking of the meaning of the words, but to allow the music to tell the story in its own way'. *Perséphone* had already received mixed reviews, with 'a certain musical weekly' brushing it aside despite Nadine Boulanger hailing it as a 'consummate masterpiece':

> Controversy is still rife around it. Maybe, as often happens in such cases, listeners, having heard 'Perséphone', will wonder why so much fuss about a work that is fundamentally simple and should leave no reasonably alert human being in doubt as to what to think of it. The ulterior course of opinion will surely be interesting to watch. No long ago, a conflict of the same order was raging around 'The Rite of Spring'. Now this work has fallen into place; and nobody but the veriest novice or incorrigible fussers would dream of making exaggerated claims for it or of denying its originality and power.[11]

In the introduction to his sweeping survey of music in the twentieth century, Norman Lebrecht writes that the music of the 1930s found the means 'to confront tyranny and subvert it', especially following the banning of Modernism in Soviet Russia from 1935 by Stalin, and the well-documented German case, in which 'Adolf Hitler ended the centrality of German music by banning its best minds and terrorizing most of those who remained into infantile submission.' Indeed, he writes, 'If German music was not heroic and national, said his cultural enforcer Josef Goebbels, it would not exist at all. Setting aside the tragic personal cost for countless musicians and their families, these edicts testified to the power and maturity of modern music. Never before had politicians tried to alter the course of music . . . In the 20th Century, music troubled dictators to the point where they had to control it.' Lebrecht also acknowledges another far-reaching influence that the growth of technology had on music at the time:

> The advent of radio and electrical records in the 1920s altered the state of music from an art that had to be actively played or consciously attended to one that could be passively absorbed while reading a newspaper, making love or brushing teeth. Erick Satie invented 'furniture music' or aural wallpaper that existed but was not noticed. It was the forerunner of Muzak and the ambient sound that cannot be suppressed in hotel elevators and grounded aircraft.[12]

Now a disparaging term, 'Muzak' is synonymous with the blandest 'elevator music' derided the world over. But the word is actually a registered trademark of a company, Muzak Holdings LLC, which still operates a distribution business for recorded 'background' music to retail outlets and other companies from its base in South Carolina where it was founded in 1934. The history of 'Muzak' helps explain the term 'wireless', a word which now has only nostalgic associations. Before the widespread adoption of radio broadcasting as a means of music dissemination, clients of Muzak Holdings and other competitors were able to receive music which was 'piped' through electrical wires. The transmission of music by electrical wires is a curiosity of early-twentieth-century technology. The original technical basis for Muzak was developed in the early 1920s when US patents were granted to one Major General George Owen Squier to transmit and distribute signals over electrical lines. Recognizing the potential for this technology to be used to deliver music to listeners without the use of radio, which at the time was in a nascent state and required fussy and expensive equipment, Squier's early tests were successful enough to deliver music to customers on Staten Island via electrical wires. But as radio, supported by advertising, gradually evolved and overshadowed the delivery of music to private households, he redirected his efforts and founded his own company, concentrating on the commercial market. Adapting the trade name *Kodak*, he called his offering *Muzak* and by 1936 was delivering music to hotels and restaurants in New York City.

A new report on the relative merits of the British and American systems of broadcasting appeared in early 1934. As is still the case, while American broadcasters existed by selling programme time to advertisers, in Britain, the system is responsible to the listeners themselves (the number of whom had risen from 600,000 in 1924 to 6 million or an eighth of the entire population in 1934 and representing an increase of tenfold in ten years), who pay for the programmes through the license fee. Though the report by the US National Association of Broadcasters (NAB) purported to be 'a full and fair discussion of the issues involved', *The Times* felt that it amounted to an 'attack' and gave little merit to the control and operation of broadcasting in Britain:

> The British system, for example, is accused of restricting the discussion of public questions; of denying debate on political issues; of neglecting public events and largely ignoring international happenings; of devoting much time to purely cultural subjects and neglecting social, economic, and political issues; of offering musical programmes inferior to those of America; of generally omitting to discuss 'up to the minute' problems; of becoming, under a system of censorship, a colourless and wasteful means of mass communication; of becoming 'an agency of political mugwumpery'; of being guilty of continuous autocratic censorship; and, in fact, of being a Government bureaucracy removed from any real contact with the great body of listeners.[13]

The assertion by the NAB that there was little in the way of the broadcasting of public events, and few international broadcasts, is a position entirely refuted by *The Times*, which pointed out that the report took 'little account' of British tastes. Listeners could be excused for preferring a relay from abroad of a new Strauss opera to the broadcast of a political speech in a foreign tongue, for example. The comment on music is, for *The Times*, particularly questionable, and it also refuted the report's assertion that American programmes showed 'definite superiority in the quality of the musical organizations presented, in the calibre and variety of programmes brought to American listeners from foreign countries . . . and in the wealth and variety of entertainment presented':

> Yet it [the NAB] complains that there is in British programmes more 'serious' music, very little dance music, and 'more music as a whole'. It is evidently no merit in the eyes of the National Association of Broadcasters that the musical activity of the BBC includes the creation of a national orchestra and several other orchestra and choruses in various parts of the country.

Aimed at American and Canadian interests, the NAB's report was surely a polemic for the preference for *commercial* broadcasting where the creation of revenue was paramount rather than the provision of a public service. It was probably not meant as a criticism of British broadcasting *per se* but served as a way of convincing American policymakers that a profit-based system was to be preferred. The long list of complaints and objections, with the benefit of hindsight, may now seem like a list of problems that may be fairly applied to American broadcasting, notwithstanding the fifty plus years of commercial broadcasting in Britain. The BBC's guiding principle, especially regarding broadcast music, has always been one of quality: only the best music from the best composers performed to the highest standards, a position that it was able to uphold even during the War.

Back in Britain, at the Olympia Radio Exhibition, £30 million worth of equipment was sold, a huge figure for the time. The event also afforded the nascent Performing Right Society (PRS) to negotiate terms with the BBC. Fees payable to the PRS by the BBC were based on the number of paid licences (6,445,000 in 1934, up from 5,150,000 in 1932 and 5,890,000 in 1933). In order to calculate the correct figure, several bases were used, all resulting in a fee of about £100,000.[14] Net license fee receipts for 1934 were just over £1.7 million and at least one MP was keen to point out the contrast between this figure and the less-than-£100,000 agreed by the two organizations, which was 'to be divided among composers, authors, and music publishers, British and foreign, on whom the BBC depends for so much of its raw material' and 'which the BBC broadcasts so lavishly and without which all its stations would be silent for many hours of the day'.[15]

Questions of copyright and performers' rights were especially ascendant during 1934. This was an effect of the increasing volume of sound film, recording and broadcasting. In May, Phonographic Performance Ltd. was established following a test case against a Bristol coffee shop and the record companies Decca and EMI (then called The Gramophone Company). Stephen Carwardine & Co., proprietors of the coffee shop, had been entertaining its clients by playing the LSO's 1931 recording of Auber's overture, *The Black Domino*.[16] Acting on behalf of the record companies, Sir Stafford Cripps argued it was against the law to play the record in public without first receiving permission from the copyright owners, and that a fee for the broadcasting or public performance of recordings should be payable. The judge agreed, and the legal principle of obtaining a license was established as an important precedent. To carry out this licensing role, EMI and Decca formed PPL after the case, which opened its first office in London's Wigmore Street in May. The company collected its first million within a year. By 2004, it was collecting over £150 million annually.

Another test case regarding copyright appeared before the Court of Appeal between Hawkes & Son (London) Ltd. (predecessors to the music publishers

Boosey & Hawkes) and Paramount Film Services Ltd. concerning the use of *Colonel Bogey* which appeared in a newsreel film of a school march-past at the Royal Hospital School in Holbrook, Suffolk. The familiar work (of just four minutes' duration) was not featured in its entirety: just 20 seconds was used. This did not breach the terms of the 1911 Copyright Act in the original judgement. On appeal, the case was acknowledged as a 'test action', and set an important precedent, 'as the defendants claimed the right to record on a sound film music which formed part of an incident which could be described as news without the consent of the owner of the copyright'. Fair Use, as the principle is now known, was the key. The defendants relied on the term 'newspaper summary' but, it was acknowledged, 'the sound film in question was neither a newspaper nor a summary'. In this case, the film of the 'incident' was made to show what happened at the opening of the school by the Prince of Wales rather than 'to reproduce the "Colonel Bogey" march". 'The function of the news reel and the journalist were identical and they should be equally protected,' came the argument.[17]

Meanwhile, EMI was also working with another partner in its early experimentation with the fledgling television industry. Between 1932 and 1934, it had been EMI's habit to conduct electronic television demonstrations in private. Compared to the progress RCA was making on the other side of the Atlantic, EMI's experiments were proving relatively disappointing. In the early part of 1934, EMI partnered with Marconi Wireless and Telegraph (MWT) to form the Marconi-EMI Television Company, the amalgamation allowing EMI to use RCA's patents, and by April 1934, after further modifications, Marconi-EMI's experimental camera, the 'Emitron', was yielding vastly better pictures than it had been able to achieve before. From its earliest beginnings, when the first public demonstration by Baird had taken place in 1925, by the 1930s the design and appearance of the television set 'played a major role' in its acceptance in the home, writes Deborah Chambers. At first, the screens were tiny, but the adoption was another pioneering aspect of British broadcasting, and by September 1939 – when television transmissions were suspended for the 'duration' – there were significantly more sets in use in Britain than either Germany or the United States. Though Britain took the lead in television manufacture in the 1930s, 'the sale of television receivers was inevitably slow in the initial years of television broadcasting. Less than 400 sets were available to receive the new service in 1936 as the range of transmission from Alexandra Palace was only 30 miles', but by the start of the War, 23,000 were in use.[18]

'Television still persists in its role as the most fugitive of all the electrical arts', ran a *Times* editorial in its August broadcasting number. Recognizing that 'pictures of much greater detail and stability' would be necessary before the public would respond and make the new medium popular, it reminded that 'a full appreciation of the great technical difficulties of its problems need not blind us to the substantial progress which has been made in recent years'.[19] The editorial refers to Professor E. V. Appleton's article on television in the supplement. Recognizing the work of John Logie Baird, whose early progress convinced the Postmaster General to 'warrant the introduction of experimental transmission' from 30 September 1929, five years on, a committee of experts and officials was set up in May 1934 to consider the progress of television in Britain. Made up of seven members of the Post Office and the BBC, the committee was instructed to advise the Postmaster General on the relative merits of the various television systems and on the conditions under which a public service might be provided. 'One of the problems considered by this committee for solution will doubtless be that of the development of a high-definition ultra-short wave television service comparable with that already provided by the BBC for the broadcasting on the long and medium wave-lengths,' wrote Appleton. In August, however, the committee had yet to report and Appleton reserved judgement: 'it would seem improper at the moment to comment on the matter further,' he wrote.[20] While the committee got to work, EMI researchers 'developed and demonstrated a complete and entirely successful system of high-definition television of undoubted entertainment value', which included 'both transmission, or broadcasting; and reception by sets suitable for use in the home'. Receiving much applause from its shareholders at this news at the AGM in November, EMI could also report that 'the satisfactory results so far obtained are of such a nature as to indicate that the story of television, like that of the broadcasting of sound, will be one of constant and sure advance'. All that remained was to wait for the action to be taken by the Postmaster General 'as a result of the committee's report', the publication of which would 'presumably be followed by the equipment of transmitting stations and the sale of television sets to the public'.[21] The Selsdon Committee finally reported its findings at the end of January 1935, and an announcement was made that two competing systems of television for the London High-Definition TV Service, Baird and Marconi-EMI, were to run side by side for six months, on alternate days. In late 1936, following the establishment of the BBC's regular service of the world's first high-definition TV service on 2 November from Alexandra Palace, EMI's system was eventually formally adopted after just two months, the Baird system proving 'troublesome for actors, directors, and other staff to use in the studio', despite is comparable picture quality.[22]

Muzak, and now Television. What other exciting technological developments were in store for an eager public in 1934? I will leave Hubert Foss to describe another experiment with technology and music, which he recalls in an early history of the London Symphony Orchestra:

> In the autumn of 1934 the Orchestra were approached by Vladimir Shavitch to co-operate in a new and peculiar method of opera presentation, the idea being to pre-record the orchestral score and chorus parts, so that all the conductor had to do in performance was to synchronise the singers with the gramophone records. In this way Shavitch believed the opera could be brought to small provincial towns without incurring heavy financial loss. The Directors were interested, but dubious, especially when the original prospect to record *Carmen* dwindled to nothing more than the Garden scene from *Faust*. At this stage the Directors began to wonder who the soloists would be, deeming it 'inadvisable for the Orchestra to be connected with a mediocre cast'. Shavitch then broke with the LSO and enlisted instead the support of Beecham and the LPO, with whose help the experiment with the Faust excerpt was performed at a London theatre in February 1935. Shavitch called the idea the 'Synchrosound System', but the Musical Times felt that 'this is too big a mouthful for these hurrying days. Let's make it snappy and call in the Synk'. It seems, however, that the 'Synk' sank, for nothing more was heard of it.[23]

Surely ordinary orchestral players found this prospect even more worrying. 'The musical profession has been suffering most severely of recent years from mechanical reproduction,' wrote a contributor to the BUF's *Blackshirt* who believed that the advance of technology was simply depriving musicians of work. This 'menace' to the livelihood of thousands revealed the need for effective organization: only fascism would 'bring this organisation into existence and grant musicians means of protecting their interests, and advancing British music'.[24] This was the serious side to developments in new methods of distribution, and now the advance of technology was displacing musicians in yet another way. In another experiment with technology, Harvey Grace, a regular contributor to *The Listener*, wrote in the 7 November issue extolling the merits that the teaching of music via wireless could bestow on 'the adult pupil'. The idea had evidently been experimented with in America for two or three months, but Percy Scholes disagreed with Grace for a variety of reasons, not least the deprivation of an income for music teachers that wireless teaching would eventuate. However, the musical advisors of the US National Broadcasting Corporation admitted that the short experiment had also shown that radio was not a possible medium for instruction'.[25]

But in 1934 there was still some sense of marvel at the innovations of the wireless. At a ceremony giving Sir Walford Davies the freedom of his native Oswestry, tribute was made to his broadcasting work. The Master of the King's Musick replied that 'wireless had done three things – it had brought the greatest music in the world to be heard in the loneliest corners of the world, it brought tens of millions into an amazing friendship, and people could hear and take part in the happenings of the world'.[26] Not everyone shared the same enthusiasm, however. Though he had nothing against the BBC *per se*, Sir Thomas Beecham was among those that doubted the BBC's role, in particular its monopoly, 'which had been created by the last Tory government through the means of a Charter'. Speaking at the Leeds Luncheon Club in early October, he claimed that 'The BBC was not a means of communicating views and opinions on politics, science or religion, but was really an entertainment bureau'. An analysis of programme output across the year could show that foreign programming and music made up 90 per cent of what was broadcast. 'That most gigantic musical entertainment bureau was not only operating free on income-tax, but was given by the state 6s from each 10s license for the purpose of carrying on its entertainment,' Beecham complained:

> The inevitable result of creating a monopoly would be, if it were continued, that in 20 years' time not a single musical institution in this country would exist, except, perhaps, for some society providing music in a cellar in London. All would be dependent upon the mechanical radio; would get their music second-hand or third-hand, and gradually the race of artists and conductors would die away. Whereas the State was helping the BBC, it was killing true music by insisting on the imposition of the entertainment tax.[27]

Sir Thomas launched another lunchtime assault on the BBC two months later. By criticizing the British broadcasting system, once again he was at pains to point out that he was not an opponent of broadcasting *per se*. But the conversion of a company into a 'semi-state organization' was 'not the right way to do it'. Not that he approved of the American or Continental systems either. But the BBC was 'unique in the world'. He had no problem with the organization itself, which was 'an institution of very peculiar character' and one which was staffed by some 'excellent friends' of his. No, his criticism was directed towards the State, which had endowed the BBC 'with certain powers that exceeded the measure and limit of such authority as it should be endowed with, and were beyond the power of any single organization in the world to administer in the national interests as regards music'. But, acknowledged Beecham, in the last six or seven years there had been what he reluctantly called an 'uplift' in the condition of British musical life:

> Some people would say it was part of the recovery from the aftermath of excessive frivolity which followed the War, and others would attribute it all to the all-beneficent, all-powerful, and all-pervading influence of their friends and broadcasters.

The lunch was held in Beecham's honour as well as that of the LPO, which over the previous two years 'had achieved a position that entitled it to rank at least with any great orchestra in the world,' said Beecham. 'Half London's musical world' was present at the lunch, at least some of the big financial names and patrons. Besides Malcolm Sargent, Walter Runciman, Lady Cunard, Lord Esher, Samuel Courtauld, Ernest Makower and his wife and Roger Eckersley were also present.[28] That 'uplift' in British musical life care of the BBC can be shown in *The Times'* broadcasting review of the year, published at the end of December. During the year the BBC, it reported, had given a main season of fourteen public symphony concerts, with a 'very large' number of 'interesting' works included in its Sunday evening symphony concerts. In addition, six concerts of the London Music Festival were given in May – three under Adrian Boult, two under Bruno Walter and one under Felix Weingartner. As well as chamber concerts given in the Concert Hall at Broadcasting House, a Proms season of forty-nine concerts was 'outstandingly successful' with audiences greater than at any time in its forty years' history. The January festival of six concerts of British music 'aroused much interest' and in all, more than 500 orchestral concerts were broadcast during the year, with a large number of chamber concerts, recitals and ballad concerts also given.[29]

An impressive record for live music. Of course, the BBC was also massively dependent on recorded music. By September 1933 a library of 25,000 records had been built up by 'a separate staff of programme builders, all of them experienced musicians with a knowledge of the full range of recorded music'. The BBC's policy was to keep two copies of every record, 'one for rehearsal, and one for transmission', though both copies were used in any transmission 'where the tune takes up two sides of the record, for it is possible by accurate timing and fading from record to record to play through, for example, a movement of a symphony, without break'.[30] This was, of course, when records were produced on shellac, and rotated at 78 rpm. Confining himself to matters of entertainment in his contribution to *The Times'* broadcasting number, author Christopher Stone could already acknowledge that from the beginning, the gramophone record was both the chief standby and chief menace of broadcasting. 'In times of peace, whatever may be the political and cultural importance of radio, its bread-and-butter functions are to provide news and entertainments,' he wrote, without elaborating on the function of radio broadcasting in times of war. 'The provision of news is a matter of adjustment within the existing purveyors of this commodity; the provision of entertainment is a matter of adjustment with the recording industry,' he writes. But why should he mention peacetime? By mid-1934, perhaps, the radio was also being considered as a tool of conflict.[31]

Indeed, in Germany, this was already the case. The reorganization of German broadcasting during 1933 had shown just how quickly Propaganda Minister Josef Goebbels was prepared to move on broadcasting, a potential tool for propaganda which he felt no one else had yet fully exploited. In July 1933 Eugen Hadamovsky, who had been a senior official of the *Reichsrundfunkgesellschaft*, was appointed its General-Director, in control of the entire German broadcasting system, and responsible only to Goebbels himself. Former directors and employees of the company were retired on the basis of the new regulations which permitted 'the dismissal of all public servants who were Jewish, alleged to be incompetent, or politically suspect'. Hadamovsky spelt out his aims explicitly, his task 'to make of broadcasting a sharp and reliable weapon for the government'. As a result, 'in less than a year German broadcasting has changed from an aggregation of privately owned companies loosely bound to a point above, into a publicly owned system of iron-bound centralization, taking instructions from the Minister of Propaganda himself,' reports the 1934 BBC Yearbook:

> The broadcasting system was in fact then, as it is now and was in the intermediate stages, an accurate enough parallel to the political organization of the Reich. Then it exhibited all the weaknesses, and all the variety, of a federal structure with considerable provincial autonomy; now it reflects in some detail the political organization of the Third Reich.[32]

In earlier guidelines were the instructions 'to respect the opinions of others; to avoid hurtful or contemptuous remarks about other states and peoples; and the statement that broadcasting served no party, admitted no propaganda.' Under Hadamovsky, this was no longer to be the case, notes the Yearbook, choosing to remain an observer at this stage. I tackle other British responses to political developments in Germany in Chapter 6. Among those that had left German broadcasting and joined other exiles in Britain was Ernst Schoen (1894–1960), composer and music theorist, and formerly programme manager of the Frankfurt Broadcasting Station, a post he held from 1929 until removed by the Nazis. A friend of Walter Benjamin since their schooldays, and a former student of Ferruccio Busoni and Edgard Vàrese, his philosophy at Frankfurt had been to 'give every listener what he wants, and even a bit more (namely, of that which *we* want)'. Schoen had written about his ideas in an essay 'Musical Entertainment by Means of Radio' in the journal, *Anbruch*. Beginning with the illusion that radio provided an opportunity to impart culture, and that what the listener merely wanted was 'entertainment', Radio Frankfurt, which was a pioneer and had a Europe-wide reputation, subtly changed the role that 'entertainment' played:

> What had previously been a decorative ornament supplementing the serious programme . . . would now have to be elevated out of the stale atmosphere of amusement into a well-ventilated, loose, and witty topicality, fashioned into a structure in which the most varied elements could be related to one another in a positive way.[33]

But what was Germany's loss was the BBC's (and, hence, the British public's) gain, in that the controller of one of Europe's most innovative and pioneering radio operations, and which had set so many high standards, was now helping to do just the same in Britain. For example, in the 1934 *Yearbook*, Schoen was able to share the experience of German broadcasting:

> There are two kinds of [broadcast] transmission cherished by all classes of listeners, viz. sport reports, which are statements of a sensational character, and light music, which is an emotional sensation. Provided always that they are not definitely boring, lectures may be acceptable as statements, if their topic is above discussion, as, for instance, in poetry, in language lessons, or in certain governmental and political speeches, and do not excite question or answer. Serious music, too, may be reckoned among the emotional sensations, as far as it is already known to the listener and does not demand a special mental effort and therefore the atmosphere of a social gathering of specially interested people.

Beginning as a technical experiment, broadcasting in Germany and elsewhere did not begin as a creative work with a style of its own, writes Schoen, but would always remain 'not an end but a means'. Broadcasting from Italian opera houses was the most appreciated because German opera directors had long resisted even the most persuasive money offers of the broadcasters. Furthermore, the ugliness of a dangling microphone in front of beautiful scenery and 'the distortion of musical beauty by the imperfect means of radio transmission', as well as, paradoxically, the presumable loss of subscribers through the competition of broadcasting, made the transmission of operas 'absolutely out of the question', for German directors. But times had changed:

> It was a big event in the history of German broadcasting when the performance of all the opera houses became available for broadcasting. It was a big event when 'Parsifal' was transmitted for the first time, a big event when Toscanini's Berlin performance of 'Aida' was radiated all over the country, when the opera performances of Bayreuth and Salzburg became familiar to every listener. And ever since then, all these transmissions, as well as those of the Scala and other Italian opera stages, have met with the appreciation of those thousands of people in more or less financial distress who form the audience of this sort of grand opera and never seem to become tired of it.[34]

For Schoen, broadcast operas should be 'strictly limited to the best of their kind in matter and performance', and regarded as *reported* art 'comparable to the reproduction of pictures in a book', rather than artistic productions in their own right.

Schoen also contributed another highly nuanced viewpoint the following year. Together with two other giants of musical criticism, Ernest Newman and Adrian Boult, he considers the whole question of broadcast music. Should music be especially written, asks Newman. Or arranged, asks Schoen. And what of the balances and control of a broadcast work – and the 'adaptation' for radio that may be required as a result? The latter was Boult's concern, as the head of music at the BBC, and although he admitted that much had been written on the performance of music and the differences between the concert hall and the microphone, for him the question of 'balance and control' represented and symbolized all the issues relating to broadcast music. For him, the art of control meant 'cutting off' the top of the fortissimos while strengthening the bottom of the pianissimos so that the sound could be adequately conveyed to the listener via loudspeaker. But the job couldn't be left to a mere technician. The services of a 'thoroughly capable musician' are required so that, for example, a crescendo can be tempered accurately 'to bring the true climax just inside the limits which are imposed on him'. As for balance in the orchestra, Boult asserts that in four years of broadcast music he could not remember 'a single occasion' on which the view of the 'balance-man' conflicted with his own, thereby ensuring the audibility of even the quietest instrumental passages, with any 'faking' restricted to the mixing of the products of several microphones together to produce a perfect 'balance'.[35]

Ernst Schoen, meanwhile, applied himself to the question of whether music should be specially arranged for broadcasting, to which he is tempted to answer simply, at the outset, No! However, after a long discussion on the merits of broadcasting music at all, in the present stage of technical development[36] Schoen was in favour of 'definite selection and even of a ruthless adaptation' of music for broadcasting purposes, for both formal and social reasons. For him, it was a question of presenting music in a way that rescued 'the man on the street' from being kept down by the forces of commercialism and entertainment. His solution was to consider ways in which 'reconsideration and re-evaluation' could enable music to play its part in making the man on the street 'fit for the world'. Among those ways was the selection of the best works, *parts* of the best works (a difficult task but not all a matter of 'taste'), careful use of 'light' music, the discussion of musical technique and its place in the broader sociological context. His list, in fact, presents a standard that can be recognized in the best of the music broadcasting that remains today: it is thus a kind of manifesto.[37]

Ernest Newman asks whether music should be specially written. 'There are few questions in this world to which a plain answer is "Yes" or "No" can be given,' he begins. But 'while the question of writing music purely and simply for wireless is full of interesting theoretical possibilities', he concludes that 'it is outside the range of practical politics'. Television was yet to help us get over the obstacle of seeing the action of opera, it was true, but ten years' evolution of television 'of the same scope and character of radio' would see to that. It was, indeed, a world of possibilities for writers like Newman to address.[38]

Not only did the BBC Yearbook (from 1935, the BBC Annual) lay down some of the technicalities of broadcasting and various statistical analyses of listenership, but it also gave the chance for the corporation to discuss several related subjects, ranging in the 1934 Yearbook from patronage in the arts to radio drama to broadcasting in rural India on the Empire Service. While not necessarily representing the views of the BBC, the contribution on the former subject began with a short introduction by the editor:

> Broadcasting not only in this country but in most others has, in the last ten years, acquired a peculiar position with respect to the Arts and the artist. Its public service character and its scale of operation naturally suggest the question of whether, and to what extent, the patronage of the Arts – in the old service of patronage, which linked a Prince Esterhazy with a Haydn – has become incumbent upon it.

The contributor's starting point was, simply, that 'Man shall not live by bread alone', with the BBC's job in the listeners' minds to provide entertainment. 'We are going through a hard time: you should therefore do your best to amuse us, so that we may forget our miseries'. Here is an acknowledgement of the dire economic conditions in which ordinary people were struggling to make ends meet. For the BBC, however, a policy of including great music, poetry, drama and prose went beyond giving the listening public something which might help it to 'rise clear of those miseries'. And although the policy had 'brought much abuse upon the BBC', in the author's opinion it was a policy that was bound to triumph, with the possibilities of music allowing it to go much further, for throughout the year the listener is provided with an opportunity to hear practically all the major classical works, as well as a representative selection of modern music.

But rather than merely being 'as much as anybody ought to expect', the BBC, in fact, also had a duty to music itself as well as to its millions of listeners, in that while presenting the music of composers 'long since dead' should it not also do something for new music?

> Most of the classical music which has now passed into the 'common heritage' of the world was written by men who enjoyed (and suffered) the benefits of patronage. Such patronage – whatever the penalties it executed in return – gave those men a certain immunity from the more mundane cares of this life. It had a further advantage in that it provided an often necessary goad to composition – for it is an outworn fallacy that genius thrives best in a garret or that it has only to whistle and divine music will come tumbling out of the skies. Sometimes that patronage, as in the case of Bach, was provided by the Church; sometimes, as in the case of Haydn, by a private person. But whoever provided it, provided thereby an incentive quite denied to the composers of the present day. And who shall say what glorious music that denial has cost us?

In a democratic age, neither church, nor 'court' or state, nor private person was in a position to provide any worthwhile patronage, with the State in particular 'too remote and impersonal' for the purpose. Only one organization had the wealth, the standard of good taste 'necessary in a wise patron', as well as the means to provide patronage, in a country which, it is admitted, had 'a wealth of potential music such as has scarcely been equalled in our history'. The 'courage and foresight' of the BBC to broadcast music of only the highest possible standard could surely be extended to patronage, 'the most ideal aspect' of the question. And while broadcasting may well have caused the demise of some second-rate choral and orchestral societies, the BBC did well 'not to respond to the plea for a direct and substantial patronage of amateur music-making':

> The right kind of musical amateur will not be prevented by wireless from making music, and the wrong kind ought not to be encouraged. As for the broadcasting

of local amateur effort, there is not the slightest excuse for multiplying a small, suffering audience into a vast one.

Besides poetry, perhaps, music could benefit from patronage from the BBC, for certainly 'no one else will – or can', and it would be 'fitting' if the role of patron could pass into the BBC's hands. As one of the greatest distributors of the arts, if most of what the BBC brought into the home was drawn from the old world, and with broadcasting being somewhat of a link between the old and the new worlds, and able to combine the best of both by living in the new world and fetching its life from the old, then why not do the same for today? Certainly, it possessed the 'courage and the power' to do something for patronage, since it would be impossible to imagine programmes without those great composers who depended on patronage. 'Is it not decent and reasonable, therefore, that the BBC should do something towards ensuring for future generations as noble an expression of our day as the music of those great masters was of theirs?'[39]

Taking up the subject of Art and Patronage in the following year, Percy Wyndham Lewis makes the case wittily for corporate patronage of the arts – especially by the BBC – in the unlikelihood of any single individual or, God forbid, the State taking up the role. There was, he argued, hardly anyone left in a condition to advance to the 'patron' stage of his personal evolution, and with the individual therefore 'out of the count', it remained to look only to the State or to corporate patronage, with the latter appearing 'to have a great advantage', since a State composed of 'highly cultivated and enlightened oligarchs', though admirable, was no longer possible. Indeed, when discussing State patronage, he writes, one must only think of 'propagandist oligarchs, such as exist at present in Russia', as indifferent to the values of art as a primitive military despotism, or far more so. An Anglo-Saxon imitation would see Upton Sinclairs or Stafford Crippses decreeing the sort of books that should be written, music composed or pictures painted. Whether desirable or not as pure politics, who could doubt that this form of reformist political fanaticism would be more deadly than Puritanism where art is concerned?

No! The greatness of pre-war (that is, pre-1914) figures such as Elgar or Beethoven represents 'an order of prestige', something which is 'apt to interfere with the smooth working of materialist dogma', be it the materialism of post-war democracy or the 'dialectical' materialism of the Marxist dictatorship:

> Yet great governments, and great nations, *quarrel* over artists, inconsistently enough: witness the hullabaloo about Hindemith and Furtwängler. Anyone would have supposed, to listen to the indignant outcries of the world press, that

the egregious Teuton had touched the most sensitive spot in the democratic bosom in laying hands upon *an artist*, a conductor of an orchestra – that *art* was a thing at all costs to be preserved, respected, and cherished, and kept inviolate from all interference from without, whether political or other.

And with the BBC just about the only large-scale British institution free from the mores of both commerce and politics meant that the public had been treated like a gentleman, 'and by its response to such treatment the public will show whether it deserves to be treated like a gentleman, or prefers to be approached as if it were some sort of half-wit sub-man':

> It has set a splendid example of what the Englishman, left to himself, can accomplish, and must have had to stand out very firmly against pressure from great interests, anxious to have a fat finger in this tremendous aerial pie.[40]

Indeed, 'The English are to-day the only nation in the world upholding not merely liberty and justice, but culture, and even its officials keep their integrity in spite of memories of war graft,' writes CRW Nevison in a companion article. 'The BBC stands today as the greatest patron of non-stop music, entertainment, commentary, information, and education, utterly indifferent to the exploiters of commerce, the political intriguers, the dictators of artistic fashions, the critics or impresarios of cliques or coteries,' writes Nevison.

> The English, through their genius for compromise in a world to-day top-sided and unbalanced through blind extremists or reactionaries, fanatics or opportunists, have set an example through the BBC of what patronage should be that makes the medieval Church appear limited in its scope by comparison.

Artists in all countries, he claims, are today giving proof of this bewilderment, with the majority accepting anything 'without choice or criticism' and a minority who 'despise public opinion, who never believe the printed word even if true ... who suspect all artists of insincerity or worse, with the inevitable result that *poseurs* and the misunderstood and the rare are exaggerated, and importance is placed upon the incomprehensible to satisfy an intellectual superiority'. Musicians and writers in particular show an overwhelming pessimism, with 'the literary man' abandoning art for 'the glorification of crime and thrills' and composers becoming 'increasingly esoteric and cacophonic', while despairing of a public that is hypnotized by easy rhythm and catchy melodies:

> It is possible on many foreign stations to realize what can happen to art if linked with commercialism. I do not say that artists of fame, established and rich already – as in America, where fantastic sums are handed out by commerce to the

successful. On the other hand, in Russia and Germany, where State has replaced all standards, artists have deteriorated into either propagandists or toadies, and recent events in Germany have proved at what cost politicians interfere with and dictate to an artist, and in Russia how quickly a nation loses face through compelling the artist to express but one theme, the glory of mechanization and the regimentation of humanity.[41]

In contrast to developments in both Nazi Germany and the Soviet Union, however, as a patron of the arts, the BBC had managed to remain very British, in making a compromise between officialdom, semi-officialdom and commercialism. 'Though governmental, it is independent; though official, it neither dictates nor is dictated to; and in the sphere of economics and politics, to the surprise of all, even the extremists, it has not entirely upheld capitalism or favoured socialism.' A comparison of European broadcasting also appeared in the 1935 BBC Annual entitled the 'Percentage Allocation of Time to the Various Programme Classes in Fifteen European Countries'. A sophisticated colour chart reveals Britain to be highly placed in the time devoted to music, though with a noticeably small concentration on opera compared to other countries. With about 70 per cent of broadcast time devoted to music (including non-'serious' music), and only Belgium and Holland devoting more time to it, the BBC was unique as an organization, and its remit much broader. There was also an Empire to service, a matter in which John Reith took a personal interest. A new orchestra was to be formed especially for use in Empire programming and the BBC was 'particularly anxious to give prominence to a wide range of musical compositions, including those of the Dominions and Colonies'. To this end, Eric Fogg, who had been recently appointed as music director for the Empire Orchestra, newly established specifically to broadcast on the shortwave Empire Service, wrote to F. Benicke Hart of the Conservatory of Music in Melbourne, W. H. Bell of the South African College of Music in Cape Town and Dr Vogt of the Toronto Conservatory of Music as well as to his equivalent in New Zealand with the purpose of seeking out composers, and forwarding publishers catalogues of chamber music and piano pieces. Canadian Leo Smith's music represented the bulk of the Canadian contribution, which was to be broadcast in February (though the Toronto Conservatory regretted to say that Dr Vogt had died in 1926). John Reith was in the fortunate position of being in Cape Town from September, and entered negotiations with I. C. Silberbauer of the South African office of the PRS, who pointed out that though it was better for a country to be unilingual, he was sure that South Africa would remain bilingual and that the most complete bilingualism possible was desirable:

> Certain people suggest that Afrikaans will not be a permanent language. I differ here for the reasons (a) it is the language of the Church of the majority of the European population of the country, (b) it is a very 'friendly' language, and (c) it undoubtedly lends itself to verse and light literature. It has been suggested to me that cultural development will be on parallel rather than bilingual lines, but I do not feel competent to express an opinion on this point.[42]

On the question of local compositions, Silberbauer said that he had been 'to some trouble' to interest overseas publishers in South African compositions. 'So far these have been mainly of light or dance music and progress has been slow,' he said, and though there was a 'considerable output of songs in Afrikaans 'composers and lyric writers suffer from the disadvantage of Afrikaans being confined almost entirely to this Country'. Reith replied that he had drawn the same conclusions from his own observations 'both before coming here and from conversations since arrival'. He imagined that many people would regret cultural development on what he called parallel lines. 'I have heard many objections to segregation in respect of language and presumably these would apply still more to culture generally,' he wrote. 'I am sure you will find the BBC interested in the popularisation of South African music. We have always been anxious to do things of this sort.' Reith sent copies of the correspondence ahead to Eric Fogg at Broadcasting House before he left Cape Town in early November with a request that he should correspond directly with Cape Town. Silberbauer was once again in touch on 7 December, reporting on a meeting he had had with the musical editor of *Die Burger* ('the principal Afrikaans medium newspaper') in which they had agreed 'that the broadcasting in England of programmes by South African composers will be a wonderful encouragement to all interested in the progress of music in this country'. Silberbauer thought that because South Africans were 'somewhat inclined to the view that their fellow countrymen are incapable of important artistic production', the effect of a BBC broadcast in England of a purely South African programme should be very good:

> Whether the whole of the programme of music by Afrikaans composers, or even only a proportion be such, the willingness of the British Broadcasting Corporation to broadcast the works will undoubtedly be very highly appreciated by the Afrikaans speaking section of the community of this Country.[43]

The music of both the Principal of the South African College of Music, William Henry Bell, as well as Vice Principal, Collin Taylor (1881–1973), 'would also have to be considered'. W. H. Bell (1873–1946) was a contemporary of both Holst and Vaughan Williams and had emigrated to South Africa in 1912. The composer of five symphonies and many other works for orchestra as well as a considerable amount of other works remains, like many British composers who worked abroad during the period, largely forgotten. Victor Hely-Hutchinson, writing in 1934, explained the 'unfortunate' phenomenon that musicians working in remote communities rarely received the world's attention they deserve from the world at large, and furthermore, musicians in larger centres are thus often ignorant of the magnificent work done by pioneers 'who blaze the musical trail abroad'. If one such pioneer, W. H. Bell, were teaching and composing in England he would be a national figure. But his residence in Cape Town ensured that the importance of his work was largely overlooked:

> As with the man, so with his music. It displays an abundance – almost a plethora – of invention; it is energetic and adventurous; it is copious and varied; it is absolutely sincere. His taste in music is catholic, and accordingly his style of composition disdains neither classical nor modern devices, but welds them into a whole stamped with an individuality and a mastery of his medium that is unmistakably 'Bell'. His music typifies the man, and while its intrinsic value is great, it also has value as the artistic expression of one to whom, for his work in spreading the gospel of music, musicians owe a debt far greater than they realise. The world of music has need for more men like him.[44]

As Jenny Doctor has explored, in July the official duties of the BBC's Music Programme Advisory panel were expanded to include reading and evaluating scores submitted for broadcasting consideration, particularly those by 'talented British composers', the panel being 'particularly concerned at the lack of broadcast opportunities'.[45] Rather than the works of composers of the Dominions and Colonies, representation of British musical interests had been a fundamental aim behind the panel's formation. 'From the first meeting of the panel, [Arthur] Bliss proved a dominant force, recommending that the Corporation take immediate steps to publicize programme policies and to enhance public perceptions of music broadcasts and the BBC Symphony Orchestra,' writes Doctor.[46] Although Bliss also proved to be a controversial figure, he continued to play an increasingly important role in formulating policy right through to the War. The formulation of only the best music from the best composers performed by the best musicians – no matter the origin – was the foundation of the BBC's music policy, which was not formally set down until 1942.

In addition to its role as the 'arbiter of taste' the BBC was also active in matters of cultural propaganda, and in fulfilling its critical purpose in influencing sentiment. This was particularly apparent in South Africa, where the battleground for 'hearts and minds' was crucial in the period leading up to the War. As early as spring 1934, John Reith was warned that the programmes of the BBC's Empire Service (which operated without state resources), were 'not satisfactorily projecting British culture or views',[47] especially in comparison to Germany, which in the opinion of the corporation's chief engineer Noel Ashbridge in August was 'determined to be the paramount nation on short waves ... in order to spread their propaganda'.[48]

If part of this projection of the British point of view could be achieved, for example, by using British music such as Gilbert and Sullivan, Purcell and *The Beggar's Opera*, which 'might please' as one contributor suggested, feedback from the BBC's earliest efforts of the Empire Service suggested that on short wave, at least, symphony concerts did not come across well.[49] This is despite the idealized image of 'the isolated British man tuning into the Empire Broadcasting station to listen to, among other things, the Queen's Hall concerts'. A 1932 edition of *World Review*, the BBC's programming schedule, imagines a scene involving dinner for one and a wireless set, on which 'Short-wave could transform the lives of these isolated British men', those who'd gone overseas to work and who, at the end of the day could hear 'the chimes of Big Ben, the news from home and two or more hours of the home programme'.[50]

Simon Potter explains how, of the tens of thousands of letters to the BBC written in response to its call for feedback on the Empire Service, those that referred to 'highbrow' music did so in a dismissive way. Not all expats were reliable, however – the 'climate' apparently having a generally adverse effect on the liver – 'nevertheless the feedback from this relatively socially elevated audience betrayed evidence of what BBC officers saw as lamentably "low brow" tastes', and that in preference to complex symphonic music, listeners preferred a dance band. Walford Davies's 'Keyboard Talks' were popular, however, but in 1935 the new Empire Orchestra focused on 'familiarity rather than novelty, nostalgia rather than cultural uplift'.[51]

The difficulty of broadcasting orchestral music on shortwave accounts for the British Council's recording programme, which was established for the express purpose of sending recordings of exemplary British music overseas for broadcasting on local medium- or long-wave stations. This was an early difficulty encountered in cultural propaganda efforts, where the technology used posed the main problem. It was 'difficult for distant listeners to enjoy complex programmes broadcast from foreign stations, particularly those involving classical music', with one BBC report pointing out that any interference (from faint whistles to rushing sounds) lessened the appeal of the symphony concert, the play or talk. This was a problem of the unpredictability of shortwave reception, and the accompanying distortion, which made stations unlistenable, 'particularly if they involved "serious" music', though 'Less highbrow fare seemed to work out best on short wave'; and this inevitably paved the way for jazz and a variety of local colour, though the resulting 'Dreams of direct contact with authentic, alien cultures did not always reflect the realities of globalization'.[52]

Further afield, the BBC's Empire Service was also competing with local broadcasters for listenership, and thus influence. In addition, questions of the high, low and middlebrow can also be heard, for example, in Australia where tastes in music continued to be especially conservative and were better suited for broadcasting on local frequencies used by the Australian Broadcasting Commission (ABC). Back home, Herbert Howells later spelt out the problem of modern music (and its 'highbrow' nature) in October 1936 in a proposed outline for a series of radio programmes in which he planned to run through the 'apparent chaos' and examine what he called the 'extremities' of modern music, adding the caveat that listeners would be induced 'to conserve their powers for what lies well on this side of *ultra*-modernity'. Outlining his proposal to the BBC's talks assistant George Barnes in 'Music and the ordinary listener: The modern problem', he provides a sincere attempt to explain to the man in the street all the new 'complexities and diversities' posed by modern music. The crux of it all, he writes, is tonality. The 'extreme' atonality and formal devices of late Schoenberg, by way of example, make the chance of 'meeting with the composer' difficult, but a compromise with the 'traditional causes' that can be found in Berg's *Wozzeck* is 'a potent sign of friendship'. For Howells, 'the *quieter* voice of modernity' can be found in the 'new counterpoint' of William Walton, 'a master of this type of appeal'. In the 'search for repose and beauty', then, we might have also found that elusive middlebrow – the man or woman that simply wants a good tune:

> [T]he inherent difficulty in Melody is that it has moved so far from the conception of this element as being immemorially rooted in 'singable' tunes. The origin of music in song is a thing 'modern' music seems bent on denying.[53]

Howells is attempting the same explanatory commentary on contemporary music as the voices of critics such as J. B. Priestley and the *Manchester Guardian's* Neville Cardus, whose views perhaps best represented those of the 'middlebrow' listener. The latter's 1958 volume *A Composer's Eleven* (referencing his cricketing background) was first published in 1945 as *Ten Composers*. Having left the *Guardian* in 1940 and making for Australia, he took up a position writing for the *Sydney Morning Herald*, where his brief was to cover a series of concerts conducted by Sir Thomas Beecham for the ABC. Cardus's *Ten Composers* was one of a range of similar publications of the time, a genre also represented by an Australian 'National Handbook' from 1934. *Music and the Listener* serves as a useful reminder of the 'Eurocentric' bias of the countries of the Empire, and its 'official' stamp was confirmed by the inclusion of a foreword by ABC chairman Charles Lloyd Jones, whose wonder at the new technology echoed something of Constant Lambert's complaint about the ubiquitous sound of recorded music on every street corner:

> Of the many forms of musical presentation, none now has wider range or force than wireless broadcasting. We have accepted all too easily, too unthinkingly, this magician – this prophet – this informer – who has stepped into our homes in the material form of a 'radio'.[54]

The handbook covered the Western canon in some detail, with chapters devoted to 'What to listen for in Sonatas and Symphonies' and to the basic question 'What is Classical Music?' as well as a brief nod to composers back home in the mother country: 'It is refreshing to be able to say that in this twentieth-century British composers have come rapidly to the front', following the injury done to 'better class music' by the success of the concert, or 'shop' ballad in the last half of the nineteenth century.[55]

Such 'light music' was the province of 'lower middlebrow' taste: sentimental songs, ballads and instrumental compositions of late Victorian and Edwardian days and appealing to what David Cardiff has called 'that self-improving section of the new universal audience brought into being by radio', those who preferred melody and a simple tune over extremes.[56] 'The impact of radio was such as to heighten rather than assuage the social antagonisms of musical tastes,' he writes. As the 'purest' of all the arts, music divided and fragmented the listening public, rather than 'fulfilling its Orphean mission of charming all ears and soothing all hearts'. The attempt, through broadcasting, to establish a common musical culture foundered on the 'implacable antipathies' of musical tastes and 'one should not underestimate the depth of hostility to each other felt by highbrow and lowbrow taste'.[57]

In the Australian example, author Keith Barry provides a short commentary on Australian composers of the day, including the 'best-known' Alfred Hill, whose works 'have a tunefulness which is highly commendable in serious music'.[58] Here, then, he unwittingly becomes the voice of the musical middlebrow, echoing the familiar complaint about the ultra-modern alluded to by Herbert Howells: the simple lack of a tune!

Thus, the BBC's efforts in educating the public had its equivalent in far-flung corners of the Empire, where the work of British composers was naturally of some significance. The *National Handbook* references Elgar, Delius, Parry, Holst and Vaughan Williams, and exemplifies perceived connections between Australian and European musical culture (including the canon of the three Bs – Bach, Beethoven and Brahms), as well as serving as a useful cue to explore the relationship between the BBC Empire Service and the ABC. Established in July 1932, the ABC was a local competitor to the BBC, and as such was an important factor in the effective dissemination of British propaganda in the dominions. As Simon Potter has explored in his recent volume on Britain, propaganda and global radio, the competition posed by ABC was further complicated by commercial interests, which also frustrated the BBC's efforts in news output. Assuming that to get the British view across, attracting listeners required the right balance between serious news, talks and entertainment programmes, the BBC relied on researching its listenership. Programming on the Empire Service was guided by analysing listener feedback, which indicated a preference for news and 'light programmes that would aid relaxation'. While the extremes of 'hot jazz crooning' and 'dull, highbrow stuff' were resisted, variety and light music received little criticism, the latter regarded as 'an antidote to the depression brought on by residence in tropical countries, away from home'.[59] As a further indication of middlebrow tastes, Simon Potter recognizes that, given the chance, 'many listeners in the UK might have expressed similar preferences'.[60]

Potter's *Wireless Internationalism* provides a helpful contextualization for the place of music in the projection of British 'soft power' in the 1930s, when the introduction of foreign language services, such as Spanish and Portuguese for Latin America, Arabic for the Middle East and an Afrikaans service for South Africa in the later 1930s, some of which focused not only providing news but also other forms of cultural propaganda such as talks, music and entertainment.[61] The first weekly news bulletin in Afrikaans, broadcast on 14 May 1939, was intended as 'an extension of an existing service to an important community in the Union in their own language'.[62] For the Arabic service, the BBC began building up a stock of gramophone records, particularly from Egypt, having previously found some difficulty in sourcing popular Arab music recordings.[63] Broadcasts in Afrikaans and Arabic had been added to the foreign language transmissions by Germany a month earlier. 'For South Africa alone, [German broadcasting service] Zeesen was able to offer a tailor-made six-hour English-language daily service, including talks and news, and was set to begin additional services in Afrikaans.'[64]

From spring 1939, the BBC's broadcasts to Germany were also combined with readings from German literature and, on Sundays, included religious services.[65] While the BBC collaborated with the Foreign Office to present these forms of cultural propaganda, the British Council had also begun its campaign of recording British orchestral music, intended for broadcast on local radio stations across the free world as a way of showcasing British talent and accomplishments in the field. Reith's 1934 visit to Cape Town to investigate broadcasting in South Africa was also an attempt to redress the balance further afield by 'projecting British culture and views'. South Africa was already bitterly divided, and by the outbreak of War, so much so that just seven parliamentary votes determined whether the country would back Britain or remain neutral. This is reflected in a change of direction in broadcasting during the period leading up to the War. By the end of the 1930s, and certainly after the war began in 1939, there was a notable shift from broadcasting to what Potter has called the 'lonely listener in the bush' to transmissions that were meant 'to reinforce the connection between Britain and its most important wartime allies in the dominions and the US'.[66]

The case of South Africa is an interesting one and was of particular concern to early British fascist groups. For Arnold Leese's Imperial Fascist League (IFL), founded in 1929, 'the Empire was definite proof of the innate superiority of the "Aryan" British race, deriving from Edwardian social Darwinism ideas about the subjugation of weak races by stronger ones,' writes Paul Stocker in his recent volume on far right 'visions' of the British Empire.[67] Given its strict racial hierarchy, South Africa 'was seen as a crucial place for the IFL', and the IFL's frequent comments on other fascist parties in the Dominions were predominantly on South Africa, singling out for praise the South African Gentile National Socialists or Greyshirts, as they were known. 'The Greyshirts were a fiercely anti-Semitic but electorally unsuccessful movement active throughout the 1930s,' and the IFL 'pledged to do all it could to promote the Greyshirts' activities in Britain, as long as they remained loyal to their British connection,' writes Stocker. 'However, as the Greyshirts began to splinter into various factions, the IFL hypocritically became increasingly irritated by the pro-German nature of many Afrikaner fascists, who harboured a dislike for the British after the resolution of the Boer War in 1902.'[68] It is in the Second South African War of 1899–1902 that the roots of anti-Semitism can be found for groups such as the IFL and their counterparts in the country itself. 'Jewish conspiracy theories pervaded every aspect of the IFL's approach to the British Empire,' with Leese 'convinced that imperial policy was beholden to Jewish financial interests' following the War.[69]

Another of British fascism's notable figures, A. K. Chesterton, whose South African background is explored in a recent volume by Luke LeCras that also sets out this aspect of Chesterton's early political beliefs including that, as far back as December 1934, Chesterton believed that 'the hold Jews had in South Africa was being strengthened by Hertzog and Smuts'. Three months later, Chesterton again accused Smuts, the general under whom he had fought in East Africa and in the Rand Revolt, of representing what he had called in the *Blackshirt* 'Yiddish finance'.[70]

Likewise, the recently founded League of Nations was seen by Leese and the IFL as 'a Jewish-dominated threat to the British Empire'.[71] Jan Smuts himself was the leading light in the League's founding. Leading the opposition to South African Prime Minister J. M. Hertzog, later Smuts' South Africa Party merged with Hertzog's United party, together forming 'Fusion' to oppose the Nationalists together. This kind of rhetoric can be traced as far back as 1900, in J. A. Hobson's now suspect *The War in South Africa: Its Causes and Effects* lay the blame for the war on a Jewish capitalist conspiracy. Hobson had been sent as South African correspondent by the *Manchester Guardian*, but though the book was popular, there was an outcry about its controversial conclusions, despite the inclusion of an interview with Olive Schreiner in which she described her heartbreak at knowing that the country was bitterly divided. When asked about anti-English sentiment among the Afrikaners in remote areas, she replied:

> You would not ask this if you had been among them. I could drive you to farm after farm where you would have found all the younger generation proud of learning to speak English and of Dressing in English fashion and learning English ways.
>
> In most of these small Dutch cottages you would find a harmonium and a book of English songs, which the daughters spent their leisure time in practising – songs mostly glorifying the British army and navy![72]

Schreiner looked forward to the day, perhaps in 25 years, that there would be no more Dutch and English in South Africa, but a fused 'Afrikander' people owing allegiance to Great Britain as their mother. 'But this hope is gone,' she said. Cecil Rhodes was chiefly to blame, she said, and sometimes the capitalists – whose goal was 'not only the mines and the towns' wealth, but the land. And when they have got the land, where is our freedom?'[73]

The roots of the subsequent rise of the far right in South Africa can be found here. By 1934 South African politics was beginning to calcify and set the scene for the National Party's disastrous post-war policy of Apartheid. General Hertzog's

United Party and Jan Smuts's South Africa Party merged in 1934 with Hertzog as Prime Minister and the National Party under D. F. Malan in the opposition. Hertzog's attitude towards universal suffrage betrays the patriarchal basis of policy towards the 'native' population, and is later summed up in a speech he gave in Pretoria in September 1937:

> I would again like to assure the native that the white man entertains for him the greatest goodwill and friendly feelings, and that the white man is quite determined to carry out faithfully that fatherly case which has been promised to the native ever since the laying of the foundations of the white man's settlement in South Africa.[74]

The need to influence was becoming ever more necessary. News transmissions in Afrikaans by both Germany and Britain did not begin until spring 1939, but the political atmosphere in South Africa was febrile. Since 1933 there had been numerous fascist movements, most of which splintered into insignificance. Oswald Pirow's Fascist New Order, for example, was founded in September 1940. Once a member of Hertzog's government, in 1937 Pirow had identified the tactics that could be used against a European invader, potentially engaging 'in a guerrilla warfare with modern equipment'.[75] But now, Pirow claimed 'that a new political order was needed to reject a wasteful and inefficient parliamentary democracy. Democracy had to be eradicated root and branch, as it could not solve the challenges facing South Africa, namely that of dealing with the black, coloured and poor white people. By purging the country from the influence of British and Jewish capitalism, a new order of society and government could be created'.[76]

Meanwhile members of the Broederbond, the highly secretive Afrikaner nationalist group that was established in 1918, had set up a new umbrella cultural organization, a further indication of the struggle for political and cultural autonomy in the country within the context of Empire. The purpose of the Federasie van Afrikaanse Kultuurverenignge (FAK) (or Federation of Afrikaans Cultural Organisations) was 'to promote Afrikaans in a coordinated way,' writes South African historian Hermann Giliomee. The FAK was established specifically to enable Afrikaners to sing in their own language. Together with the publication of the *FAK-Volksang-bundel vir Suid-Afrika* (Collection of People's Songs for South Africa), the FAK funded a competition for the composition of a national anthem in Afrikaans that could be sung alongside 'God Save the King'. In 1938 the government chose M. L. de Villiers's setting of C. J. Langenhoven's poem 'Die Stem van Suid-Afrika' as the national anthem.[77] It remains officially a part of the

National Anthem to this day, South Africa enjoying a hybrid anthem of *Nkosi Sikelel' iAfrika* and *Die Stem* from which a final verse is used in English translation.

At the same time, as Stocker explores, the BUF 'portrayed themselves as the only true defenders of Empire able to bring about a unified imperial unit to defend its white peoples from subversive activity,'[78] but South Africa posed a problem. Fascists in the country were also pro-German with Afrikaners not necessarily disposed towards the 'goals' of British imperialism, and even some English-speaking South Africans often 'lukewarm'.[79] Ultimately, South Africa's immediate fate was determined by just seven votes after a parliamentary debate on South Africa's neutrality in the event of an outbreak of war. As Richard Steyn has shown, 'that the debate took place one day after Great Britain had declared war on Adolf Hitler's Germany was itself a quirk of fortune', but the narrow majority in favour of supporting Britain 'was to change the course of the country's history'.[80] South Africa's political divisions would be resolved only well after the War when the Nationalists assumed power in 1948.

During the 1930s, bringing programmes of the highest quality to listeners 'continued to be challenged on nationalist grounds,' writes Jenny Doctor. Tensions between the BBC and the Music Advisory Committee escalated in autumn 1934 over nationalism and the use of foreign artists. The question of foreign artists was a perennial source of squabbling among BBC staffers, as well as the Music Advisory Committee. As early as May 1933, the issue was providing much animated discussion, but it was not until October 1934 that some serious facts and figures were laid down. Sir Adrian Boult stuck to the existing procedure of procuring the finest artists available, and where artistic considerations were equal, to give preference to British players, but not everyone agreed, with some members thinking it the duty of the BBC as a national institution 'to use British artists only in public as well as studio work'.[81] But Adrian Boult was able to show that 'over the previous five seasons, the BBC had more than adequately supported native musicians' and that international artists' broadcasts provided models of excellence for local musicians, encouraging improvement of British performance standards'.[82] A BBC memo of 20 November recognized that though it would be possible to employ only British artists for all its work, this would inevitably result in a lower standard of performance, the importance of the Corporation's concerts, thereby having less value and giving less prestige to those employed there:

> If Foreign Artists are to be used, they must come into the programmes on the basis of the use of the finest available artist for each occasion. It is most satisfactory

that in the past the Corporation has been able to employ British Artists in very fair proportion to artists from all other nations together. Comparison with each other nation separately gives an overwhelmingly British performance in almost every case.[83]

A breakdown of British and foreign artists shows a consistent preference for British conductors and singers; foreign instrumentalists, however, consistently outnumbered their British counterparts for every season from 1930 onwards (excluding the Proms). Overall, it could be shown that for the complete 1933–4 season ('Period beginning of Symphony Concerts to end of Promenade Season 1934') for individual artists (and excluding members of the chorus etc., all of whom were British), the proportion was about five to one.

> The appearance at public concerts of the greatest artists from all countries is the strongest force in setting a high standard, the effect being exactly similar to that of the visits of famous foreign orchestras to this country, by which a standard has been set and maintained, to the vast improvement of orchestra playing in this country.

That autumn, the Corporation presented its 1934–5 schedule in the *Radio Times*, the cover of the 12 October issue emblazoned with the headline 'The Broadcast Music Season Opens'. In a regular column entitled The World We Listen In, Filson Young attests that 'The contents of the number of the *Radio Times* in which this article appears afford an impressive body of evidence as to the musical activities of the BBC. I think listeners take these activities too much for granted. The number of hours daily, day in, day out, throughout the year devoted to music conforming to a very high standard of performance, is formidable.' Indeed, the *Radio Times* boasts that twelve LSO concerts were to be broadcast every Wednesday evening from the Queen's Hall between October 1934 and April 1935 beginning with Sir Thomas Beecham conducting Delius's *A Mass of Life*:

> The reasons for including Delius's great and lovely work The Mass of Life are twofold. One reason, naturally, is its intrinsic merit, and the other is that the lamented death of Delius earlier in the year calls for the tribute that both performers and listeners are anxious to pay to one of the world's greatest contemporary composers.

A week later, the same consideration of Holst's recent death took the form of a performance of his *Planets* suite. Stravinsky's *Perséphone* was to have its first English performance at the fourth concert of the series and the BBC Symphony

Orchestra was to travel for the first time since its creation in 1930, with visits planned to certain provincial cities and to the Continent. 'With the exception of the annual visit to Canterbury the Orchestra has never yet played outside London, and it has been felt that, since the Orchestra is obviously national property and not confined to London, listeners in the various Regions should have an opportunity of hearing this fine body of players at first hand.' The regular Sunday evening concerts were to continue for twenty-four consecutive Sundays. Elgar's *The Spirit of England* was to be performed on Armistice Day. The contemporary concert (the first already described, of Prokoviev's music) was to continue with a performance of Hindemith's *Mathis der Maler*. The forthcoming Proms Winter Season was promising to 'become a regular feature of the year's music', the 'almost extravagant popularity' of the autumn season having led enthusiasts to ask why it should not last as long as football, beginning with the first league match and ending with the Cup Final. 'To that there is no answer, excepting that neither orchestra nor conductor could stand the strain even though they had nothing else to do.'[84]

Giving an overview of prospects for broadcast music over the coming months, *The Radio Times'* opening editorial commented that when the broadcasting of music is a daily affair throughout the year, it may seem strange to call a particular period the Music Season, and to refer to the dates on which it begins and ends. 'But it is almost a tradition that the first symphony concert of a series begins the season and the last ends it. Actually the season is longer than that, and may be said to begin with the first of the Sunday Orchestral Concerts, which will be given this Sunday evening [14 October 1934].' A glance at the Sunday line-up of programmes reveals a broadcast schedule made up entirely of the relay of religious services and music on the National Programme (1500m), with the 9.30 pm slot on the regional transmitters 'radiating' the Sunday Orchestral Concert, the first concert of the fifth series: an all-Beethoven programme with the BBC Orchestra conducted by Adrian Boult. Highlights of the season were to include, 'for the first time in the broadcasting history of this country', a concert of music conducted by 'the world-famous' Toscanini. The BBC was also to revive 'after a lapse of years' what it called Studio Opera. 'Then there are the visits that the BBC Symphony Orchestra will make to provincial cities. Listeners outside London have not before had an opportunity of hearing the Orchestra in the concert hall, and since these concerts will in effect be Symphony Concerts supplementary to the London Symphony Concert Season, the opportunity should be particularly welcome. In March, too, the Orchestra will visit Brussels. Thus not only will British listeners be enabled to confirm their opinion of the BBC Symphony Orchestra at first hand, but for the first time in history the Orchestra will present its credentials as one of the finest in Europe to a Continental audience.'[85]

It is striking to note just how high a proportion of broadcast time was devoted to art music (half the time on Sunday devoted to 'serious' music, for example, and well over a third overall, with broadcasting hours still only from 10H45 to 23H15 in 1934). The remainder of the Sunday schedule was made up of religious programming. There is, incidentally, one aspect of the BBC's output that remains firmly in its past. Towards the back of the same issue of the *Radio Times*, there appears a half-page advertisement by the BBC Publications Department. It publicizes 'two important new religious pamphlets,' *The Way to God*, 'undoubtedly one of the most important yet issued by the BBC,' and consisting of 'very full synopses of the series of 19 lectures to be broadcast from 7 October 1934 to 21 July 1935', and *The New Christendom*, containing 'notes on the lectures in the new series of talks, an essay by the Rev. E. Shillito and many illustrations' in 'a study of the extension of the Christian message today'. This was a time when officials of government and other institutions believed in the concept of Christian civilization, one which went a long way later in the decade in challenging the forces of totalitarianism.

In this chapter we have traced the role the BBC played in the dissemination of music during the year. We have explored the arrival of various new technologies, and the commercial and technical considerations that became increasingly important as a result. There is another musical pioneer whose work merits some special acknowledgement in the importance of recorded music at the time. Louis Boyd Neel, who had been an amateur musician, but had recently made the brave step of taking up music as a full-time profession, can be credited with achieving several 'firsts' during the year. He was to conduct the first music heard at the new Glyndebourne opera house in 1934, in private performances, at John Christie's invitation'.[86] Boyd Neel's orchestra had its first real success with a concert (their second, and this time broadcast by the BBC) at the Aeolian Hall in Bond Street on 24 November 1933, at which Kathleen Long was the soloist in Mozart's A Major Concerto (K.414) and J. S. Bach's D Minor (BWV 1052). 'Evidently the BBC were pleased with the results, for it was not long before we were asked to go on the air again, and we had our second broadcast on 18th February 1934,' writes Boyd Neel in his memoir. The orchestra had just been chosen to play under Ernst Bloch, in a concert of his own works, to be staged once again at the Aeolian Hall. Boyd Neel's first meeting with the composer was 'rather unusual', he recounts. On arriving in London, Bloch took to his bed in the Langham Hotel (now part of the BBC) with a chill, and Boyd Neel was obliged to visit him in his room:

> I found him propped up in bed, smiling benignly on various satellites who were waiting on him. As soon as I was introduced, he proceeded to give me a long dissertation on the harmonization of Bach's Chorales, telling me that everything a student wanted to know about harmony was to be found in these masterpieces. Apart from an afternoon spent many years later with Sir Donald Tovey, I have never had such an illuminating music lesson.[87]

The Boyd Neel Orchestra can be credited – as a string ensemble – with reviving neglected masterpieces such as Dvorak's *Serenade for Strings*, and its recording contract with Decca (which ran until 1979) persuaded Boyd Neel to give up his medical career for good in 1934. The first recording was of Holst's *St. Paul's Suite*, followed by the Respighi's *Ancient Airs and Dances* (which the orchestra had played at their first concert), the Elgar *Introduction and Allegro* and music by Mozart, Handel and Grieg. The orchestra also gave the first ever performance of Benjamin Britten's *Simple Symphony* in May 1935:

> The 'Simple Symphony' is a *tour de force* for one so young to have composed, for the original pieces date from when he was aged between nine and twelve.[88]

Its composition in 1934 was something of a petulant gesture by the then frustrated and impatient composer, whose 'boyish' Cantata *A Boy was Born* was coincidentally 'sung by the BBC on the day of Elgar's death'. Britten's later pacifism is well known. Norman Lebrecht writes that this was largely due to his association with Frank Bridge and their names cannot be separated. 'Like Britten, Bridge was born and died within sound of the sea; he was a loner, a pacifist and an explorer. Neither composer can be understood without the other', writes Lebrecht. Britten's tuition was tended by Bridge, 'the most cosmopolitan and forward-looking of English composers' who 'instilled in Britten a hatred of war and a cognizance of Europe'.[89] It is Britten's *Variations on a theme of Frank Bridge* that immortalizes the connection between the two composers. Boyd Neel was also the first to record Vaughan Williams's *Fantasia on a Theme of Thomas Tallis*, with the composer present and who said afterwards that he was completely satisfied with the results. Boyd Neel regarded this 'wonderful' work as 'perhaps the greatest of all achievements in string orchestral composition', though achieving the desired effect had its challenges:

> Problems of recording it were immense, because we had to strive for the impression of the music being played in a vast cathedral nave, preserving at

the same time the wonderful effect of the echo orchestra, which in a church or concert performance should be at some distance from the main body.⁹⁰

High praise, and so early on, when Boyd Neel published his first memoir in 1950, especially when the man and his music were beginning to become unfashionable, though Hubert Foss's biography of Vaughan Williams appeared in the same year. The *Tallis Fantasia* was written expressly for performance in Gloucester Cathedral, so having the composer present at the recording was particularly useful in the studio setting.

Vaughan Williams was a kind humanitarian, and aware of social issues, as another letter written in 1934 illustrates. It concerns the aspirations of a young friend, an employee of the Ford Motor Company, who approached him for advice on pursuing a career in music, and with whom Vaughan Williams had been corresponding:

> His last letter to me seemed discontented and very emotional. Personally I feel that he ought to try to throw himself more into his work at Fords and not take it for granted that it is a necessary evil – In his last letter he speaks for example of sordid everyday drudgery and talks of his life as being a stereotyped copy for the millions of lives led by our population.⁹¹

Perhaps Vaughan Williams's friend was hoping to emulate Boyd Neel who, as we have seen, abandoned his medical career for the world of music. There is one final anecdote that illustrates how 1934 very much represents the beginning of a new world in music and technology. A recording of Elgar's *Mina*, written for light orchestra, was presented to him on disc in February 1934 at his home in Worcester. It was the only way he could hear the results of his efforts and the recording enabled him to make comments. *Mina* was to be his final completed work, as just eight days later he died, but the composer had been working on a much bigger work. Alas, his long-awaited Third Symphony remained incomplete, and he left behind just a few sketches and fragments. It is to the subject of 1934's unfinished symphonies that I turn next.

Notes

1 Doctor, 1999: 281.
2 Ibid., 332.
3 Richards, 2001b: 160–1.
4 Gardiner, 2011: 512–13.

5. *The Times'* Broadcasting Number, 14 August 1934.
6. BBC WAC – National Anthem, R27/267 – November 1934.
7. Walford Davies, 'Musical Education, Beauty Made Audible, Listeners and Performers', *The Times*, 14 August 1934, p. xviii.
8. Lambert, 1966: 201.
9. Ibid., 200.
10. *Gramophone* magazine, August 1934.
11. M-D. Calvocoressi, in *The Listener*, 28 November 1934, p. 896.
12. Lebrecht, 1992: ix,
13. Broadcasting in Britain: An American View; Very Little Merit Allowed, *The Times*, 30 January 1934, p. 16.
14. BBC WAC – R20/136/1 – PRS Fees.
15. BBC and Composers (Letter by Lord Elmsley, M.P.), *The Times*, 19 October 1934, p. 10.
16. Carwardine's Bristol tea-room played the recording in February 1933, which gave rise to the test case in which the High Court of Justice ruled in favour of record companies who won the legal right to prevent public performances of their records (see *The Times* of 14 & 15 December 1933, p. 4).
17. Court of Appeal: Musical Copyright and News Film, *The Times*, 27 April 1934, p. 4.
18. Chambers, 2011: 359–75.
19. British Broadcasting, *The Times*, 14 August 1934, p. 13.
20. Television; Translation of Light and Shade, Stages in a Complex Process, *The Times'* broadcasting number, 14 August 1934, p. xxiv.
21. Company Meetings: Electrical and Musical Industries. A Year of Further Progress, *The Times*, 17 November 1934, p. 19.
22. Source: www.bairdtelevision.com, accessed 25 April 2014.
23. Foss, 1954: 146–7.
24. The Professions Must be Organised, Alexander Raven, *The Blackshirt*, Issue 75,p. 4, 28 September 1934.
25. *The Listener*, Volume XII, Issue 307, 28 November 1934, p. 915.
26. Sir Walford Davies: 'Honorary Freeman of his Native Oswestry', *The Times*, 28 September 1934, p. 12.
27. Sir Thomas Beecham on the BBC: 'Monstrous Monopoly of the Air', *The Times*, 2 October 1934p. 16.
28. Sir Thomas Beecham and the BBC: 'Criticism of Excessive Powers', *The Times*, 4 December 1934, p. 11.
29. Broadcasting Events in 1934; Review of the Year, *The Times*, 29 December 1934, p. 8.
30. The Function of the Sound Record, *BBC Yearbook 1934*, pp. 119–21.

31 Gramophone Records; Broadcasting and Sales, Artists Contracts, Christopher Stone, *The Times*' broadcasting number, 14 August 1934, p. xviii.
32 The Re-organisation of German Broadcasting, *BBC Yearbook*, 1934, pp. 295–8.
33 Benjamin, 2008: 398.
34 Broadcast Opera in Germany, Ernst Schoen, *BBC Yearbook* 1934, pp. 67–71.
35 Music for Broadcasting (3) Adaptation in Performance? Adrian Boult, *BBC Annual* 1935, pp. 175–7
36 That is, acoustics, transmitting apparatus and 'stereoscopic' hearing, which would present the listener with all the advantages of direct listening, 'a standard which yet seems as utopian as that of unlimited television' (!).
37 Music for Broadcasting (2), Should it be Specially Arranged?, Ernst Schoen, *BBC Annual* 1935, pp. 171–4.
38 Music for Broadcasting (1), Should it be Specially Written?, Ernest Newman, *BBC Annual* 1935, pp. 168–70.
39 The Maecenate of the Microphone, C. Henry Warren, *BBC Yearbook* 1934, pp. 61–5
40 Art & Patronage (1), Wyndham Lewis, *BBC Annual* 1935, pp. 184–7.
41 Art & Patronage (2), C.R.W. Nevinson, *BBC Annual* 1935, pp. 189–92.
42 BBC WAC R27/91 – Empire Music. That no mention of any other language used in South Africa hardly needs comment. Today there are no fewer than *eleven* official languages, including Afrikaans, in a country of only 50 million. The politics of language and, by extension, of culture in general and music in particular, has acute resonance in the South African context.
43 BBC WAC R27/83 – Dominions Music.
44 'Symphony from South Africa', *Radio Times*, 16 November 1934.
45 Doctor, 1999: 208.
46 Ibid., 289.
47 Potter, 2020: 94.
48 Ibid., 95.
49 Ibid., 175.
50 Quoted by Potter, 2020: 181. Ninety years on, this may not be the province of 1932 listeners alone. I freely admit to tuning into BBC Radio 4 care of 'wireless' after a day's work in my South African home to listen to, among other things, *P.M.*, the chimes of Big Ben, the Six O'clock News and *Just a Minute*.
51 Potter, 2020: 183–6.
52 Ibid., 210–16.
53 Foreman, 1987: 194–7.
54 Barry, 1934: 9.
55 Ibid., 111.
56 Cardiff, 1991: 214.
57 Ibid., 221.

58 Barry, 1934: 113.
59 Potter, 2020: 187.
60 Ibid., 188.
61 Ibid., 111.
62 *The Listener*, 14 May 1939.
63 Potter, 2020: 122–3.
64 Ibid., 95.
65 Ibid., 141.
66 Ibid., 200. I have explored the case of film as propaganda in *Culture and Propaganda in World War II*, especially the sole Ministry of Information-funded feature film *49th Parallel* (1942), which was scored by Vaughan Williams in his first foray into film music. It was specifically aimed at the United States, though by the time of its release, the Americans had already been dragged into the War.
67 Stocker, 2021: 32.
68 Ibid., 34–5.
69 Ibid., 33.
70 LeCras, 2020: 43.
71 Stocker, 2021: 34.
72 Hobson, 1900: 102.
73 Ibid., 103.
74 *Cape Argus*, 17 October 1937.
75 *Johannesburg Star*, 17 October 1937.
76 Mouton, 2020: 164.
77 Giliomee, 2020: 150. C. J. Langenhoven (1873–1932) was a leading player in the development of Afrikaans literature and cultural history.
78 Stocker, 2021: 35–6.
79 Ibid., 39.
80 Steyn, 2020: ix.
81 Doctor, 1999: 294.
82 Ibid., 295.
83 BBC WAC R27/432 – Public Concert Policy.
84 Another Season of Broadcast Music: A First Glance of the Plans for 1934–1935, *Radio Times*, 12 October 1934, pp. 90–1.
85 *Radio Times*, Volume 45, Issue 576, 12 October 1934, p. 87.
86 *Gramophone* magazine, July 1972, pp. 178, 183.
87 Boyd Neel, 1950: 16–17.
88 Ibid., 23.
89 Lebrecht, 1992: 51.
90 Boyd Neel, 1950: 22.
91 Ralph Vaughan Williams to Bernard Van Dieren, 20 October 1934 in Cobbe (ed.), 2008: 232.

2

Unfinished symphony

The death of Elgar in February left only the barest sketches of a new symphony on which he had been working for several months. 'A few bars had been orchestrated, but only a moderately complete sketch of the first movement and fragments of the others are in existence,' reported *The Times*.[1] Elgar's Third Symphony was a BBC commission, and the planners intended to build the second London Music Festival around it, as well as another major, and eagerly anticipated a new symphony by William Walton.[2] 'Don't let anyone tinker with it,' Elgar pleaded in late 1933. 'No one could understand . . . no one must tinker with it.' For a moment, he even thought that perhaps it was better if it were burnt.[3] In August, the manuscript was handed over to Adrian Boult at the BBC at Broadcasting House by Elgar's daughter. 'No attempt, however, will be made to put the work into a form suitable for performance,' assured *The Times*. With the death of Elgar, and the eventual delay in the first performance of Walton's new work, writes Stephen Lloyd, '1934 turned out to be one of unfinished British symphonies. Holst's death in May left only a single movement – a scherzo – from an otherwise incomplete work.[4]

Announced for performance on 22 March 1934 with Jan Smeterlin, Arthur Bliss's new piano concerto had also been proving difficult to complete. Writing to Leslie Heward in September 1933 to complain that his new piano concerto was 'not going at all well', he blamed the delay on having 'so many things apart from music to attend to this summer that I could not concentrate on it'.[5] The work was eventually first heard at the New York World's Fair six years later, in June 1939, part of the British Council Music Advisory Committee's contribution to that event.

Distractions of one kind or another were also Walton's difficulty. Following his earlier success with *Belshazzar's Feast* in 1931, William Walton had been agonizing over his new symphony. Expectations of its imminent birth were high throughout 1934, and Hamilton Harty had expected to perform it as early as

April 1933. The symphony was begun in February 1932, after Harty had asked Walton to write one following a performance of the Viola Concerto with the conductor and Lionel Tertis as soloist by the Halle Orchestra in Manchester in January.[6] Walton's relationship with Imma von Doernberg, which can be said to be the emotional background to the symphony, was the main reason for its continued delay. Suffering from writer's block because he had not yet resolved his turbulent love affair, he simply could not complete the symphony's final movement. A new date of 19 March 1934 was set but in the previous summer, Walton had also accepted a contract to write music for the film *Escape Me Never*, adding to the distraction of his failing relationship. But even the film score had its difficulties, and Walton complained in January 1935 that 'The film people kept me hanging about chiefly owing to their stupidity & inefficiency & in the end I had to write all the music in four days'.[7] Eventually confessing to have already burnt three finales, he refused to 'pump out' a 'brilliant, out-of-the-place pointless & vacuous finale' in time for the first performance in December 1934.[8] Despite the break-up of (or perhaps even because of) their relationship, Walton left the dedication to Imma intact.

If 1934 is the year of the British 'Unfinished Symphony', it coincides with an Austrian film of that name, directed by Dr Willy Forst, released the same year in London at the newly opened Curzon Cinema – its first screening. Shown privately at the end of February, *The Times* considered *The Unfinished Symphony* an 'interesting and unusual' film and 'an extremely good choice' for the occasion. A Gaumont-British production directed by Willi Forst and Anthony Asquith with Austrian actor Hans Jaray (1906–90) playing the composer, the film was, for *The Times*'s reviewer, 'a good example of the strength of the alliance that sensitive acting and photography and classic music may eventually build up between themselves', and for whom the music was the most important part. Despite not quite true to the life of Franz Schubert 'as history knows it', the film 'never forgets that music must be at the source of its inspiration, and, even when Schubert's affairs most irritatingly intrude, the director . . . keeps the music which belongs to the Schubert story consistently in the front of his mind'.[9]

At the start of his career, Alistair Cooke was a film critic for the BBC from October 1934 to March 1937. His review of the film gives an early indication of his powers as a broadcaster and journalist:

> Composers in films have their own venerable tradition. The legend is that no musician is really a musician until he forgets what two and two make and begins to leave his hat around. It's a pity that Schubert's charm, in the very agreeable *The*

Unfinished Symphony, should be rooted in this particular bed of roses. Because even apart from the fact that he writes music when he thinks he's writing arithmetic, and apart from his habit of feeling his hat all the way round to make sure of the brim, Hans Jaray *has* a charming manner, charming enough to scare Gary Cooper or Leslie Howard into thinking it's going to be impossible to be a successful film actor if all you have is good looks, acting ability, and a British English or an American English accent. Hans Jaray is, like all the Schuberts we have seen or ever shall see, petulant, plump, very modest, rather simply gallant and writes his music mainly has an accompaniment to his love affairs. I should have been thankful for just one scene showing him working from nine till twelve straightening out some stiffish bit of orchestration. But no – Hollywood and Elstree are agreed that musicians are impractical, childish people, that the cabinets of England meet only to arrange some scandalous marriage, that everybody before 1800 always wore fancy dress and laughed whether there were any jokes or not, that . . . the people of central Europe . . . spend their days and nights singing and dancing and drinking in an orgy of gaiety.

For Cooke, *The Unfinished Symphony* could be enjoyable 'if the music of Schubert means to you your childhood, or pleasant Sunday evenings or any other period of your emotional history', but 'If you are fond of Schubert's music not so much as a memory teaser but in a musical way – I'm not so sure'.[10] Cooke's review of another new musical film in 1934 appeared in the winter 1934/35 edition of Sight and Sound. The acting in *The Merry Widow* (speaking intervals, he called them, in this 'opera film') didn't seem up to much, and neither did the direction ('Mr Lubitsch's very personal contribution to that new type of musical film I warned you about some time ago – I mean the disguised opera'[11]). Cooke's critique of Ernst Lubitsch's direction is scathing. 'He is – like his films – glib, mischievous and amusing', but the original has satire and the epoch in which it is set, the 1890s, was one 'to enjoy or despise', but not 'to snigger at'.[12] *The Merry Widow*, freely adapted from Lehar's ebullient operetta for Hollywood audiences, starred Jeanette Macdonald and Maurice Chevalier, the English lyrics were by Rogers and Hart, musical adaptation by Herbert Stothart and it was produced and directed by Ernst Lubitsch. Chevalier opens the musical numbers singing 'Girls, Girls, Girls' in his inimitable style. The film contains considerably more dialogue than the original and to modern eyes is surely so dated as to become unwatchable, even for Chevalier nostalgists. In fact, it is so loosely based on Lehar's work that it becomes a standard narrative film, in the musical genre typical of its era, with musical embellishments and interludes that diverge widely from the original, Lubitsch taking as much liberty with the score as he does with the libretto. Lubitsch's success in leading *The Merry Widow* in the direction of camp kitsch in a film that is almost entirely devoid of the wit and charm of the operetta, and which puts Chevalier, as Count Danilo, centre stage, almost at the expense of the Merry Widow herself. *The Times'* reviewer was also rather indifferent. Despite 'some lovely photography' and the 'cunning pattern of black and whites' in the background for the waltz (an 'unusually effective spectacle'), Lubitsch's inspiration sometimes 'altogether deserts him'. Despite her 'admirable' singing, Jeanette MacDonald's acting 'lacks sparkle and her animation seems a little forced'. In Danilo's part, played by Maurice Chevalier, on the other hand, it was 'easy to understand why he was so popular with the girls of Maxim's'. In summing up, 'Lehar's music, of course, wins half the battle for any version of *The Merry Widow* before the filming has begun, and Lubitsch has given it a sumptuously expensive setting. It is all very glittering, very magnificent, and very gay, but, for Lubitsch, it is a conventional production, and a few more moments of his acid and individual wit would have been worth all the magnificences.'[13]

So much for *The Unfinished Symphony* and *The Merry Widow*: conventional, kitsch and, ultimately, unmemorable and without much to redeem them. However, cinema also presents another opportunity for music in 1934. To the exciting innovations of the year – whether wireless, television, *Muzak* or even 'Synk' – and the new experiments such as the two-week Glyndebourne festival (and even smoking concerts) or, simply, the joy of recoding music that had been neglected or, worse still, forgotten, we can also add another exciting development in 1934: the whole new genre of Film Music. Following fast on the tails of Max Steiner in Hollywood whose score for *King Kong* constituted a breakthrough in scoring for films, William Walton was asked in the summer of 1933, while he was struggling to complete his momentous new symphony, to score music for the film *Escape Me Never*, one of the first British films to feature original music.

'Is cinema music stagnating?' asked a *Times* report on 26 May. Use of pre-existing music was all very well, but for many, the possibilities of existing music as an accompaniment were limited, and the development of film music could never follow the rapid progress shown by film itself during the last fifteen years. In the opinion of the public as well as of film directors, music was little more than a 'necessary evil'. The report is of a musical experiment conducted in Berlin. The Institute of Wireless Experiment there (and recently closed, presumably by the new regime)[14] hosted a class (what we would call a workshop') by Paul Hindemith for the creation of music for silent films. Music for sound film, meanwhile, offered even less scope for the composer, and the writer admits:

> The technical side of the film music, its instrumentation, style, or formal laws, cannot be treated in this short discussion, which is no more than an attempt to suggest in outline how music may be used with the film, and how, in fact, it may become something more than a 'necessary evil'.[15]

How wrong Hindemith was, in fact. Far from stagnating, film music was just about to expand and in Britain it was to get a 'shot in the arm' from none other than William Walton, as Max Steiner had done the year before in Hollywood with his score for *King Kong* in 1933. Meanwhile, at a farewell luncheon given by the English Speaking Union in honour of the secretary of the Motion Picture Producers and Distributors of America, Carl Milliken (the 'right-hand man of its president, Mr Will Hays'), Lord Lee of Fareham, vice-president of the Gaumont-British Picture Corporation, set out his vision for the future of British film, where 'we had made a great mistake sometimes by going for ape-like imitation and parrot-like repetition of the efforts of other countries'. But he saw a change coming. He believed the ideal film of the future 'would have perfect photography, really fine illustrative music, some simple and self-explanatory theme and little or no talk'.[16]

Some 'really fine illustrative music' appears in Walton's score for the melodrama *Escape Me Never*, which was released in 1935. Walton, who can thus be credited with writing the first British film score, was paid £350 (a considerable sum in those days), but found the pace of work arduous. 'Walton always professed to find composing music a great struggle and effort; the fact remains, however, that when driven to it he *could* provide high quality music quickly to order,' writes Christopher Palmer.[17] He was required to write two sequences, the first accompanying a scene floating down a Venetian canal at the film's opening sequence, and the second, music for a Russian ballet. 'For a first film score,' writes Stephen Lloyd, 'Walton's *Escape Me Never* is remarkably accomplished and effective. At first it "nearly drove me to a lunatic asylum" but "much to my surprise I soon found myself writing five to ten minutes' music a day without too much difficulty", he later admitted.'[18]

Walton was commissioned to write the music by Dallas Bauer,[19] head of the BBC's drama department, and who also acted as producer of the film, which was directed by Paul Czinner. Czinner's wife Elisabeth Bergner was nominated for the Academy Award for Best Actress for her role in the film. The couple subsequently involved Walton in two other film productions, *As You Like It* and *A Stolen Life*, in which the music for the Russian ballet turns up again as background to a newsreel. Written by Margaret Kennedy and based on her 1930 novel *The Fool of the Family, Escape Me Never* was written for Bergner who had starred in the original West End run of the play at the Apollo Theatre. *Escape Me Never* was remade in Hollywood in 1947 with Erroll Flynn and Eleanor Parker, with music by Erich Korngold who had settled in the United States having fled the Nazis from his native Austria.

Edited by David Lean, the British production of *Escape Me Never* also secured the services of Muir Mathieson as Music Director. Muir Mathieson, whose first film was as Assistant Music Director in *The Private Lives of Henry VIII* (1933), went on to direct Mischa Spoliansky's music in both *The Private Life of Don Juan* and *The Scarlet Pimpernel* (both 1934). In a sparkling career in film music that spanned more than thirty years, Mathieson went on 'to arrange, direct, conduct, and occasionally compose, the music for almost one thousand films between 1934 and 1970'.[20] Among the first of those films was *The Rise of Catherine the Great*, which was also directed by Czinner and starred Elisabeth Bergner. Alexander Korda had approached Mathieson via the Royal College of Music (RCM) when his Musical Director, Kurt Schröder, left London Films in 1934. He needed a conductor 'who could demonstrate to his Musical Director how to beat time in seven for the score of *Catherine the Great*'.[21] Mathieson was only twenty-two and this for him seemed 'an amazing proposition', as well as being highly flattering, not to mention lucrative. This was heady stuff and, as he said himself, the salary was very tempting. It is tempting to imagine the reaction of his fellow students at the RCM, and even the staff:

> Although Muir rightly believed in the artistic integrity of his composers, working with them cannot always have been easy. There were initial and continuing difficulties, but part of Muir's success lay in his ability to talk to composers on their own level. For their part they respected him, valued his judgment and were excited to find themselves part of a team with an outcome that would bring pleasure to a vast audience.[22]

Despite Muir Mathieson's reputation for xenophobia, his work exemplifies the perceived need to raise standards in British film production in the 1930s. 'The only constant in terms of employment criteria for composers, under Mathieson's direction in the 1930s, was the requirement that they be respected musicians beyond the film studio gates,' notes Alexis Bennett in an overview of collaboration between directors and musicians in British studios, particularly at London Films, home of the Korda brothers.[23] Bennett shows how a certain tension existed behind British film scoring, specifically between 'realistic' commercial interests and craftsmanship, especially in classical musicianship. Muir Mathieson was also a 'champion' for British composers and believed that they should be given the opportunity to write scores that benefited both 'concert music' and the film industry. Bennett has explored the cosmopolitan atmosphere of Denham Studios, home of London Films, where Mathieson gained a reputation 'as a broker of composer-director collaborations' despite what some saw as an 'anti-foreigner' stance. Mathieson, in fact, frequently hired foreign composers to write for London Films. If he preferred to hire British composers and 'actively avoided booking foreign composers', as some have claimed, this is refuted by his inviting Austrian émigré Ernst Toch, and his one-time teacher at the Royal College of Music, Australian Arthur Benjamin, who was brought in to score the music for *The Scarlet Pimpernel*, together with Mischa Spoliansky. Spoliansky had been active in the Weimar period but had fled Berlin shortly after Hitler's rise to power in 1933. His career had already given rise to questions of popular appeal set against inaccessibility, the Berlin *literati* objecting to 'crude' cabaret, but its *kleinkunst* proving too highbrow to please broad audiences. Later he was credited for writing music that did not sink to the level of the 'lowest common denominator'.[24]

Mathieson thus exemplifies the priority for quality in musicianship over simple concerns for preferring second-rate home-grown fare. Resisting the commercial pressures that also required British filmmakers to fulfil their legal obligations for a certain percentage of British-made films (the cheap so-called 'quota quickies'), film collaborators in the 1930s also managed to balance entertainment value with 'a sense of craftsmanship and conscientiousness' in the music scoring process. A key figure in this regard, Mathieson was responsible for this process at London Films, employing composers 'most of whom he seems to have appreciated for their reputations beyond film scoring', and, indeed, writes Bennett, 'immigrant or exiled composers thrived in Britain', often under Mathieson's guidance.[25]

Alexis Bennett has also noted that the period was 'significantly under the influence of John Reith's strong ethos of public service broadcasting, drawn partly from his strict Presbyterian upbringing', finding parallels with John Grierson of the GPO Film Unit, and Mathieson himself. Later, the tension emerges again between sheer commercialism in the process of making *Things to Come* (1936), during which composer Arthur Bliss and author H. G. Wells became 'disillusioned' with Korda. The film, writes Bennett, is 'an early example of a composer being given relative freedom and early involvement on a picture', and in this case, the author also had a keen interest in presenting a certain 'message to mankind'. Wells felt that Korda did not have 'much of an ear' and disliked the Hollywood practice of scoring the film after it had been cut. In this he had Grierson's support (writing 'Balls!' to the notion in a letter to Arthur Bliss!).[26] As Bennett notes, Mathieson shared Wells's 'didactic streak', but I have shown elsewhere how this attitude served film music well in British films, which have far less 'mickey-mousing' than their Hollywood counterparts of the time. Vaughan Williams later confessed a complete inability to write music for films in the Hollywood style. His first score, written reluctantly only after Muir Mathieson's repeated badgering, is a fine example of the outcome of this inability.[27]

Another Korda film, meanwhile, *The Rise of Catherine the Great*, was released in London in February. Not to be confused with *The Scarlet Empress*, a Hollywood production directed by Josef von Sternberg (the working title of which had been *Catherine the Great*) and released in the United States in September, it premiered in London in May. 'Shoving contemptuously to one side the countless rather stiff and unloving paintings of Catherine made in her lifetime, the delirious, dream-come-true 1934 movie *The Scarlet Empress* remains the definitive account of how she came to power – albeit one with a loose hold on historical detail,' writes Simon Winder. 'The movie is so vivid and brutal that it almost blocks out completely the real Catherine, but it would be a gloomy pedant who did not revel in *The Scarlet Empress* and admit that watching [Marlene] Dietrich dressed in a sort of satellite dish covered in pompoms eying [sic] up the strapping troopers brings history to life.'[28] Perhaps the BUF's reviewer at the time of the film's release was a 'gloomy pedant'. Apparently confusing the two films, the reaction to *The Rise of Catherine the Great* was not favourable, Alexander Korda 'not merely content to suppress or pervert history', but going so far as to rewrite it. Strong words, indeed:

> When the prostitution of history is the ambition of every producer from Islington to Santa Barbara, and a lecherous Catherine I turns our scrambled eggs over and over with a Kansas City accent, it is a divine relief to watch a film star who is a human being.

That human being was in the person of Gracie Fields, in her new film *Sing as We Go*, which offered a study on the 'lighter side' of 'the cotton land's misery' and the 'heroism' of its workers: 'Singing with the visions of endless dole queues before them, they march out of the closing factory, careless and gallant.'[29]

That same year, an adaptation of another play by Margaret Kennedy with a musical theme was being shown in cinemas. Michael Balcon recalls how in the silent version of *The Constant Nymph*, filming a full-scale orchestra had proved extremely challenging:

> In the natural effort to attain the visual effect impossible on the stage we had an elaborate climax in which Ivor Novello conducted a full-scale symphony orchestra in the Queen's Hall. We had hired the Queen's Hall and the orchestra and Novello had been painstakingly coached to make the correct movements as conductor. But not a note of music![30]

Basil Dean, meanwhile, retells how the same scene was handled in the 1934 production, where the interior scenes were filmed at Shepherd's Bush, except for the performance of Lewis Dodd's Symphony at the Queen's Hall:

> Here Balcon was as lavish as he had been in the case of the silent version, engaging the London Symphony Orchestra to play music especially composed by Eugene Goossens and John Greenwood. The sequence was so much more satisfying now that the orchestra was actually being recorded, even though Brian Aherne obviously knew less about conducting an orchestra than did Ivor Novello. Today that portion of the film would have an added poignancy, reminding all music lovers of the loss of their much loved concert hall.[31]

Dean also commissioned Rutland Boughton to write music for his production *Lorna Doone* together with Cecil Armstrong Gibbs. 'Music was needed to heighten the romance of the film so I commissioned Rutland Boughton, well remembered for his opera, *The Immortal Hour*, to write Lorna's theme song,' he recalls. 'Dr. Armstrong Gibbs contributed incidental music for the fight between John Ridd and Carver Doone, and for Jan and Lorna's night-ride to London to appear before King James II (*sic!*).'[32] The film, first shown at the Adelphi Theatre on the Strand at Christmas 1934, was Margaret Lockwood's first speaking part.[33]

That December, the world was to hear for the first time the symphony that Walton had been working on since February 1932, the completion of which he had been so distracted from. Whether it was his bitter break-up with Imma von Doernberg, or the diversions afforded by his work from *Escape Me Never*, London audiences finally got the chance to hear it on 3 December. 'What a Work!' wrote Sir Henry Wood after its first performance: 'It was like the world coming to an end, its dramatic power was superb.' For Walton himself, the First Symphony was 'the climax of my youth' and of all the major works which first made their appearance in 1934, this is, indeed, the one that stands out. The sheer audacity and breadth of Walton's First Symphony is, on first acquaintance, nothing short of breathtaking. The first movement's relentless drive and energy almost reaches fever pitch, and he hammers home the point. Much has been said of the second movement, *con malizia*. Even Adrian Boult eventually withdrew from conducting the Symphony – 'all that malice' was just too much. And the anguish of the third movement – '*con malincolia*' (correctly, in Italian, *con malinconia*) – is the ultimate expression of Walton's passion. It has the 'pathétique' element, the subjective experience of loss and despair, despite its beauty. This is a young man's passion, an expression of utter desolation. How can we fail to be moved by it? But we are saved, so to speak, with the onset of the final movement, in which the much-needed breakthrough finally emerges. At last, it's as if we have seen through all our pain, and we arrive, if a little battle-scarred, triumphant and resolute, ready to face the world.

Walton marked his score 'Con Melancolia' in error. In fact, any of *Con Melanconia*, *Malinconia* or *Malenconia* would have done. The mistake in the use of the Italian term can be put down to an error by the Oxford University Press (OUP) in a letter to the BBC concerning the symphony, in which the third movement is described incorrectly as Adagio con melancolia. Another corrected mistake occurs in the description of the fourth movement, marked as *Maesto – Brioso ed ardentemente* (which should, of course, be *Maestoso*).[34] Arnold Bax also used the incorrect marking for the opening of his Fifth Symphony, first performed in January 1934.[35] Aptly chosen for the heart-wrenching music of Walton's symphony, it is useful to speculate where he might have picked up the term. Hildegard of Bingen and Chopin use it, and the finale of Beethoven's Op.18 No.6 String Quartet is marked *Con Malinconia*. And the largo of his Piano Sonata Op.10 No.3, was 'explained by Beethoven himself as the "description of the state of mind of a melancholic". Some other works from a more recent era (Messiaen and the 1990s 'cross-over' *Symphony of Sorrowful Songs* by Goreski are all given as examples of the expression of melancholy in music in Jacky Bowring's 2008 book *Field Guide to Melancholy*). Schubert's *Die Winterreise* and Tchaikovsky's last three symphonies also come to mind, but there is one work that must surely stand apart – Walton's First Symphony, perhaps together with the extraordinary closing passage in his 1929 Viola Concerto. The latter deserves mention simply as the composition of a young man of only twenty-seven years. But the Adagio of the symphony is the perfect expression of melancholy, and on a much broader scale.

Early response to Walton's symphony included some comparison with Schubert. His good friend, the pianist Angus Morrison, later recalled that Walton would have liked to write something like the slow movement of the Schubert C Major String Quintet: 'That sort of timeless serenity was not in Willie's make-up, but the agonized bitter-sweetness of the movement as it finally emerged, certainly was.' Stewart Craggs comments that although the two first movements are in many ways totally unlike, 'present-day views of Schubert would incline more towards agonized bitter-sweetness than to timeless serenity: perhaps Walton was closer to his goal than Morrison realized'.[36]

That first audience, however, was deprived of the resolution eventually afforded in the final movement. Hubert Foss recounts how negotiations had been going on for some months with the symphony's publisher OUP, where Foss was in charge of the Music Department. 'Excitement over the new work had risen so high that when the composer found himself unable to complete the last movement in time it was decided to take the unusual step of performing the other three movements only' for the first performance. But it was immediately apparent that the symphony was 'destined to be one of the most significant and universally admired works' of the decade. The LSO, for whom the work was the season's highlight, were afforded four rehearsals for the work because of its difficulty. In the event only two were found to be necessary.[37]

The full symphony was scheduled for performance at a Courtauld-Sargent concert in the spring of 1935, but it was a full year after the first LSO performance that it was finally performed in its entirety by the BBC Symphony Orchestra under Adrian Boult. The BBC still likes to claim the work's first performance (as the BBC Symphony Orchestra was claiming eighty years later at the Proms, evidence that some rivalry continues to remain among orchestras), but the sense of excitement at its first incomplete hearing surely heralds its true birth. 'No doubt the composer felt that it would not be fair to the London Symphony Orchestra to withhold longer what is ready for it,' commented *The Times'* review the following day. 'Whither does all this lead and what sort of a movement can bring the solution of the many issues raised in the first three?' it asks. The first movement 'builds to a vigorous climax through a long sequence of rhapsodic episodes. The macabre *scherzo* without the definite contrast of a trio is no less continuous. The slow movement, including some passages of quite entrancing melodic arabesque, is the most interesting of all, but not affording any mental relaxation. Is that what the *finale* is to do, and has relaxation been delayed too long? That is what we must wait to discover.' Otherwise, 'further rehearsal,' felt the reviewer, 'might smooth away some of the asperities of this hearing' though nevertheless, 'the composer was called and warmly applauded at its close'.[38]

The difficult birth of this symphony and the rather testy relationship with the BBC goes back to September 1933. Adrian Boult expressed his gratitude in a letter to Walton for the reassurance that the symphony 'will be ready for performance' on 15 December 1933. But before year end, William was writing from Weston Hall in Towcester that, 'Having been ill, I wrote to Sir Hamilton Harty telling him that it had put me so much behind [. . .] with my Symphony that it would be best not to announce it for performance on March 19th' (as originally planned), and expressing Sir Hamilton's wish that it would be reserved for him; a BBC performance was not therefore necessarily possible and certainly finishing it on time for the March 1934 performance was doubtful anyway. Boult replied on 12 January that he had read Walton's letter 'with some apprehension'. This was not unfounded. In February, Walton wrote, 'There is, I am alarmed and disappointed to tell you, quite definitely no hope of my finishing this Symphony in time for its intended performance on March 19th,' apologizing profusely for the inconvenience (Boult was hoping for the second performance for the BBC in May, and this meant that Harty would still get the first performance). 'I am extremely sorry if this causes you much inconvenience, and I am sure you will realise that it is a rather painful situation for me to live down,' he wrote. However, by March he was writing to Christabel Aberconway that 'The Symphony progresses slowly and steadily & I've now completed the 3rd movement. You know how rarely I am pleased with anything I write, but with this particular movement I think (I hope I'm right) I've brought off something a bit A1 extra'. In June he sent all three movements to Ernest Newman: 'I am most grateful to you for taking an interest in the work,' he wrote, 'and I can assure you that any criticisms you may like to make, adverse or otherwise, especially the former, will be more than welcome.' By July Walton was feeling 'pretty gloomy' about the progress of the final movement; writing to Dora, wife of Hubert Foss, his publisher at OUP, he told her that he was at the end of his tether: 'As a matter of fact I'm not at all sure that I shan't have to begin this movement all over again & only a chance remark of the gardeners wife as she brought in the famous ham saved me from destroying it already. "How pretty your music is getting – it sounds just like a great big band."'

By August, he had had a reply from Newman, who had given him cause for 'satisfaction and encouragement'. Sir Hamilton Harty, who was to conduct its first performance had seen only the first two movements at this stage, but to Walton seemed 'sympathetic & understanding' towards the work. Newman had advised 'most careful handling to secure an adequate performance', but Walton was 'hoping for the best' as Harty was insisting on extensive rehearsals, 'not because the notes are in themselves so difficult, but so as to give the players a chance to get inside the work'. But by the end of October, the fourth movement was still unfinished, when Adrian Boult telegrammed Walton saying that he would like to include the symphony as the 'centre attraction' of a Winter Promenade Concert taking place on 10 January. Walton could only reply, 'So sorry second performance of symphony reserved for Courtaulds.' On 13 November, there was again some disappointment that the second (incomplete) performance was reserved for the Courtauld/Sargent/LSO concert, set for 4 April 1935 (the first having been scheduled for 3 December 1934).

'We regret to hear your decision relative to the Symphony. You will of course realise that it caused us a certain amount of unpleasantness,' advised Boult. 'May I ask whether you would let us give the first performance of the complete work?' he asked, hoping to include it in the London Music Festival scheduled for May 1935. 'I fear we must leave it at this and wait until the work is quite finished before doing anything more about it; but the matter will certainly not be forgotten,' wrote Boult in an internal memo. And indeed, the circumstances surrounding the symphony's first performance never have been quite forgotten. In the Proms 2014 120th season, the BBC was still boasting of giving the first complete performance.

With regard to its composition, Walton wrote to Patrick Hadley on its difficult birth, 'I persisted in finding something which I felt to be right & tolerably up to the standard of the previous movements. This involved me in endless trouble & I've burn't about 3 finales, when I saw that they were'nt [sic] really leading anywhere or saying anything.' The difficulties made Walton feel a bit 'oopset' about the prospect of the Symphony's first performance, which the committee of the LSO had urged to go ahead, as 'another postponement would be fatal', despite Harty's willingness to wait until the following March, or to perform the work without a finale. 'It being pointed very forcibly, by my friends and advisers, that it was the lesser of two evils, I concurred. Anyhow I'm certain that it is better for it to appear like this, than with a bad or artificial finale.'

The first three movements are Walton expressing his anguish. To Christabel Aberconway he was referring to the symphony as his 'unfinished' – which was not now worrying him too much, though as it stood the end was 'a trifle on the gloomy side'. This, of course, is the slow *andante malinconia*. But now, when the inspiration for this emotional expression of a failed relationship was behind him, was he to finish the work appropriately? The last movement is different from what has gone before, and it ends on that heroic note. But in November it was still in gestation. In the composer's own words, 'The only things that can be said about it are, either "Thank God, there's not a finale" or "What a pity there isn't one" or the more subtle ones may say "I wonder what the finale will be like".' This letter reveals much about Walton's inner world. His concern was that the finale should continue what he calls the emotional and spiritual tone of the first three movements rather than the 'notes', which may be 'bad enough' – a typically self-deprecating remark. He was satisfied with the first three movements – they were 'as good as they could be' – and if he could only complete a finale that was as good, the whole would be 'a bit of orlright'.

'When Walton completed his First Symphony in 1935 after Imma had left him for another man, he dedicated the work to her,' writes Stewart Craggs. Its first three movements – in turn furious, spiteful and depressive – can be seen as charting an emotional relationship that was breaking up in extreme bitterness. The finale, on the contrary, radiates a triumphalism that appears to express Walton's state of mind – exhilarated, free-wheelingly optimistic and not a little relieved – at the start of his new life with Alice, Viscountess Wimborne. But Walton's dedication, if at least partly ironic, was also honest. Without Imma, the First Symphony would not have come to life as we know it.[39] In her biography of Walton, his wife Susana provides some fascinating insight into the relationship and, in particular, some comment on the *con malizia* and finale. In early 1933 Walton, still in Italy, wrote to Hamilton Harty, apologizing for the slow progress he was making. 'I hope and think that it promises to be better than any work I've written hitherto,' he wrote, 'but that may be only an optimistic reaction to the months of despair I've been through when I thought I should never be able to write another note.' He was not just feeling gloomy about Imma, however:

> I must say I think it is almost hopeless for anyone to produce anything in any of the arts these days. It is practically impossible to get away from the general feeling of hopelessness and chaos which exists everywhere.[40]

Walton was absorbed by Imma and, writes Susana, 'was impressed by Imma's apparently extraordinary power to heal. Once, when he broke his nose in an accident, she made the bruise and swelling disappear overnight by laying on her hands. The symphony dragged on by fits and starts for three years and William decided that Imma's healing powers could also help with his work.' Perhaps Walton was the quintessential tortured artist. '"Symphonies are a lot of work to write," William told me. "Too much. One has to have something really appalling happen to one, that lets loose the fount of inspiration".'[41] Sure enough, by 1934 Imma, Walton's 'first true love' had left him for Tibor Csato, a Hungarian doctor. This left him without his muse and frustratingly thwarted in his attempts to complete the symphony. It was an acrimonious break-up and the depth of feeling especially in the second movement of the symphony – *con malizia* – is palpable. Walton kept the dedication to her, but began his relationship with Alice, Viscountess Wimborne, twenty-two years his senior, which was to last until her death from cancer in 1948. Susana Walton recounts her husband's explanation of the problems he had, and which delayed his finishing the symphony, the completion of which was 'undoubtedly' inspired by Alice Wimborne:

> I changed horses, so to speak. A great mistake to change horses crossing streams. Imma left me, and I found beautiful, intelligent Alice. She was very kind, full of all the virtues. Moreover I even got on very well with her husband, Lord Wimborne, a Privy Councillor, who had been Viceroy of Ireland. One of England's richest industrialists, he had been a steel magnate. The family seemed to like me, I don't know why.

They remained in Amalfi, where Walton struggled to finish the symphony. Of Alice, Walton later recalled: 'She was a few years older than me, a grand hostess, very rich and very musical ... Alice was very good at making me work and would get very cross if I mucked about.'[42] Alice gave sumptuous parties after each 'first' performance, those of the first three movements in December 1934 and of the complete symphony a year later. Testament to the closeness William enjoyed with another friend and collaborator, Constant Lambert, Susan Walton retells the story of another solution to being 'stuck' in the final movement:

> [W]hen I got to the middle of the movement I was stuck, so I rang up a friend at the other end of London to ask if he had any ideas ...

'The "friend at the other end of London" must have been Constant Lambert,' writes Susana. Paul Harper-Scott has named Constant Lambert, together with Cecil Gray, as two of Walton's most influential and sympathetic friends.[43]

No volume (not even this modest one) that discusses politics and music in the 1930s can ignore Harper-Scott's book 'Revolution, Reaction and William Walton', published in 2012. By the author's own account, it is essentially a work of philosophy, but its emphasis on Walton and modernism means it cannot go without comment if merely to acknowledge that his choice for his case study of William Walton is more or less arbitrary, 'because he's a completely ludicrous figure', not at all modernist and that even he 'cannot resist of the force of ... the "Truth" that is emerging in modernist music'.[44]

This volume is, rather, a survey of contemporary views of Britain and its music in the 1930s. It is for the scholar who is interested in this enthralling period and, I hope, will also have some appeal to the music lover as well as to the general reader interested in the cultural history of the 1930s. I would therefore advise the reader who wishes to seek a way forward, beyond the discussions of 'our imperial and demoralized political economy' and of 1930s English music in the context of communism, to turn to Harper-Scott, in the hope that this will help us provide a quilting-point 'to supplant neoliberalism'[45] or to find a way to heighten awareness of the present 'struggle between humanity and techno-capitalism'.[46] These are matters that concern us now. What concerned the people of the 1930s?

There is much presented on politics in the work, but it is not my intention to even attempt to represent its salient points, though I confess a profound bafflement at much of its content. 'In literature,' he writes, 'writers such as Eliot, Forster, and Woolf turned their back on the faithful modernist experiments of the earlier decades of the century and resurrected old genres such as the medieval pageant play (Eliot, *The Rock*; Forster, *Abinger Pageant* and *England's Pleasant Land*) or even, in Tolkien's case, brandished medievalism as a full-blow [sic] fantasy.'[47] Harper-Scott's book ends with an extensive commentary on Walton's First Symphony, aligning it with the 'death of the modern project' in Britain. There is a vision of England in Walton's music:

> With the attainment of various motivic and harmonic *telé*, Walton turns the vestigially faithful-modernist fragmentation of the opening into a characteristically reactive-modernist virtue: the restricted ambition of the Tolkien/Eliot English vision. The new community presented in all of Walton's music is a vision of an England whose ethical reach is drawn into itself, no longer morally and politically policing the world but withdrawing into a positively construed insular carapace. In his post-war music [i.e. post the First World War], the First Symphony's traversal of the motion from the faithful to the reactive subject is presumed: already as a starting point, and in the social-democratic world the trace of the communist Event is denied: 'Yes, we have to do something about our impoverished and demoralized political economy, but Communist modernism is not the way: we can rebuild our society – not as if nothing has happened but in a less radical way than that'. We do not customarily hear post-war austerity and practical coping anticipated in 1930s English music ... but ... its response to motions of history is not as conventional as some have presumed.[48]

Harper-Scott makes the work a mere reaction to communism. He writes that in the First Symphony, 'We can almost hear the music declare: "I was once an *enfant terrible* and involved in modernism – look at the first three movements – but what I'm doing now proves that this was the folly of youth".'[49] But Stephen Lloyd has described the symphony as 'fastidious craftsmanship that shows through every bar of the finished score',[50] and although there are Sibelian influences, he writes, Walton's 'remarkable' First Symphony 'could have been written by nobody else. In performance . . . its effect is shattering. After the cumulative power of the first movement, and the nervous tension of the scherzo (marked, famously, *Presto, con malizia*), there is a slow – at time[s] stormy – movement of great beauty, yet with an uneasy undercurrent of unrest, as suggested by its direction *Andante con malincolia*. The jubilant, almost triumphant, finale was surely the only way to release the listener from the stern grip of what is arguably the finest post-Elgar English symphony.'[51]

Incidentally, while Norman Lebrecht can acknowledge that Walton's symphony – especially its finale – 'reflects a change of mistresses from Baroness Imma Doernberg to Lady Alice Wimborne', and is thus a personal document, the parallel in Vaughan Williams's symphony of the same year is overlooked, finding Vaughan Williams's Fourth Symphony 'a furiously dissonant commentary on political events',[52] rather than a personal document. This is the oft quoted but unsound explanation of the Fourth. He also dismisses Walton's First Symphony, which 'came out rather like Sibelius' Fifth turned sour', the composer, living 'in considerable comfort', and later enjoying 'a languid Mediterranean existence among friends'.[53] Lebrecht (who, to be fair, acknowledges his one-sidedness) also writes off Delius's double concerto as 'simply tedious'.[54]

It must be said, however, that on attending the first complete performance of Walton's symphony, Britten didn't think much of it, either, writing in his diary: 'A great tragedy for English music. Last hope of W. Gone now – this is a conventional work, reactionary in the extreme & dull & depressing.'[55] But we can forgive Britten his youth. He was also rebuked at the time by Grace Williams for his comments on Vaughan Williams's *Five Mystical Songs*, a performance of which he attended in 1934. He wrote that the work had finished him entirely:

> [T]hat 'pi' and artificial mysticism combined with, what seems to me, technical incompetence sends me crazy. His correspondent, Grace Williams, rebuked him sternly for this: 'Now don't malign poor old Uncle Ralph and call his mysticism artificial. There's nothing artificial about the man: I swear it; and I happen to know him pretty well. Those songs are absolutely sincere and *well scored*.'[56]

There is a parallel between the appearance of Vaughan Williams's Fourth Symphony and Walton's monumental First. Both appear after a similar gestation period. In August, Vaughan Williams wrote to Adrian Boult: 'as regards my symphony I have been writing it for about 3 years now & I believe it is finished. I have made a 2 pft arrangement and I will get that played through.'[57] Adrian Boult heard the arrangement on two pianos in November, noting the timing of each movement – 7¼, 8½ and 14 minutes – 'the Third and Fourth Movements are played without break'.[58] Some of Vaughan Williams's difficulties with the symphony are expressed in a letter to Arthur Bliss, whose advice (particularly after the death of Holst) he relied upon and which led him to make certain alterations to the score:

> I can't *cut out* that recapitulation of the 2nd subject *slow* at the end – but I have led up to it differently... [and] now I have made a more emotional climax and a gradual diminuendo to the soft end... I believe that will be all right.
>
> I am going to alter the end of the scherzo – but cannot yet see the right way to do it...
>
> You mustn't think your advice has not been valuable because I have not exactly followed it – when I give advice to my pupils I tell them that they can do one of 3 things
> (a) accept it blindly – bad
> (b) reject it kindly – bad but not so bad
> (c) think out a 3rd course for themselves – sound.[59]

The usual Uncle Ralph self-deprecation and humour is clearly in evidence here! But the similarities are striking. Both symphonies were written over a period of three years. The sonata form of the first movement of each makes them conventional, in a sense. But both symphonies are violent and stormy. Though their idioms are entirely different, the experience of hearing them for the first time provoked similarly strong reactions, even shock. They are the two large-scale British works from 1934 that remain in the repertoire. The relentless pounding rhythm and driving force behind the first movement of the Walton couldn't be further from the quiet of Vaughan Williams's 'soft end'. And rather than a reaction to political events of the day (Harper-Scott's 'Communist modernism' for Walton, and the political scene in Europe as has been endlessly ascribed to Vaughan Williams's symphony), both were conceived, arguably, with the subjectivity of both composers' relationships with women: Adeline on the one hand and Imma on the other, both men suffering in their own way and expressing their anguish in the music.

Vaughan Williams called his removal to The White Gates in Dorking, due to Adeline's ill health, an 'exile'. Though born in Gloucestershire, and schooled in the countryside, living in rural Surrey was not the city life that he relished. He loved young people and evidently loved life. Being married to the invalid Adeline, despite his loyalty to (and fear of) her, frustrated him. There is no romanticism, let alone pastoralism in his Fourth Symphony. But it is passionate nevertheless, and very angry. Anthony Payne has called it 'shatteringly dissonant'. The composer himself was cagey about it: that it reflected 'unbeautiful times', though not as a definite picture of anything external such as the condition of Europe, but, rather, it 'just occurred to him that way', a view he expressed in a letter. After Adeline's death in 1951, Vaughan Williams smashed up her chair, and certain relics associated with her as well as photographs of her family were destroyed.[60] Following the deaths of Elgar, Delius and Holst, Vaughan Williams was 'devastated', writes Simon Heffer, who points out that besides George Butterworth, there had never been anyone else with whom he discussed his work and that musically, no one had ever been as close to him as Holst, the F Minor Symphony 'the last work on which Holst would have any immediate influence',[61] though he did turn to Arthur Bliss as we have seen.

> Vaughan Williams also became depressed about the worsening situation in Europe, watching Mussolini 'thundering at the door', as he told Maud Karpeles, and noting the growing tensions in Austria with a sense of foreboding . . .
>
> For all his denial of a programme for the symphony he was writing, it stretches credulity too far to believe that one as conscious as he was of what was happening abroad, and with such well-formed opinions on it (he complained to Maud Karpeles that 'the funny thing is that it seems to be our pacifist party in England who are crying out for us to intervene') could have kept it entirely separate from his music.[62]

Adeline's health as well as his own – a cut on his foot exacerbating an earlier leg injury – contributed to his sense of frustration, impatience and anger in the new symphony. As much as speculation suggested that the F Minor was a reaction to the world situation and the horror of war, there is also another consideration:

> Some of his friends even suspected that his wife's increasing frailty and the realisation that she would never again be active were the main spurs to his anger, even more than the futility of war and international conflict.[63]

This must surely be the answer. Vaughan Williams constantly refuted the idea that the symphony was about war. And it makes sense. The symphony was written between 1931 and 1934. War was not yet inevitable; commentators have been too keen to impose a programme on the work that only makes sense in retrospect. It is surely the personal expression of a man of feeling and conscience, not afraid of his own anger. Ursula Vaughan Williams's account of the Fourth is also often quoted. 'His own story of the genesis of his Fourth Symphony was that he had read an account of one of the "Freak Festivals" in which a symphony, he couldn't remember who had written it, was described in detail,' she wrote. 'So without any philosophical, prophetic, or political germ, No.4 took its life from a paragraph in *The Times*.' But Hugh Ottoway warns that 'The composer's stories about his works should be treated with caution', adding that if *The Times* story was true, 'then the underlying impulse, the pressure to create, must already have been very strong indeed'.[64] In an article in the Journal of the Ralph Vaughan Williams Society, Geoff Brown has unearthed *The Times* number in which the story is based. It is the final report on the July 1931 (the ninth) annual festival of the International Society for Contemporary Music (ISCM) – the so-called 'Freak Festival' – and it appeared on 1 August.[65] *Times* critic H. C. Colles wrote that only Webern's symphony 'blazed a trail into the future'. Going on to give an account of the trends in modern symphonic writing, Colles describes it thus:

> Prodded into activity by dissonance, soothed by sentiment, overwhelmed by the power of a battering climax.

'If that does not describe the Fourth Symphony to come, nothing does,' writes Geoff Brown. He is in agreement with Ottoway, however:

> It would be wrong to make too much of this. Indeed it might be wrong to make anything of this. VW would surely have written his Symphony in F Minor if he had never read *The Times* at all: the very most the article could have done would have been to lend support to an already existing notion for a symphony containing dissonant battering.[66]

As Michael Kennedy has noted, after its first performance, there was much reaction, but at the time, he writes, 'nobody related the symphony to the state of the world in 1935. Colles, indeed, talked of its "gaiety"; others, though finding it grim, did not look to fascism for an explanation. This myth developed later, and some of his friends propagated it.'[67] It is Frank Howes who was the first to do so in a letter in which he said, 'In No.4 the prophet sees the nature of naked violence triumphant in Europe – and in No.6 there is similarly a prophetic warning of what will happen to mankind if it persists in its foolish, wicked wars.'[68] The 'electrifying and cataclysmically powerful' symphony was the first to be identified by a number alone, writes Michael Jameson, 'but its vitriolic angst and destructive power render any extra-musical synonym redundant. The new symphony sounded (to those who would listen) its own threatening alarum, and as Frank Howes observed "the prophet sees the nature of naked violence triumphant in Europe".'[69] Even Mellers concurs with the most common interpretation of the symphony; that it was a prophecy of the Second World War is borne out by the fact that it was composed alongside *Dona Nobis Pacem*, the text of which explicitly concerns war, suggesting that the Fourth was, indeed, a product of the decade's turbulence:

> It could not have been otherwise, for Vaughan Williams could not regard the battleground of his art as separable from the outside world. No less than the Cantata, the Symphony is an appeal, if not for peace (that comes in the Fifth), then at least for the renunciation of war – in a psychological rather than material sense. Certainly war's horror is incarnate in the first bar.[70]

In her biography, Ursula Vaughan Williams provides a useful retrospective for the end of 1934, which sums up both recent musical developments and the political scene in Europe:

> That winter Ralph was given the John Clementi Collard Life Fellowship – a single award held previously only by Sir Edward Elgar and given '*honoris causa* for outstanding services to British music'. John Barbirolli was conducting operas at Sadler's Wells; Robert Helpmann had a great success dancing Satan in *Job*; there were the first performances of Williams Walton's unfinished symphony; and *A Boy Was Born* by Benjamin Britten, then aged twenty-one, was published. But on the continent there were sinister portents: the November number of *The Music Review* reported an attack on Paul Hindemith in *Die Musik* and commented: 'The folly of confusing music and politics is not only childish, it is tragic. Dr. Furtwängler whose word carries some weight in musical matters in Germany has published a protest against the application of political standards in the world of art'. It was still officially a time of peace, at any rate in England, but elsewhere a time that was beginning to make demands of heroism.[71]

Besides working on the F Minor Symphony that year, Vaughan Williams was also quietly working on several other works. *Six Teaching Pieces* for pianoforte appeared in three books. They included three two-part inventions, the Valse Lent, Nocturne and a Canon. Various arrangements of English folk songs, among them *An Acre of Land, John Dory, I'll Never Love Thee More, The Ploughman, Tobacco's but an Indian Weed*, and most famously, the *Fantasia on Greensleeves* adapted from the opera *Sir John in Love*, his version of *The Merry Wives of Windsor*, which was composed between 1924 and 1928. The folk song *Lovely Joan* – a tune found by Vaughan Williams while collecting songs in Norfolk – is the basis of the middle section. It received its first concert performance at the Queen's Hall on 27 September by the BBC Symphony Orchestra and was conducted by the composer himself. The September 1934 prom was the first concert performance of the piece – and the last, at least until eighty years later in a 2014 Prom, which also featured the Fourth Symphony. The English folk song continued to inspire him. Vaughan Williams contributed to a large volume of folk songs from Newfoundland, and an unpublished work, not performed until 1937, was written for the English Folk Dance Society Masque. Other new works that year included the *Suite for Viola and Small Orchestra*, dedicated to Lionel Tertis, receiving its first performance at the Queen's Hall on 12 November with Malcolm Sargent conducting the LPO, and with Tertis as soloist. Music for *The Pageant of Abinger* consisted of various hymn tunes arranged for a performance by the Band of the 2nd Battalion of the West Yorkshire Regiment (known as the Prince of Wales's Own) on 14 July 1934. E. M. Forster provided the narrator's speeches.

After the first performance of his symphony in December, William Walton attended a rehearsal of Vaughan Williams's F Minor. During the rehearsal, he overheard Constant Lambert telling a fellow musician, Arthur Benjamin, that it was the greatest symphony since Beethoven. 'Walton's own symphony had been ground-breaking, compelling, intense and exciting; but what Vaughan Williams had at last more than proved was that he could match those trends and qualities among the younger generation without being seen to imitate them,' writes Simon Heffer.[72] If earlier in the year Lambert was lamenting the state of 'music in decline', this, then, was the kind of music he wanted!

In *Music, Ho!* Lambert had written a useful comparison between the nationalism in the music of Elgar, Vaughan Williams and Walton. Vaughan Williams's style, he wrote, is based on material without classical or international precedent and which, without being necessarily folk song in the picturesque way, is intimately connected with the inflections and mood of English folk music. But it cannot be said to share the freedom from provinciality shown by Elgar and Walton:

> Elgar's music is as national in its way as the music of Vaughan Williams but, by using material that in type can be related back to the nineteenth-century German composers, Elgar avoids any suspicion of provincial dialect, even though his national flavour is sufficiently strong to replace certain countries – France in particular. Similarly Walton (who, reacting against the music of the immediately preceding generation, has far more in common with Elgar than with Vaughan Williams), by using material that can be related to Handel on the one hand and to Prokofieff on the other, addressed an international audience in easy terms without losing his national and personal qualities.[73]

On the other hand, another new composition by Vaughan Williams, *The Pilgrim's Pavement*, a hymn for soprano solo, mixed chorus and organ, with words by Margaret Ridgely Partridge, was written for and read at the dedication of the Pilgrim's Pavement in the central nave of the Cathedral of St. John the Divine, New York City, on 11 March 1934. The work, Andante Moderate, is, interestingly, in D Modal Minor, and connects it to both Vaughan Williams's symphony in that key (his Fifth) as well as a new symphony which had been performed in the New Year, that of his brother-in-law R. O. Morris. I explore Morris's symphony in the following chapter.

Notes

1. 'Elgar's Last Symphony: Unfinished MS. Handed over to the BBC', *The Times*, 11 August 1934, p. 10.
2. Lloyd, 2001: 114.
3. Northrop-Moore, 1984: 820.
4. Lloyd, 2001: 114.
5. Foreman, 1987: 167.
6. Lloyd, 2001: 112.
7. William Walton to Christabel Aberconway in Hayes (ed.), 2002: 97.
8. Lloyd, 2001: 118.
9. The Curzon Cinema: 'Unfinished Symphony', *The Times*, 1 March 1934, p. 12.
10. Tarzan Meets Schubert, The Cinema, BBC, 19 November 1934 (transcript) in Cooke, 2001: 23.
11. *The Listener*, Volume XII, Issue 311, 27 December 1934, p. 1066.
12. Cooke, 2001: 32.
13. New Film in London: 'The Merry Widow', *The Times*, 26 November 1934, p. 10.
14. The closure of the institute was again, perhaps, to Britain's advantage.
15. Cinema Music: Recent Experiments, *The Times*, 26 May 1934, p. 10.
16. Raising Film Standards: British and American Efforts, *The Times*, 30 May 1934, p. 12.
17. Sleeve Notes from CHAN8870, (C) 1990, Christopher Palmer.
18. Lloyd, 2001: 149, quoted from an interview in the *Sunday Telegraph* of 25 March 1962.
19. Bauer and Walton also later collaborated on *Salute to the Red Army*, the pageant staged at the Royal Albert Hall during the War to mark the twenty-fifth anniversary of the army of the Soviet Union.
20. Hetherington, 2006: 41–2.
21. Ibid., 37.

22 Ibid., 48–9. Mathieson went on to persuade Vaughan Williams to write for the Wartime Ministry of Information-sponsored film *49th Parallel*, the composer's first of many forays into film music.
23 Bennett, 2015: 15.
24 Ibid., 18.
25 Ibid., 19.
26 Ibid., 16.
27 I explore the music for *49th Parallel* (1942) in *Culture and Propaganda in WWII*.
28 Winder, 2011: 244–5.
29 A Gracious Act, 'Sing as We Go', Gracie Fields' New Film, *The Blackshirt*, Issue #74, 21 September 1934, p. 8.
30 Balcon, 1969: 37.
31 Dean, 1973: 186–7. *The Constant Nymph* was remade in Hollywood in 1943 with Charles Boyer and Joan Fontaine. Korngold again provided the music.
32 Ibid., 233.
33 *Lorna's Song* is the only film music composed by Rutland Boughton. A recording was released in September 2020 by Albion Records, sung by the star of the film Victoria Hopper, who is featured on the cover image.
34 OUP letter to the BBC dated 26 September 1935 (BBC WAC, Composer file WAL).
35 Lloyd, 2001: 139, note 90. The most accessible of Bax's symphonies, it is dedicated to Sibelius, and it was first performed in a fortnight of concerts arranged by the BBC in the New Year.
36 Craggs, 1999: 78.
37 Foss, 1954: 146.
38 London Symphony Orchestra: William Walton's New Symphony, *The Times*, 4 December 1934, p. 12.
39 Hayes (ed.), 2002: 55.
40 Walton, 1989: 76.
41 Ibid., 86.
42 From the film *The Haunted End of the Day* (1983). The recent publication of Chips Channon's diaries in full reveal how waspish he could be. Walton was Sacheverell Sitwell's 'yes-man' (31 July 1935), and Alice Wimborne 'the silliest woman in London Society' (15 August 1935).
43 Harper-Scott, 2012: 224.
44 Interview published in *The Oxford Culture Review*, 10 December 2012 (accessed online 29 July 2020).
45 Harper-Scott, 2012: 252.
46 Ibid., 253.
47 Ibid., 230. E. M. Forster's *Abinger Pageant* was accompanied by music written by Vaughan Williams and first appeared in 1934.

48 Ibid., 249.
49 Ibid., 222.
50 Lloyd, 2001: 110.
51 Ibid., 139.
52 Lebrecht, 1992: 368.
53 Ibid., 374.
54 Ibid., 93.
55 Lloyd, 2001: 145.
56 Heffer, 2000: 41.
57 Cobbe (ed.), 2008: 229.
58 BBC WAC, file note dated 6 November 1934.
59 Ralph Vaughan Williams to Arthur Bliss, 6 November 1934 in Cobbe (ed.), 2008: 233.
60 These claims are made in the 2007 BBC film *The Passions of Vaughan Williams*.
61 Heffer, 2000: 82.
62 Ibid., 83.
63 Ibid., 86.
64 Ottaway, 1972: 29.
65 The ISCM or IGNM (Internationale Gessellschaft für Neue Musik or International Society for Contemporary Music), the Schoenberg-dominated society propagating serial music, was founded in 1922 by Professor Edward J. Dent, who was president from its foundation until 1938. In 1936, the ISCM festival was held in Barcelona, the year the Spanish Civil War began, and in 1939 in Warsaw. One wonders if Cyril Scott linked these coincidences in any way. I discuss his esoteric views on music's 'secret influence' later.
66 Geoff Brown, *The Times* and the Fourth Symphony, *Journal of the Ralph Vaughan Williams Society*, Issue #21, June 2001, pp. 15–16.
67 Kennedy, 1980: 245.
68 Quoted in Ottoway, 1972: 29.
69 Jameson, 1997: 67–8.
70 Mellers, 1991: 163.
71 Vaughan Williams, 1964: 203.
72 Heffer, 2000: 84.
73 Lambert, 1966: 135.

3

Musical experiment and fashion

A popular seasonal presentation and one of the first musical events of the year, Rutland Boughton's opera or, rather, choral drama *Bethlehem*, based on the fourteenth-century Coventry Nativity Play, was staged, ten performances of which were to be given at Church House. In this 'dramatic fantasia on Christmas Carols,' wrote *The Times*' reviewer, 'Boughton has firmly brought together in his music the double strand in the nativity play – the sacred mystery and naive rusticity', a coming together of modern music and the atmosphere of the medieval mystery play through the carol as intermediary, the total effect of which was 'something wholly English'.[1] During Christmas week, scenes from Bethlehem had also been relayed from the Pavilion at Bath for the BBC's West Regional programme.[2]

Meanwhile, the BBC's series of six concerts of British music also got underway on New Year's Day, broadcast live from the Queen's Hall under the baton of Adrian Boult. The varied programme featured Constant Lambert's *Rio Grande*, the *Cockaigne* overture by Elgar, Delius's *Song of the High Hills* (with Isobel Baillie, Eric Greene and members of the Philharmonic Choir), with several other songs by Roger Quilter and Cyril Scott, as well as Alexander Mackenzie's overture *Britannia*. Most importantly, the concert included the first performance of R. O. Morris's symphony in D. Though he was 'not a young composer,' wrote *The Times*' reviewer the following day, R. O. Morris's music 'has been slow to find its way'. Indeed, the names of R. O. Morris and Alexander Mackenzie (as well as Rutland Boughton) remain unfamiliar to twenty-first century ears, and the prominence of their music during the first week of 1934 is thus even more intriguing.[3]

Reginald Owen Morris (1886–1948), who had a reputation as a great teacher, joined the Duke of Cornwall's Light Infantry at the outbreak of the First World War with his friends George Butterworth and Geoffrey Toye. He married Emmie Fisher, sister of Adeline Vaughan Williams in February 1915.

None of his music has ever been performed at the Proms, and very little seems to have been made commercially available. The Lindsays's recording of two of his *Canzoni Ricertati* (Nos. 1 and 6) for String Quartet appeared in 1993 care of ASV Records. The sleeve notes acknowledge Morris as 'a leading authority on Sixteenth Century contrapuntal music' and Professor of Counterpoint and Composition at the Royal College of Music. Probably written during 1934, Morris's book *The Structure of Music* was published in December 1935 by OUP and was an important contribution to the understanding of music at the time. In two parts, Harmonic Forms and Contrapuntal Forms, and one of several works on sixteenth-century counterpoint, Vaughan Williams rated the volume very highly. Morris's students included Edmund Rubbra, Gerald Finzi, Constant Lambert and Michael Tippett. In her biography Ursula Vaughan Williams tells how Vaughan Williams, his wife Adeline, Emmie and Reginald Morris were all living together at 13 Cheyne Walk in September 1926 when R. O. was appointed Director of the Department of Composition of the Curtis Institute of Music in Philadelphia, though by 1928 this had not worked out and the Morrises returned to England. Organized in 1930, a concert of Morris's works was 'something on which Ralph had set his heart. He felt that R. O.'s diffidence obscured the real value of his music behind his reputation as a teacher and scholar, so he concentrated on making the evening a success to the last details,' writes Ursula. After the concert Adeline wrote of the performance:

> We have been back five days after a most delightful and exciting London season. The climax was the Morris concert – lovely. We feel so satisfied – we were so happy about the music itself – the hall was almost brimming over – afterwards there was a party at the Edwin Fishers' new house ... you can guess how Uncle R went 'all in' and when after having run the gamut of every delicacy and drink he came upon smoked salmon and began all over again. He was very anxious about the concert – looked a wreck. Morris was angelic, a surprise to us all! It was most warming to my heart to see him on the platform bowing to the outburst of shouts and clapping – a real ovation, not a sham one at all – how well one knows the difference![4]

R. O. Morris's D Minor Symphony deserves some investigation, because Vaughan Williams's major Dorian-mode work, the Fifth Symphony, did not appear until 1943. It is easy to speculate that it was written with the memory of R. O. Morris's 1934 premiere in mind. The symphony was four or five years in gestation. The use of the Dorian D key of this symphony was a deliberate evocation of an English Elizabethan past. Surely R. O. Morris was attempting the same thing. According to *The Times'* review of the first performance of Morris's symphony, 'the Dorian cut of the opening tune of this symphony makes one expect him to acknowledge considerable indebtedness. But the tune is no sooner proposed than one realizes that the debt has been paid off. The composer is free; the three movements develop on lines which are as different from those of Vaughan Williams as from those of the other two English masters' (i.e. Elgar and Bax). The reviewer's prediction, that it is music 'to be heard again', a symphony 'which should presently take its place a mong its companions of this programme as something to which an audience returns with the assurance of pleasure in its finely drawn lines', is perhaps a rare misjudgement in H. C. Colles's speculations despite its qualities:

> Music which always interests because of its clarity, its moderation, and its shapeliness. There is nothing extravagant, nothing redundant. Innumerable points of beauty arise from the development of its simple ideas.[5]

The series of British music concerts continued apace. *The Times'* review of the Queen's Hall concert of 8 January, conducted by Adrian Boult, provides a useful contemporary view of various works which, though not receiving their first performance, 'offered the opportunity of renewing acquaintance with several [works] which have not had frequent performances'. Lord Berners's *Fantasie Espagnole* 'made a lively, if rather un-British, climax' to the concert, Benjamin Dale's *Romance* for viola and orchestra and three songs by Dresden-based Roland Bocquet were the 'slight' things that made up the second half. Two songs from Rutland Boughton's *The Immortal Hour*, and Eugene Goossens's *Sinfonietta* were heard in the first. Vaughan Williams's *Flos Campi* was 'still apt to leave its hearers wondering what it is about', especially with reference to the quotations from the Song of Solomon. *The Times* critic's advice was to forget about the words and, rather, 'listen to Mr. Lionel Tertis's viola, and to the other instruments and voices in relation thereto [as] Mr. Tertis gives the whole work continuity and substance and brings out the growing beauty of the latter part'. The major work in the concert was Arnold Bax's 'vigorous and highly coloured' Fourth Symphony, which for *The Times* was probably more likely to become popular than any of Bax's earlier symphonies:

> Though one has a fear that in trying to achieve a more forthright style the composer risked dropping into the commonplaces of melody, disguising them with elaborate orchestration. Certainly the work is not on a level with the majestic third symphony, but possibly it represents a stage through which he had to pass, and no modern British composer has shown a more remarkable capacity for growth than has Bax.[6]

The public got the opportunity only a week later to hear whether that capacity for growth had materialized in the first performance of the composer's Fifth Symphony, 'the most important musical event of the week', at the Courtauld-Sargent concert conducted by Sir Thomas Beecham on 15 January, and to be repeated the following day, at the Queen's Hall.[7] And, indeed, its first 'vivid' performance received a more than cordial reception since, according to *The Times*, the composer seemed to have made up his mind 'more definitely' than any living composer that the traditional symphony suited him best, and that the ground plan of this new work was 'exceedingly simple and free from any attempt to speak in an unknown tongue', but nevertheless containing passages of very full scoring, without using an excessively large orchestra. Bax 'has always had an enormous sense of orchestral effect, but with maturity he has learned to keep it under control', comments the reviewer, and 'the first impression of the work is that, while it is full of details which further hearings will make more perspicuous, the ground plan is exceedingly simple and free from any attempt to speak in an unknown tongue'.[8]

Like Vaughan Williams's Fourth and Walton's First, Bax's Fifth Symphony was begun in 1931. Immediately recognized as 'a substantial addition to the repertory of the larger orchestral works', *The Times* doubts that it would 'arouse the sort of popular enthusiasm evoked by Tchaikovsky's "Pathetic" in the late nineties, or by Elgar's First Symphony in the early nineteen hundreds'. Though melody, then, 'suffers' with the new music, Bax's new symphony was not without it, though to generate the sort of enthusiasm reserved for Elgar or Tchaikovsky he would need to be 'a franker melodist than Bax ever has been or is ever likely to become'. There is some melody to be had, as *The Times*' review of the performance testifies:

> The first movement is naturally the most elaborate and full of diversified interests; the second is a reverie over a melody of haunting beauty, with some exquisite features of scoring; the third begins with a dance measure which takes the place of a Scherzo, but gradually evolves into a movement of high purpose and exalted feeling.

The Times devoted a column to Bax's music from which the references to Tchaikovsky and Elgar come, with further commentary on the new symphony:

> Those of us who have watched Bax's development through the last quarter of a century regard this symphony as the ratification of a position which he has been slowly gaining, and which seemed promised to him when Sir Henry Wood produced his Third Symphony at Queen's Hall nearly a year ago.

In the process of writing five symphonies Bax's gathering ideas show how 'constructive thought' had displaced 'decorative effect', his latest symphony especially allowing listeners to begin to know Bax's voice as 'something distinct' from the 'generic voice' of modern composers:

> Someone described him as a composer who seemed 'to have gone modern against his better judgment.' The comment had just this much appositeness, that in all his work of the immediately post-war period, and particularly in the short choral pieces . . . there was a certain sense of straining after harmonic effect, as though he feared to put what he had to say into the simplest musical terms. While others had to labour to attain technical versatility, Bax was so accomplished that he had to learn what he could afford to do without, to shed excrescences and to exercise self-criticism.[9]

But a survey of Bax's symphonies at the Proms reveals, once again, a very meagre history. The Third has received nine performances (the most, of all seven symphonies), the last of which was given in 1944 – extraordinary for what *The Times* called a 'majestic' symphony, and for one of the works chosen by the Music Advisory Committee of the British Council to represent British music in its recording programme during the War. Even *The Tale the Pine Trees Knew* last appeared at the proms in 1945, *Tintagel* in 1989, *Overture to a Picaresque Comedy* appeared in 1994 (the 100th Prom season). The Fifth, perhaps the most accessible, has been heard just twice: on 11 September 1945, and again on 24 July 1984. But Bax is another unsung British composer of recent times. Why? Of all his works, *Tintagel* has had the most appearances but the last was twenty-five years ago, in 1989. *Roscatha* was heard on 25 August 2014. Julius Harrison's contribution to Victor Gollancz's Musical Companion of 1934 recognized Bax as 'possibly one of the most original composers the world has ever seen'. Symphonies have one thing in common with trees, he wrote, 'they are planted for future generations'. He was hoping as much for Bax's symphonies. Harrison's wishes are yet to be fulfilled, it would seem. Or perhaps Harrison was too quick to fill the gap left behind by Elgar, Delius and Holst? In this section of *The Musical Companion*, commentary on Bax takes up more room than all the other contemporary composers put together, Vaughan Williams having completed at that time only three symphonies. But Lewis Foreman's 1983 biography, revised in 2007, was received with much acclaim.[10] Releases of recordings of his music have done something to rescue Bax from neglect, but his decline in popularly since the 1980s is inexplicable, nonetheless. 'With a perfect command over resources of every description,' Harrison writes of the Fifth, Bax 'exhibits characteristics that can be likened to those of no other composer', and has an equal facility of reproducing the beauty or strength of 'all probable combinations of musical sounds' in his own way at almost any given moment:

> Since 1921 he has written five symphonies which are now acknowledged the world over as extremely important contributions in the history of the symphony. Romantic in origin, yet never unduly sentimental, they avow no programme. But at the same time there is in them some definite conflict or outpouring of the emotions in certain well-defined channels that stamps them with the hall-mark of greatness.

Harrison acknowledged that though the 'immense power' of the climaxes was sometimes coupled 'to a certain type of cacophony', they did not, however, 'fall on the ear with that sense of grating so nerve-racking in other modern works'. But he did concede that though the symphonies' 'fine qualities' were being appreciated in 1934, he feared that it would take many years before the happy stage when 'their many beautiful points' could be dissected by 'the man in the street' for 'indeed they are very beautiful, full of lovely themes and touches that cannot possibly be appreciated in full measure at one hearing'.[11]

The Times' reviews of the new music being performed during the festival certainly did not pull any punches, but as earlier reviews have shown, it was fair, and gave credit where it was due. Did it make any obvious blunders? That Bax's symphonies sank into relative obscurity and are now largely forgotten is maybe one contradiction to the initial reception. Its review of two new works at the fifth concert of the season, at which 'Mr. Frank Bridge conducted his "Rhapsody Phantasm" for pianoforte and orchestra', shows how cutting it could be:

> We wish it were possible to say something in commendation of this work, but, apart from an effective, if not very original, climax at the end, the music is as vague as its title. The material of it is undistinguished and its treatment turgid.[12]

Evidently, the concerts were not very well attended. However, the last of the six concerts attracted a 'better audience' both in numbers 'and in the signs its members gave of a lively interest in the proceedings'. Attributing the size of the audience to the presence of choral works, *The Times* suggests that 'English audiences have more faith in their composers' writing of choral music'. Walton's *Belshazzar's Feast* and Holst's *The Hymn of Jesus* were 'brilliantly displayed'. Among other new works was E. J. Moeran's Rhapsody No.2, 'a skillful work' which to *The Times'* critic, suggested 'rather too much of the earlier manner of Vaughan Williams', hoping to find Moeran's 'own voice emerging decisively in his newer things'.[13] A review of the series of six BBC Concerts as a whole appeared in a more substantial piece in the same issue of *The Times* on 13 January, which prompted a correspondent to comment upon the smaller audience at the fifth of the series:

> 'That the audiences were so small until the last concert led many otherwise well-wishers to see only failure in such a scheme, and even to scent hostility and perhaps resentment over such expenditure of time and money on the part of the BBC,' and indeed whether it was wise to have six concerts at such close intervals of time (two days apart).

But the BBC, in organizing the concerts, had 'laid the public and musicians alike under a debt of deep gratitude', for 'where in any other country would one find the broadcasting authorities public-minded enough to be responsible for so ambitious, and at the same time so idealistic, a scheme? And where, and in what other country, could they have found so fine and varied a mass of contemporary music, so modern though not merely fashionable, so alive without being extravagant, and above all so conscious of a tradition without being reactionary?' He issued a clarion call to music in Britain, supposedly *Das Land Ohne Musik*:

> We have been suffering from an inferiority complex too long over our music, and the public attitude is still to some extent that of a prejudiced hearer who has not yet developed the speculative sense in his growth and progress in musical understanding.[14]

The fortnight, which for *The Times* had shown 'an impressive demonstration of what living native composers are doing, and have been doing during the last 20 years or so, with an orchestra', included music by Bantock, William Wallace and Alexander Mackenzie, as well as Elgar's First Symphony and works by Ethel Smyth, which 'saved the programmes from modishness'. The performance of several new symphonic works showed British composers 'working on parallel lines with their contemporaries elsewhere'. What *The Times* called their 'community of outlook' was all the more interesting because it appeared at a time when national differences were being 'exploited consciously and often to the point of absurdity in other walks of life'. Eschewing the programmatic forms of composers such as Berlioz and Richard Strauss, the British also refused 'for the most part' the subjective point of view which resulted in the sophisticated emotionalism of Tchaikovsky and of Scriabin'. But the one difference between British composers and their Continental counterparts was that, even in the younger generation (Lambert and Walton), writers of orchestral music were 'very much more held by what is generally called the classical tradition', contemporary British works sounding 'comfortably old fashioned', with composers deciding that 'the past has produced a body of experience not lightly to be set aside'. A mistrust of new theories was, for Lambert and Walton and others like them, 'their most British quality'. And while they may toy a little with polytonality, atonality or even the twelve-tone scale, 'they would never pursue any of them with the relentless logic which has produced the post Schönberg school'. With very little of the music played in the fortnight 'experimental, and none of it iconoclastic', the effect of the new technologies was, again, very much in evidence. The BBC was credited with helping audiences learn 'just what modern symphonic music is', through 'its sane and thoughtful presentation'.[15]

Ethel Smyth's setting of H. B. Brewster's 'The Prison – a Dialogue' for soprano with soloist Elsie Suddaby and Stuart Robertson was performed under Thomas Beecham in a concert of the BBC Orchestra and the Philharmonic Choir on 3 January. According to *The Times*' reviewer, Smyth fought 'unflinchingly' for a hearing of her music which to some extent had failed to find interpreters 'in order to live'. 'But now that the battle is won,' wrote the reviewer, with a concert that also included the concerto for violin and horn, the Choral Scherzo 'Hey, Nonny No' and the overture to *The Wreckers*, 'her most representative opera'. The applause called her repeatedly to the platform: 'we may be content to join in congratulations on this well planned celebration of Dame Ethel Smyth's career'.[16]

Further testament to the BBC's important place in presenting music was arranging a further six concerts (the first three conducted by Boult, and the last three by Bruno Walter) for the London Music Festival for the opening weeks of May. Apart from a performance of Tchaikovsky's Op.23 piano concerto, the concert of 9 May was devoted to English music, and in particular the winning overture of a *Daily Telegraph* competition, the only new work in the entire programme. Composed in 1929 and dedicated to Percy Grainger, the winner, Cyril Scott's *Festival Overture* was premiered by the BBC Symphony Orchestra at the Queen's Hall conducted by Sir Adrian Boult. The competition's runner-up was *Metropolis*, said to be an abstract picture of London, by Frank Tapp (1883–1953). The overture depicts a 'serious London', and the only specific pictorial reference is a bell in F sharp inspired by St. Martin-in-the-Fields. The third prize was awarded to Arnold Cooke's *Concert Overture No.1*, which Cooke (1906–2005) said was Inspired by Hindemith. His harp quintet of 1932 was performed with the legendary harpist Maria Korchinska and broadcast in late 1934. All three competition winners were later performed at a Proms concert on 30 August, Cooke's first appearance at the Proms. The overtures were performed in succession at the beginning of the concert which also included Grieg songs, Opp.25 and 48, Prokoviev's D Major Violin Concerto (No.1), Borodin's Second Symphony in B Minor, Handel's Organ Concerto in B flat Major HWV 290 and *The Damnation of Faust* by Berlioz.

The Proms season of 1934 can be regarded as a useful barometer for British music in 1934. In addition to the forty-nine summer concerts, beginning on 11 August, a further twelve took place from New Year's Eve into January 1935, at which much of the summer's outing was repeated, apart from a few notable exceptions. Proms winter seasons enjoyed two short-lived periods from 1932, and again after the War from 1947 for five years. The 1935 winter season, beginning on 31 December 1934, repeated much of what had been performed in the summer, but with some more notable departures. Ethel Smyth's *Entente Cordiale* was performed on 3 January, Walford Davies's *Solemn Melody* on the 5th, Bridge's Christmas dance *Sir Roger de Coverley* on the 6th, Holst's *The Perfect Fool* Op.39 and two songs by Ireland on the 7th. Vaughan Williams's *Tallis Fantasia* appeared again on the 10th together with Bantock's *Songs of the East*, Set 3, Ireland's *The Forgotten Rite*, Elgar's Violin Concerto and Delius's *Dance Rhapsody No.1* again. Lambert's *Music for Orchestra* appeared on Friday, 11 January.

Analysis of the 1934 season reveals that – overall – the Proms repertoire remained consistent with the previous forty years: Wagner overtures, Brahms, Tchaikovsky, Beethoven, Mozart and Bach, naturally. But there were some notable departures. Nicolas Medtner, not yet resident in England, featured in the fifth Prom with his *Six Pushkin Poems*, Op.36. The season began with Elgar's *The Kingdom*, Op.51 and, in the same concert on Saturday, 11 August, Holst's *The Planets*. The death of those two composers determined the selection, though Delius was not to make an appearance until a few days later. *Cynara* was performed on Friday, 17 August, with the first half of Thursday's concert on the 23rd devoted entirely to his works – *Fantastic Dance*, the double concerto for Violin and Cello, *Idyll*, the Piano Concerto in C Minor and *Brigg Fair*. A *Dance Rhapsody No.1* was performed at the Last Night on 3 October.

Most, if not all, the Proms were twice the length they are today. Holst's *A Somerset Rhapsody*, Op.21 No.2 was played alongside an extraordinarily long programme that included Brahms's D Minor *Serenade*, Op.11, his Second Piano Concerto and First Symphony, together with John Ireland's *Mai-Dun* and Debussy Nocturnes. On 7 September, two Beethoven symphonies (1 and 5), the Overture to *Fidelio*, Op.72, the Second Piano Concert, Walton's *Sinfonia Concertante* and Berlioz's *Symphonie Fantastique* were performed. The music of contemporary

British composers peppered the season. Naturally, the music of Ireland, Bridge, Bax and Balfour-Gardiner appeared together with Vaughan Williams – whose music was featured in just one concert on Thursday, 27 September, when six of his works were played in a concert that also featured an arrangement by Henry Wood of Handel's Organ Concerto in D Minor and Herbert Howells's *Procession*, Op.35. In this concert the public was to hear for the first time Vaughan Williams's now famous *Fantasia on Greensleeves*. The *Tallis* Fantasia opened the programme and was followed by *The Running Set*, *The Lark Ascending*, *Songs of Travel* and *A London Symphony*.

Relatively new to British audiences at the time, the music of Jean Sibelius was a particular highlight of the year's Proms season and heralded a continuing obsession with his music. 'Fashion may be foolish, but it has its value if it leads to a temporary boom in a composer like Sibelius,' wrote *The Times*' reviewer after a September Proms concert. 'There has been enough talk about him and sufficient recent performances of his music to stimulate public curiosity about him.' The composer 'remains himself, like no one else, and his music [is] like clear cold water in a dusty world'.[17] To what, or whom, do we owe our familiarity with the music of Sibelius? Sir Thomas Beecham did as much for Sibelius as he had done for Delius. But also, Lambert, in *Music, Ho!* as well as Vaughan Williams pointed to Sibelius as the greatest living symphonist. 'It is becoming increasingly the opinion of the musical world that Sibelius is the greatest composer since Beethoven,' wrote Ralph Wood in an article on Beethoven which appeared in the July edition of *Music and Letters*. 'And this is accompanied by the feeling that Sibelius is *like* Beethoven, and the first man to be so.' Wood explains why this is so, giving four 'concrete reasons':

1. That Sibelius's harmonic vocabulary is on the whole exceptionally restrained, simple, conservative and sparing.
2. That he often seems as careless of placating the ear as Beethoven at his deafest.
3. That his 'form' and 'content' are, indeed, utterly indivisible – and, technically speaking, his 'forms', as unorthodox as his 'materials', are, quite often, the reverse.
4. That his symphonic movements have a unity, an emotional grip and an all-through sweep, unapproached by any other but Beethoven.[18]

Form and Content were the subjects of the Philip Maurice Derricke Lecture for 1934, given at Lady Margaret Hall. It is hard to imagine *The Times*, or any other daily newspaper of any weight reporting so fully on a lecture on such an obscure – and non-general – subject as an aesthetic philosophy of music. But this is what *The Times* does in 1934, contrasting the lectures with that recent publication, *Music, Ho!* Donald Francis Tovey's lecture on 'Musical Form and Matter' (equivalent to Lambert's Form(al) and Expressive Content) was published by OUP in early September. The lecture was subsequently published in *The Main Stream of Music and Other Essays*. In the lecture, Tovey likened tonality to perspective in painting. 'Whereas perspective is an optical science which exists whether painters chose to recognise it or not,' he writes, 'tonality is wholly the work of musicians, and, in the classics from the time of Alessandro Scarlatti to that of our modern atonalists, has been intimately associated with certain clearly defined art-forms and rhythmic schemes.'[19]

Tovey regards this a dangerous difference. If tonality in music (the equivalent of which in painting is perspective) represents, as Simon Rattle has said, order and social hierarchy, then the debate about modernity in music has even more political significance. Tovey also comments on how tonality is understood and appreciated as much by the educated musician as by the layman despite the latter's 'lack of facilities' to explain key relations and remember parallel cases. Appreciation of tonality is universal but as inexplicable as describing the taste of a peach, of describing the colour red (and not just to a blind man). Tovey also explained that the contrast between programme and absolute music is like that between form and matter, classical and romantic art, pattern and emotion where 'in any satisfactory work of art, form and content become one', in which 'the creative process would seem to be essentially one of integration'. He uses the analogy of an amoeba that absorbs or digests its food 'by simply coming into contact with it and extending itself around it', absolute music wholly absorbing its subject matter thus. 'And so, it would seem, all music is, either more or less, programme music.' *The Times* again:

> When, therefore, Professor Tovey speaks of absolute music he does not mean music which has no subject matter, but music in which the subject-matter is wholly digested. This is even more important than he, for the purposes of his argument, need insist upon, for subject-matter, however completely digested, is responsible for the greatness or otherwise of a work of art. Greatness is not the same as perfection.[20] Music contains many perfect miniatures in its vast literature, and what is perfect is perfect, be it small or great. But difficult though the category of greatness may be to define, it is one which musicians cannot do without. Those works are great which deal with exalted subject-matter. A prelude by Debussy is no less perfect, but it is less great, than a symphony by Beethoven.[21]

But what has all this got to do with politics, you may well ask. Programme music is, for Lambert, the most obvious and shameful when it is applied to nationalism in the jingoism sense, and usually through words, the most easily applied matter to the formal music. Vaughan Williams's *A London Symphony*, on the other hand, is absolute music in which its subject matter has been digested, but which also has some 'national' meaning. The symphony was performed at the Latvian National Opera House at Riga for the first time in March 1934, under the baton of Albert Coates, who had given the first performance of the revised 1920 version of the work. Vaughan Williams was famously cross with those that attempted to impose a programme on his work. Albert Coates's 1920 programme on the *London* symphony infuriated him. This is despite Coates's keen evangelizing of the composer's works abroad, especially in his native Russia.[22] What seems to be the trouble is a certain triviality present in those programmes, a tendency to simplify what are, on the surface, clear references to London down to a picture-postcard level. But in a recently discovered 1940 letter to the *New York Times*' chief music critic Olin Downes,[23] Vaughan Williams explained that one person's London is not the same as another's:

When Coates first wanted to do the symphony in America, he saw that the American public must have a detailed programme or they would not listen to the work – & then his wife had written one. When I saw it I was horrified – but what was I to do? I modified the worst parts & let it go (weakly I realize now) imagining that it would appear once and never again – But when I found it was being attached to several performances I did my best to scotch it.

I want the symphony to express the spirit of London – if my music does not do so, it will not help to say that a certain bit 'means' the Thames or Bloomsbury etc. – if it does represent the spirit, then the detail can be left to the hearer's own imagination – The eternal peace which surrounds the music, the turmoil I have tried to express in the music – to some the river may give that – to another not.[24]

Vaughan Williams may not have been fully cognizant of the reason for Coates's insistence on a programme. Coates knew that, given he was staging a production of the symphony in the United States, a programme would provide the necessary explanation for that audience. In a postscript, he added that his hope was that 'people who know London will recognise in my music the same emotion which London gives them, and those who do not know London will get an emotional picture of what London means to some people'. But Vaughan Williams did admit that he 'made a few suggestions (besides the obvious Big Ben & the street-songs) which may help people get in the right mood'. In presenting this letter for the first time Allan Atlas presents too the inevitable discussion about absolute and programme music. But the *London* is both 'expressive' and 'absolute'. Indeed, the chimes of Big Ben attest to a programme, but 'is Vaughan Williams suggesting a kind of "absolute" music to which the listener can attach a programme of his or her imagination?' asks Allan Atlas.

> And is a composition to which the listener attaches his or her own program (whether invited to do so or not) any longer 'absolute' music, at least, for the listener? In the end, the idea of program music – from the occasional literalism of a Richard Strauss tone poem to the 'merely' suggestive/evocative *La Mer* by Debussy to the after-the-fact programmatic appropriation of Beethoven's Fifth Symphony (one 'meaning' for the Allies, quite another for the Nazis) – is filled with many shades of grey.[25]

Like the contrasts between form and content, absolute and programme music, identified in Tovey's lecture, the difference between 'Modern' and 'Contemporary' music is provided in *The Times*' review of a concert of Russian music, which took place at the Queen's Hall on 26 January:

> A distinction has to be drawn between 'modern' and 'contemporary'. If to 'contemporary' is given a strictly temporal sense, then 'modern' is a stylistic epithet, but if 'modern' is applied to time, then 'contemporary' becomes geographical, and means 'in the Central European style'.[26]

These distinctions were useful in explaining some of the music played at Broadcasting House in a series of concerts broadcast by the BBC. Prokoviev's suite from *The Gambler* was contemporary in the latter sense, for instance. Miaskovsky, on the other hand, was a 'contemporary' composer in time, but neither modern nor contemporary in style, using the idiom 'derived from Tchaikovsky and Rachmaninov'. In contrast, Shostakovich was both contemporary *and* modern. The first performance of Prokoviev's new piano concerto by the BBC Orchestra under Bruno Walter took place as part of the same series on 31 January 1934 with the composer himself at the keyboard, 'dashing off its spluttering fireworks with easy nonchalance'. *The Times*' reviewer called it a 'dry biscuit', though. The programme note 'explained that his music should be clear to any mind disabused of the romantic nonsense of the nineteenth century'. But the reviewer, probably H. C. Colles, nevertheless despairs: 'We modern men cannot feed forever on cocktails and dry biscuits.'[27]

In a *Radio Times* preview of another Prokoviev premiere later in the year, Constant Lambert recalls the occasion on which, expecting something quite revolutionary – such as when Glazunov was 'driven from the hall' on hearing the Scythian Suite – he, instead, was quite disappointed to hear music that was lyrical and even pastoral in nature, instead of being 'blown out of my seat'. However, on reflection, what seemed then a 'regrettable weakness' from a composer who was supposed to have been the natural successor to Stravinsky now seemed to him 'the most attractive feature in Prokoviev's music':

> In an age when composers have for the most part developed every element of music save the melodic, it is a great relief to find a writer who, in spite of his brilliant orchestral camouflage, does not disdain an appeal through line alone.

In fact, Prokoviev's distinguishing mark is his 'melodic line'. And though present in Stravinsky ('with whom he has often been thoughtlessly classed'), the line itself 'is earth perfunctory or deliberately borrowed' despite the harmony, rhythm and orchestration. However, that is not to say that Prokoviev is pure melody. His melodic line 'has none of the cosy yearning of the German song writers'. It is 'cold and refreshing, like a mountain stream' and though derived from Russian folk song has 'no facile nostalgia about it'. Prokoviev 'possesses a horror of jazz which expresses itself in a complete avoidance of cross accent or syncopation. As a result we get a little tired of the continual pounding of common time'. Lambert is writing in anticipation of the first British performance and broadcast of Prokoviev's Third Symphony Op.44, 'the most important work of his to be played here' on Friday, 19 October, from Broadcasting House, with the composer himself at the podium. The Symphony was followed by a suite from the ballet music *Chout*, Op.21:

> The two most immediately attractive movements appear to be the andante and the scherzo, the first a beautiful piece of sustained lyrical writing, starting with a theme as simple and singable as a folk song; the second, a fantastic caprice, mainly for divided strings, which shows Prokoviev in his most Disney vein.[28]

To Lambert's ear, Prokoviev's lyrical side 'recalls pastoral beauty of flowers and trees' but the 'grotesquerie' in *Chout* (The Buffoon) recalls a Walt Disney cartoon, Mickey Mouse at his most surreal. 'One feels that chairs and coffee pots are joining in the dance and that the piano is playing itself without the aid of human agency,' he writes, seeming to anticipate Disney's *Fantasia*, which was to be released in 1940. 'I think it is worthwhile pointing out that he, like Disney, is an artist who has created a world of his own.'[29]

The British Music Festival in the New Year, the London Festival in May, the Proms from August, and now a festival of Russian music were all innovations. In the same week as the latter, the 30-strong New Orchestra of London gave their first concert at the Aeolian Hall. Conducted by Joan Bickers, its members were 'the recent product of the musical colleges of London'. With the programme including George Butterworth's *On the Banks of Green Willow,* 'this was altogether an excellent first concert which should augur well for the success of the new orchestra'.[30] Shortly after this concert, Grace Burrows conducted the Women's Symphony Orchestra at a Queen's Hall concert on 2 November, which included Franck's D Minor Symphony, works by Sibelius, Bax (his *Romantic Overture* 'in which the composer pays the sincerest form of tribute to the dedicatee, Delius'), and Bantock:

> This policy of giving stable fare amplified by a greater number of out-of-the-way works than the regular orchestras are prepared to undertake is the chief artistic justification of a body such as this. For it cannot be claimed that the standard of playing is brilliant enough to compete in these days with the other London orchestras.

It wasn't due to Burrows's skills as a conductor. Her 'directions' were both 'decisive and well-conceived'. Rather, it was a matter of the violin playing:

> The lower strings and the wind are reliable, but the violins are half-hearted, and it is in soft even more than in loud passages that one wants more rosin on their bows.[31]

The new season seems to have been particularly rich with regard to experiments in music. In November, a new idea for chamber music concerts, 'run not for profit but for giving young musicians of proved ability a chance to take their place alongside artists of established reputation', began: the smoking concert, 'in which the attempt is made to reproduce the atmosphere of friendliness and informality which the nature of chamber music really requires'. Held at the Princes Galleries in Piccadilly (though perhaps better suited to the nearby Ritz), the atmosphere of the concerts was of a style much in vogue: 'Smoking is encouraged, refreshments are obtainable, the audience sits not in serried rows but in groups around tables, the eminent persons who have sat to eminent portrait painters look down from their frames on the wall upon the eminent persons in the audience.'[32] A dubious response to another 'modern' trend, surely.

Meanwhile, Anthony Tudor had succeeded in staging three of Holst's *Planets* suite as a ballet, though not to *The Times*' satisfaction: 'But though this ballet failed to realize the splendid idea of its creator, it showed that there is beyond doubt in 'The Planets' the making of a first-class ballet. Is it too heartless a suggestion to make that Mr Tudor scrap his present composition and begin from the beginning again?'[33] But 1934 was a period of innovations and new fashions, some of which endured, and some of which were quickly forgotten. On 5 January, George Dyson had addressed the forty-fourth annual conference of the Incorporated Society of Musicians (ISM) as well as the Conference of Educational Associations meeting at University College, Gower Street, on the same day, on the subject of 'modern musical idioms', referring to the taste for 'extreme fashions' in music. He had noted a trend in which the only new works that appeared to have some chance of life showed 'a much less revolutionary idea of musical expression', as in the past. 'Ten or 15 years ago there were works by which people were completely carried away; if anyone wanted to-day to clear Queen's Hall quickly these works would be put in the programme,' he said, to the sound of laughter.

> Ever since the normal, simple harmonies of our musical system were fixed, possibly 400 years ago, most of the changes in music – and certainly anything that could be called a revolution – had been in the direction of greater complication. This was due to the fact that, if an idiom was used a great deal, it became commonplace and the man who wanted to say something original [that is, out of the standard 'major and minor system'] was compelled, willy-nilly, to go outside the ordinary range of ideas.[34]

'Whether it was musical logic in the classical sense was a matter for debate,' remarked Dyson. Certainly, Constant Lambert believed that by 1913, when *The Rite of Spring* was first performed in Paris, music 'had already reached the absolute limit of complication allowed by the capacity of composers, players, listeners and instrument makers', and there was nothing more complicated to be found in the music of the 1930s.[35]

At the ISM's annual dinner at the Hotel Great Central, Marylebone, a government representative (H. Ramsbotham, Parliamentary Secretary to the Board of Education) and the chairman of the BBC, J. H. Whitely, were present. The latter referred to the current series of Queen's Hall concerts of British musical works, 'the first time such a thing had been attempted'. He hoped that 'it would receive adequate support from the public generally. At the same time, he would never give way to the idea that no foreign artists should be allowed to perform in England. Music was too sacred a thing to be affected by political frontiers.' That speech got cheers as did several others: 'If fame could be measured by the number of those that become acquainted with a work of art, the composer had outstripped all his competitors.' This was some consolation, because, though his reward was great in this respect, if a composer depended on the income received from the publication and performance of his works, he could scarcely afford to be a member of their society – something 'nothing short of a scandal'.³⁶

In President W. Gillies Whittaker's opening address, he had remarked that a swift and great change in politics since before the war had taken place in 'the conditions of musical matters'. There had been a huge falling-off of private music students and there were very many other changes taking place. 'People bought radio sets and motor cars instead of pianos and concert tickets. They built garages instead of drawing rooms.' The effect on the music profession was devastating. Young people were 'whizzing' from place to place rather than settling at home, indulging in cultural recreations. 'When they listened to music at all, it was not to an occasional Strauss waltz, but to hour after hour of decadent jazz.' These were some of the negative aspects highlighted. The positives, however, were also to be noted. For example, 'over 200 festivals and half a million competitors annually' (under the auspices of the Competitive Festival Movement) 'were an amazing answer to the charge that we were less musical than other nations'. Further still, 'Music had now ceased to be the property of the exclusive few and had become the property of all.' Whittaker also pointed out that 'non-professional music activity had been one of the characteristics of our national life', exemplified in the latter part of the nineteenth century by the profusion of glee clubs, choral societies and amateur orchestras:

> Our plant is not dead, it is merely delicate and drooping. Is it not our business to attempt to revive it? Can we not visualise a growing band of union between ourselves as professional musicians and the amateur forces in this country?³⁷

Vaughan Williams had always referred to music in Britain as a 'tender flower', but the idea that England was a 'land without music' persisted with evidence from the most unlikely places. 'What is the matter with the English artistic consciousness that it has never produced a work of art comparable to that of the Europeans?' asked a contributor to the Vassar News, a campus journal published in Poughkeepsie, New York, following a performance of English music at the University in February 1934.

> English compositions are charming but beside those of European composers they are almost trivial. They lack the element which seems to make some works of art 'great' – the confusion and subsequent resolution, the strain and relaxation which produces physical disturbance in the listener and leaves him the feeling of Katharsis [sic!]. Most strikingly was this illustrated in last Thursday's concert of compositions from the periods of flourishing English musical talent. The Elizabethan songs and music for the harpsichord were even more delightful,

and as moving as European compositions of the same period and nature; the misfortune lies in the European composer's never having gone beyond the conception which he so perfectly expressed in them.

Here we see reference to the brilliance of and equality to the Tudors as far as music is concerned; an acknowledged reference point among British composers of the early twentieth century, though news of the 'musical renaissance' had apparently not entirely impressed.

> English contemporary music shows no further organisation of experience. That the English composer has taken advantage of the development of musical vocabulary is evident in the tonal and rhythmic material of Vaughan Williams' *Merciles Beaute*, and to a lesser extent, Arnold Bax's *Moy Mell*; but he has failed to pass the serene sentimentality glorified by the Elizabethans.

To be fair, the review owned that it was 'perhaps unfair to make so broad a statement, using as an instance last Thursday's program, which was entirely made up of short pieces' and that an upcoming performance of British music 'might show that the English [are] capable of really great art'.[38]

For the time being, German music was bound to dominate. Wagner's music even found its way into the Aldershot Military Tattoo of 1934, with one observer asking what the innovation of a potted version of *Tannhäuser* had to do with the army. Perhaps it demonstrated the army's technical mastery of the staging of such events, though the opera's themes of the conflict of sensuality and spirituality, as well as the victory of good over evil, could perhaps be seen 'to underline the continuing Christian emphasis of the Tattoos'.[39]

In November *The Times* was pondering 'what to do with Handel', which was a question 'still unsettled'.[40] With forty operas lying unperformed, why dramatize the oratorios? The question of Bach, on the other hand, had been answered: 'we perform him in conditions as like as possible to those for which he wrote', performing cantatas, for example, in Church (especially St. Margaret's, Westminster). Wagner, Beethoven and Bach continued to inspire, and not just musicians. *The Musical Times* reported in May 1934, for example, the inspiration for artist Josef Weisz, whose progress as a sculptor was hindered for the lack of objective form that would satisfy his creative expression. He found it, at last in, music, in particular that of the 'crystal-clear and mathematically correct music of Bach':

> In that way lay the Universe ... the secret of all true creation, the urge to create ... and the need of a form based on the fundamentals of cold legitimacy.[41]

A sculpture of Bach in the pose of Rameses II is the result. 'L. S.' writes that Weisz 'professes to trace the rhythmical pattern begun in the Egyptian pyramids and continued in early Grecian art and Gothic architecture, and finally "crystallised" in the music of the Master', who thus showed him 'the way to Plastic Art'. The inspiration of Bach is described in the writings of Cyril Scott (described by Eugene Goossens as 'the father of modern British music'), whose book on music first appeared in 1933, and was reprinted in May 1934. *Music: Its Secret Influence throughout the Ages* begins with an analysis of the effects of Western music from Bach and Handel upon the minds and emotions of mankind. Although the book concentrates on the effect of music on the emotions, Scott is at pains to point out that he does not intend 'to imply that music operates on the emotions only: there are several types of music which operate on the mind. Thus we shall see in due course that Bach's music had a very definite effect on the mentality – for, in accordance with our axiom, as Bach's art is of an intellectual type, it produced an intellectual effect.'[42] But it is not just about the mind, even as far as Bach's music is concerned. 'The keynote of Bach's genius,' writes Scott, 'was *profundity*, yet not an arid profundity, dull, unattractive, fit only for the entertainment of technicians, but one replete with high inspiration and inventiveness.'[43]

Since this chapter concerns the experimental in music, it follows that it would not be complete without mentioning the question of the ultra-modern. It is difficult when thinking about the stature of J. S. Bach and the standards he set for the Western canon not to consider how far removed some of the new music was from, say, the Second Viennese School. For one rather famous layman, who was giving a speech on great hymn tunes at the annual Armistice Festival at Westminster Chapel of the United Welsh Churches, the key to the understanding of modern music was quite simple (as well as amusing):

> I keep a large number of pigs and I can tell you now about modern music: If I take a piece of paper the next time I go when feeding is on and put down in the old notation every squeal, every grunt, I turn out as good a specimen of modern music as you can get.[44]

No doubt this was a commonly held view of the time. As Jenny Doctor explains in her volume on ultra-modern music and the BBC, the Corporation routinely avoided provoking controversy and maintained a non-interventionist policy as far as the broadcast of music of the Second Viennese School was concerned. Arguments about the 'cacophony' as opposed to 'symphony' of music, derived from a *Radio Times* article of 21 April 1933, continued to rage. Schoenberg's and Webern's music was less represented as a result. As Jenny

Doctor has traced, performances of the music of Alban Berg, for example, began to gather momentum at the BBC, outside the 'streamlined format' and 'routine presentation' of the Corporation's concerts of contemporary music that were the norm.[45]

> In the early 1930s, as at the end of the previous decade, Schoenberg's music was the focal point of BBC attention. However, the inaccessibility of his 12-tone idiom, as epitomised in the BBC performances of the Variations for Orchestra, Op.31 [the 'Cacophony' of the *Radio Times* article], finally drove critics and the public to reject his music outright. With Schoenberg's permanent departure from Europe in autumn 1933, BBC interest in his post-war output quickly waned. Attention shifted to his friend and colleague, Berg, who had been all but ignored by the BBC during the 1920s. Broadcasts of Berg's music prevailed from the time that excerpts from *Wozzeck* were first transmitted in 1932.[46]

The BBC's 1933–4 series had begun with an all-Schoenberg concert, but the main event was planned for March 1934 with the first British performance of Alban Berg's opera *Wozzeck*, in which the BBC abandoned its usual stance, and 'the attention accorded to Berg more than made up for this deficiency'. Not only was its performance, which took place at the Queen's Hall as part of the BBC Symphony Concert series on 14 March 1934, 'the most important BBC event of the season', but it was also 'one of the most significant BBC events to take place during the first decades of the Corporation's existence'. *Wozzeck* rehearsals began in early March on six consecutive days (excluding Sunday) in a studio and then at the Queen's Hall. The performance was conducted by Adrian Boult:

> Given the investment in time and money for this one performance, it is not surprising that the Corporation mounted an unusually intense publicity campaign, launched on 11 February, when Boult conducted a Sunday orchestral concert including the popular Three Fragments from *Wozzeck*, as well as Webern's arrangement of the Schubert Dances, D.820.[47]

After the successful concert performance at the Queen's Hall, a number of excerpts were included in a Proms performance in August. 'Sir Henry Wood is never happier than when presiding over an international assembly, which included in this case delegates from Italy, France and Britain, as well as from Russia and Austria, giving to each a fair field and no favour; nor is he ever more alert than in instructing his Promenade audiences in new thought and modern ways.' On this occasion, fragments of Alban Berg's *Wozzeck*, performed by May Blyth, 'represented contemporary music'.[48] Hopes for a fully-fledged stage production at Covent Garden gathered pace for the rest of the year. 'This would afford the general public a long over-due opportunity of judging from a proper angle the most outstanding work of the post-war epoch.'[49] Geoffrey Toye at Covent Garden was initially not interested in staging it at the Opera House, but the idea that the BBC had taken over the theatre began to interest him, or, at least, if some sort of cooperation deal could be worked out to stage it the following year. By July, negotiations with Covent Garden were proceeding apace, especially 'if the BBC were to supply the Orchestra, Chorus, Soloists and Conductor'. On 12 September Toye wrote to the BBC to report on enquiries it was making:

(1) To see whether we could buy the complete production, including scenery and costumes, from some large German opera house.
(2) To find out whether Dr Erhardt has ever produced the opera, and where.
(3) To find out from Mr Christie whether Dr Ebert will be in London and available for producing 'Wozzeck' should we require him [to].

Costumes from Covent Garden's own wardrobe might do, if the 'complete production' was not obtainable from Germany. But on 16 October, he wrote that he had 'entirely failed to get any production of Wozzeck from Germany or Austria so far. Berlin have dispersed their production, and I gather from them that it was only a "frame-up" anyway. Vienna, on the other hand, will be using theirs at that particular time, according to Clemens Kraus, so we cannot get anything from them'. Geoffrey Toye promised to try Frankfurt and Stuttgart. However, he wrote again on 29 October admitting to drawing a blank from 'all continental enquiries with regard to the production' with Vienna, Berlin, Strasbourg and Frankfurt unable to supply the scenery and costumes, even on hire.

> I have had a boy in here called Alistair Stewart with some sketches for 'Wozzeck' and I propose showing them to Adrian Boult. . . . Of course this would be a much more expensive way of doing it.

Toye subsequently put Alistair Stewart in touch with Adrian Boult. By December, Otto Erhardt had agreed to produce *Wozzeck* at Covent Garden with Stewart's designs and progress was being made on coping with the speed of scene-changes and the like. Writing from Dresden on New Year's Eve to Adrian Boult, Erhardt had gone as far as to arrange for the relevant sketches to be sent to Vienna for the purpose of production, aligning his letter 'With all my good wishes for the New Year to you and your works, and looking forward to a brilliant cooperation with Wozzeck'. Ernardt worked closely with Alban Berg. The former wrote again from Vienna on the first of February to Boult, expressing his disappointment that Geoffrey Toye had informed him of financial difficulties. Clearly something had gone wrong. Covent Garden was not prepared to finance a new production, and the German opera houses were not prepared to supply the necessary materials (in view of Berg's work being classified as *Entartete Musik*, this is not surprising). To begin with, it was a postponement – and for the BBC and Adrian Boult (writing on 14 February 1935), the reason was

> that it is impossible to justify any expenditure on the stage side of the matter. From the point of view of our listeners we could give 'Wozzeck' from the studio equally successfully. It is thus impossible to proceed further with a Covent Garden production, to our great grief. It is most unfortunate, of course, that it has been found impossible to come to an agreement. Will you please tell Mr. Berg that I certainly hope that there will somehow be found some other opportunity for me to conduct 'Wozzeck' again?

Further elaboration was necessary on 26 February:

> The difficulty is that we as a broadcasting authority, existing on the money paid for wireless licenses by six million licence holders, must be careful how we spend that money on anything that will not be within reach of all those six million licence-holders.

The production fell through, with Covent Garden clearly unwilling to meet the production costs. The BBC recognized the value and importance of *Wozzeck*, and the regret expressed by Adrian Boult was genuine. In his regular column in the *Sunday Referee* of 18 March, Constant Lambert had commented that 'It is a grotesque comment on English musical life that Alban Berg's "Wozzeck", the finest opera of recent years, should have received its first English performance not on the stage at Covent Garden but in concert form at the Queen's Hall'.[50] For Lambert, Alban Berg was 'a typical individualist and romantic, making no compromise with his audience, writing at rare intervals works for his own satisfaction, Berg is yet the only atonal composer who is in any way in touch with the general public, having achieved with his opera *Wozzeck* a far greater success than is usually vouchsafed to the musical "extremists"'.[51]

> Since the advent of Hitlerism, however, music of the Alban Berg type has been completely banished. Even in the case of an atonal composer who was neither

a Jew nor a Communist, his music would be banned on the grounds of idiom alone, such sounds being officially classed as 'intellectual Bolshevism'.

There was even room in Lambert's mind of the possibility of counter-revolution in Germany:

> Were there to be a Communist counter-revolution in Germany – and more unlikely things have happened – no doubt atonalism, though hardly a popular idiom, would be encouraged on the grounds of its 'revolutionary' label.[52]

For those on the extreme right, failure to produce *Wozzeck*.. at Covent Garden during the following season came as something of a blessing. For members of the BUF, the opera 'epitomized the fascist equation of Jewish creativity with an ugly, unintelligible modernism', writes Roger Griffin, with one contributor to *The Blackshirt* expressing relief that Covent Garden audiences would be spared the 'threat' of *Wozzeck*, calling it 'another modern Jewish perpetration'.[53]

In April, the ISCM met in Florence where the highlight of a chamber music event was a performance by the Kolisch Quartet of Vienna of the *Lyric Suite* by Alban Berg, 'the now famous composer of *Wozzeck*'.. The concert contained other contemporary works, and *The Times*' correspondent provides a useful barometer of British conservative attitudes towards much of the new music:

> While all were ostensibly 'contemporary' in style, that is to say, free and easy in their attitude towards established notions of tonality and harmony, none was wantonly freakish.[54]

I explore British attitudes, specifically those pertaining to political developments in Germany, in the following chapter.

Notes

1 'Bethlehem'; Rutland Boughton's Choral Drama (Reviews), *The Times*, 1 January 1934, p. 10.
2 *The Listener*, Volume XII, Issue 311, 27 December.
3 His most performed work, Mackenzie's *Britannia*, Op.52 was performed at the Proms forty-eight times between 1895 and 1940. The last outing was scheduled to be performed at the Proms on 25 September 1940, but due to bombing raids, the concert was cancelled. *Columba*, Op.28 was last performed as long ago as 1919 and the *Scottish Concerto*, Op.55 at the Last Night in 1943.

4 Vaughan Williams, 1964: 185.
5 'British Music: a New Symphony', *The Times*, 2 January 1934, p. 8.
6 'British Music: Vaughan Williams and Arnold Bax', *The Times*, 9 January 1934, p. 8.
7 'Music This Week: New Symphony by Bax', *The Times*, 15 January 1934, p. 10.
8 'Arnold Bax's New Symphony: A Vivid Performance', *The Times*, 16 January 1934, p. 10.
9 'Bax's Music: from Tone Poem to Symphony', *The Times*, 20 January 1934, p. 8.
10 According to the Oxford Dictionary of Music, Bax's autobiography *Farewell, My Youth* (1943) is one of the best books by a composer.
11 Harrison, 1934: 255–60.
12 'British Music: BBC Orchestra's Concert', *The Times*, 11 January 1934, p. 8.
13 'New British Works: BBC Concert', *The Times*, 13 January 1934.
14 Contemporary British Music: To the Editor of *The Times*, Evlyn Howard-Jones, 37 Eaton Tce., SW1, *The Times*, 20 January 1934, p. 6.
15 'British Music: Modern Symphonic Tendencies', *The Times*, 13 January 1934, p. 8.
16 *The Times*, 4 January 1934, Dame Ethel Smyth's Music: A Broadcast Concert. Ethel Smyth's *The Boatswain's Mate* premiered at the Proms in 1934.
17 'Promenade Concert: The Music of Sibelius', *The Times*, 5 September 1934, p. 10.
18 Ralph W. Wood, 'The Meaning of Beethoven', *Music and Letters*, Volume 15, Issue 3, July 1934, pp. 209–21.
19 Tovey, 1947: 166–7. Tovey wrote a violin concerto for Pablo Casals in 1934. He was knighted in 1935, in which year appeared the first of six volumes of his *Essays on Musical Analysis*.
20 The reference to perfection comes from another point made in Tovey's lecture: the unique possibility afforded to music for expressing perfection. *The Times* again: 'This perfectibility is established in a beautiful piece of argument about the difference between science and art, a characteristically Toveyan digression which, with others like it, the reader would do well to pursue for himself.'
21 'The Content of Music: Form and Matter in Union', *The Times*, 8 September 1934, p. 10.
22 Coates was born in St. Petersburg (in 1934 called Leningrad) of English and part-Russian parents in 1882. He died in Cape Town in 1953. 'Whirlwind conductor, he assisted at the birth of Russian Modernism as conductor at St. Petersburg's Maryinsky Theatre (1911–19), cultivating a public taste for Skryabin and encouraging Prokoviev to write operas. After the revolution, he wandered far and wide, deputizing for Beecham in London, forming the Rochester S. O. and teaching at the Eastman School (1923–5), finally settling in South Africa' (Lebrecht, 1992: 73).
23 It is possible that Olin Downes and Vaughan Williams met in one of the composer's trips to the United States, where he delivered the lectures published as *National Music* in 1934.

24 Vaughan Williams to Olin Downes, reproduced in the *Journal of the Ralph Vaughan Williams Society*, Issue #60, June 2014, pp. 4–5.
25 Ralph Vaughan Williams and Olin Downes: New Uncovered Letters, Allan W. Atlas, *Journal of the Ralph Vaughan Williams Society*, Issue #60, June 2014, pp. 4–5. This 'after-the-fact programmatic appropriation' alludes to the meaning attached to a work in the years, decades or even centuries following its first appearance. In the case of Beethoven's Fifth, its *Wirkungsgeschichte* took on an especially significant meaning during the Second World War, as Atlas mentions here and as I explore in my book on wartime culture and propaganda.
26 'Modern Russian Music: BBC Concert', *The Times*, 27 January 1934, p. 8.
27 'BBC Orchestra: A New Concerto', *The Times*, 1 February 1934, p. 12.
28 'Notable Music of the Week: A Prokoviev Contemporary Concert, Constant Lambert', *Radio Times*, 12 October 1934, p. 92.
29 *Fantasia* (1940) was based on Disney's earlier success with the *Silly Symphonies* series, such as *The China Shop*, which was released in 1934.
30 'The New London Orchestra: First Concert at Aeolian Hall', *The Times*, 13 October 1934, p. 10.
31 'Women's Symphony Orchestra: Bax, Bantock and Sibelius', *The Times*, 3 November 1934, p. 10.
32 'Music Lovers' Smoking Concert: First of a New Series', *The Times*, 21 November 1934, p. 12.
33 '"The Planets" as a Ballet: Mr Tudor's Interpretation', *The Times*, 3 November 1934, p. 10.
34 'Fashions in Music: The Search for New Ideas of Expression', *The Times*, 6 January 1934, p. 8.
35 Lambert, 1966: 70.
36 *The Times*, Music as a Profession: Difficulties of Executants and Composers, 4 January 1934, p. 8.
37 Music for All: Professionals and Amateurs, *The Times*, 3 January 1934, p. 15.
38 *Vassar News*, February 1934.
39 Richards, 2001a: 236.
40 'Dramatic Handel: A Scheme for Presentation', *The Times*, 3 November 1934.
41 A Modernist's Tribute to Bach, 'L. S.': *The Musical Times*, Volume 75, Issue 1095, May 1934, pp. 406–7.
42 Scott, 1958: 41.
43 Ibid., 57.
44 Mr Lloyd George on Hymn Tunes, *The Times*, 10 November 1934, p. 8.
45 Doctor, 1999: 260.
46 Ibid., 334.
47 Ibid., 271.

48 Promenade Concert: A Modern Programme, *The Times*, 15 August 1934, p. 8.
49 From a BBC Internal Circulating Memo dated 16 March 1934 (BBC WAC R27/405/1).
50 'Wozzeck! At Last!' quoted in the list of Lambert's journalism in Lloyd, 2014: 402.
51 Lambert, 1966: 256. Alban Berg, meanwhile, did not live 1935 out. He died that year on Christmas Eve in Vienna from complications arising from blood poisoning, caused by an insect bite. He was just fifty.
52 Lambert, 1966: 257.
53 Griffin, 2004: 54.
54 'Contemporary Music: Works by Young Composers', *The Times*, 5 April 1934, p. 8.

4

Responding to Germany

From 1934 every German citizen was required to raise his/her right arm in the Nazi salute on hearing the Horst Wessel song. Already being sung in translation in England by members of the BUF, the song held a special significance for devotees. Miranda Seymour tells the story of Ariel Tennant and Unity Mitford's visit to an Austrian castle near Vienna in the summer of 1934, where Unity 'could hear the voices of imprisoned Nazis calling to them from deep within, far down below'. Lying down on the roof, she began to sing the Horst Wessel song, 'but terribly loudly, and over and over'.[1] Unity was regarded as the most extreme of her clan. The song's appearance was ominous for Constant Lambert who believed that, from a musical point of view, the direct association of political feeling with a piece of music was the 'lowest and least desirable form of nationalism', though it was nevertheless necessary to acknowledge its existence and not to regard it as a regrettable side show:

> No political pamphlet or poster can get a hundredth of the recruits that are enrolled by a cornet and a bass drum; and it is doubtful whether the [Great] war would have lasted six months without the aid of that purest of the arts, music, whose latest gift to civilization is the notorious Horst Wessel Song.[2]

There were many other British travellers in Germany and Austria that summer – Germany still being regarded as an appropriate destination for completing an education. Christopher Sidgwick, a teacher, spent four months in Germany that summer, too, and published his observations on his return in *German Journey*. Attitudes to and experiences of music were ever present. Writes Miranda Seymour,

> Sidgwick's tour of Germany included moments of unexpected comedy. He found it hard to keep a straight face when, having delivered a talk on British foreign policy to a school group of Hitler Youth, he was thanked by a heartfelt rendering of 'Pack up Your Troubles' and 'It's a Long Way from Tipperary'. He

was mildly amused (while regretting the predictable absence of Mendelssohn) to find Saxon King Alfred the Great gazing down on him from a plinth in the Valhalla, Nuremberg's new temple to Teutonism.[3]

The concerts arranged for the traditional visit of the Berlin Philharmonic to London at the beginning of 1934 included, unsurprisingly, several major symphonic works of the German canon. The Queen's Hall concerts of 22 and 23 January featured Schumann's Fourth Symphony, Beethoven's Seventh and Brahms's Third. On the following Sunday, the BPO played at the Royal Albert Hall, performing Richard Strauss's *Tod und Verklärung* and four pieces of his *Couperin Suite*, in honour of the composer's seventieth birthday. Clearly there was some anticipation of some public reaction to the recent developments at the BPO. Whatever the fears, they appear not to have materialized, and Thomas Beecham's call for 'a more than usually warm welcome' for the BPO was heeded, as *The Times* reported. When Furtwängler came on to the platform, he was received 'most cordially', the 'magnificent playing' of the orchestra arousing genuine enthusiasm:

> There never has been any doubt that the Berlin players would be received at Queen's Hall with the appreciation that their past performances have merited; suggestions to the contrary seemed as absurd as special appeals on their behalf were unnecessary. Nevertheless ill-mannered people do sometimes get into concert halls, and it is satisfactory to record that there were none present last night.
>
> Beethoven was superbly played from first to last, and the coda of the finale was worked up so brilliantly that, when the ending was reached, even an audience which must surely know that symphony by heart seemed taken by surprise, and to be asking themselves whether it was really over before they dared move a hand.[4]

The performance of Beethoven's Seventh at another Queen's Hall concert the following week provides a useful contrast. The London Philharmonic's performance, under Bruno Walter, followed an 'exquisite' rendering of the *Pastoral*, which had been performed after the *Coriolan* Overture in an all-Beethoven concert. However, the reviewer in *The Times* found the Seventh 'rough by comparison', suggesting that 'Perhaps another rehearsal was needed to finish Herr Bruno's conception', and 'Fine as much of the playing was it was a long way behind the perfect mastery displayed in the "Pastoral"'.[5]

There exists a huge contrast between public pronouncements concerning Nazi involvement in the Arts at the beginning of 1934 and at the end of the year.

The Berlin Philharmonic was about to appear in London on its regular annual visit, but a change in the orchestra's financial structure had just taken place. On 15 January, with the approval of Hitler himself, the eighty-five members of the BPO who owned the Berliner Philharmonisches Orchester GmBH, agreed to sell their shares to the German Reich, officially transferring the body to the State, the orchestra having been already renamed the *Reichsorchester* the previous November. As Misha Aster has written in his history of the *Reichsorchester*, the City of Berlin transferred its share gratis. The change was received with a 'tremendous sense of relief, tinged with a new kind of uncertainty', writes Aster. With their shares transferred to the Reich, the players 'gave up their earlier self-directing, self-governing rights'. Not only was the orchestra's continued existence now guaranteed, but it was also the orchestra's wish to engage with the Nazi Ministry of Propaganda and 'to serve it in future'.[6]

But there were misgivings. In anticipation of the Berlin Philharmonic's annual visit, Sir Thomas Beecham felt obligated to write to the press in January to clarify the position of the orchestra and of its conductor, Wilhelm Furtwängler, who was 'the crucial figure in the marriage between the Berlin Philharmonic and the German Reich', and it is to Furtwängler's position that Beecham addressed a letter to the press the following week. 'Nothing could be further from the truth', he wrote, that the orchestra had been deprived of its independence, and that Furtwängler had abandoned the principle of separation of music and party politics. From Beecham's point of view, the orchestra that was to appear the following week was 'precisely the same' as that which had visited the previous year, with no changes made nor any racial discrimination permitted to prevail. Indeed, prominent Jewish players, such as the orchestra's leader and two principal cellists, had been retained. This 'triumph of artistic impartiality over nationalistic dogma' was due entirely to the 'sane judgment and personal influence' of Furtwängler, he wrote, suggesting that the orchestra and its conductor 'should be given a more than usually warm welcome'. Keen to emphasize that his letter should not be regarded as criticism of German politics, he wrote that his plea was 'solely for the fitting recognition of moral courage and the maintenance of an ideal, things which the English public has always been the first to recognise and honour'.[7]

But in his recent biography of Constant Lambert, Stephen Lloyd has shown how misgivings were not easily allayed, with Lambert 'not prepared to be so trusting'. On reviewing an earlier visit in February 1932, the composer and critic had largely confined his comments to the quality of the orchestra's playing and to Furtwängler's technique.[8] 'This time, however, he was at his most outspoken,' writes

Lloyd. 'Carefully avoiding the word "Jew", in his regular *Sunday Referee* column, 'he began by challenging the cultural composition of the orchestra', noticing that 'most Germans of international repute, and almost all German composers of merit are either voluntary or (more often) involuntary refugees'.[9] Asking a number of questions in relation to the retention of some Jewish players, Lambert noticed that 'The list of players was not so colourful as it used to be', though with the leader of the orchestra Simon Goldberg's name at least among them.[10] Beecham's assurances, indeed, proved to be premature. Was it simply wishful thinking? Early signs of a more profound and lasting change in Germany included the removal of Mendelssohn's likeness from the gallery of the Berlin Philharmonie. The Kreisler cadenzas and Mendelssohn's Violin Concerto could be played only in private.[11] Syzman Goldberg, the principal concertmaster (violin) was the first to leave the orchestra in 1934; Joseph Schuster, first solo 'cellist', was next. Schuster was not forced to leave as such but was asked to sign a new contract. But anticipating a new wave of anti-Semitism, he chose to leave for the United States later in the year. Similarly, a statement from Goldberg reveals as follows:

> Being Jewish and Polish, I knew that I would have no easy time under the Hitler regime. I took the initiative myself and dissolved the contract with the Philharmonic. I wanted to pre-empt my dismissal and the internment of myself and my wife. It was not easy, because I was being threatened, with refusal of an exit visa. I was told to make a statement to American journalists in a press conference, that I was leaving the orchestra, because I could not pursue my solo career and my work as concertmaster simultaneously. This is why I fled Germany in 1934 head over heels.[12]

Gilbert Back, first violinist, left the orchestra in 1935. Nikolai Graudary, first solo cellist, also left in 1935, both also heading for America. These are the four who left the orchestra for political reasons. It was a matter of pride, in fact, to the Nazi Administration that no Jew had been recruited into the orchestra since 1930 and it was committed to removing any Jewish presence. The basis on which Jews were excluded from German cultural life was revealed by Josef Goebbels almost immediately after the Nazis' assumption of power in 1933. In a speech delivered to the chamber of culture (*Reichskulturkamer*) in 1934 he declared that Jews were 'unsuitable' to manage Germany's cultural heritage. Together with composers who were explicitly excluded from the profession because of their race, there were also others who voluntarily emigrated, as the experience of the BPO members shows.

Of the composers who continued working within the official structures of the Third Reich, possibly the most prominent was Herbert Windt, if his involvement in the film work of Leni Riefenstahl can be used as a measure of his prominence. Riefenstahl's first film, *Victory of Faith* (1933), a record of the 1933 *Parteitag* was suppressed due to its depiction of Ernst Röhm and his cronies, who were executed in 1934, soon after the film's release. Herbert Windt recycled much of his music for the film for the following commission, *Triumph of the Will* (1934). I have commented elsewhere on some of his music, particularly the sequence in which Hitler is shown arriving in Nuremberg.[13] It has been called 'probably the most significant piece of music in the film'.[14] Although Windt went on to write for another forty-six films during the Third Reich, his disability and disfigurement prevented him from becoming a 'trophy-artist' for the Nazi ideal and he had a somewhat patchy relationship with the authorities. In a similar vein to the spectacular event depicted in *The Triumph of the Will*, in the packed Berlin Sportpalast that April, the first 'spring concert' devoted entirely to military and patriotic music was given by the SS and attended by Hitler and several of his ministers. Included in the programme was one work which *The Times*' correspondent seems to have considered particularly noteworthy, a 'Solemn Summons'. With music by Richard Strauss, the 'mystic' words by Rudolf Binding, he notes, 'were printed in the programme in a peculiar squat type without capitals, apparently meant to give the impression of something especially Germanic'.[15] He provided a rough translation without further comment, the words presumably speaking ominously for themselves:

> great nation's holy vengeance
> – deep in sleep, dulled in serfdom –
> waked by a single call: awaken!
> as though rejuvenated it already rises.
>
> are we then really now awakened
> out of sleep and almost out of death?
> nation, a giant, who stirred
> when a holy and stern commandment reached him.

While the Nazi elite were enjoying their 'feast' of marches and 'patriotic songs' at their spring concert, Germans at the other end of the political spectrum were attending the annual gathering of the ISCM. Its president, E. J. Dent, wrote from the Hotel Helvetia to Herbert Thompson, music and art critic of *The Yorkshire Post*, on 4 April:

> I created much amusement at the opening ceremony by making a speech (in answer to the Prefect of Florence, who made the usual oration all about Mussolini) in which I emphasised the dangers of nationalism and the necessity

of free thought and speech for the artist. It was the sort of thing that no Italian would dare to say now, but I gathered that they were all enormously pleased to hear someone else say it!¹⁶

Dent admits that he 'carried it off' by paying homage to Florence and Italy as 'the homes of music'. And despite watching the audience becoming nervous, he qualified risky words such as 'revolution' with the adjective 'musical'. The German audience (largely Jews and Communists) liked his speech though Dent expected that 'it would have been more risky to make such a speech in Germany itself'. Persecution of the Jews had upset the Society's finances with the German section refusing 'to pay for anything at all', and members from other countries objecting to paying for the refugees, several of whom were on the programme. For fear of trouble with the Nazi authorities, Paul Hindemith, who was to have played in one of his own works, had refused to attend. Hindemith was about to be embroiled in a full confrontation with the Nazi authorities, as we shall see. Dent describes one of several 'amusing incidents' which highlight the complications brought to bear on music because of Germany's political situation:

> [Y]esterday a work was played by a young Jew from Breslau who is living at Strasbourg. I put him down as belonging to 'Germany'; but [Alfredo] Casella objected, as *he* doesn't want to risk any rows with the Nazis himself, for fear his own music should be boycotted there. Casella therefore put the young man down as coming from 'Paris' – to which *he* objected; so finally he was ascribed to 'Germania Indipendente', which I thought a very amusing alternative name for Alsace!!¹⁷

The next Festival was likely to be in Carlsbad ('a very Nazi place'), though the authorities there were 'tremendously keen to have us'. Yes, Germany was a serious matter but, ironically, because of Nazi meddling in the arts, especially in music, Germany was in danger of becoming guilty of a charge usually levelled at England:

> As to the Germans, I think they are hedging. The patriot mediocrities who are now running music in Germany hate modern music, and therefore hate our Society, because we don't perform their works, but I gather that in higher quarters there is a strong desire to keep in with us, because they are afraid of Germany being musically boycotted and considered as 'das Land ohne Musik'.¹⁸

The Nazis were only just beginning to cement the finer points of their ideology in 1934 and convert them into practical measures. It was the year in which they made clear to themselves, and to the world, what they believed, and who they regarded as the torchbearers of those beliefs. Writing from Germany on 6 May, *The Times*' Berlin correspondent was able to name the men who had become associated with Nazi attitudes and, by extension, those whose beliefs had become synonymous with those of Hitler himself:

> Houston Stewart Chamberlain, Schiller, and Wagner have been chosen by Herr Hadamovsky, the young Nazi Director of the Reich Broadcasting Corporation, as the three masters whose works best correspond to National-Socialist feeling in political philosophy, poetry, and music.[19] For the next six months transmissions of excerpts from Chamberlain and Schiller and of Wagner's music are to form 'the artistic and intellectual summit of the broadcast programmes'. Chamberlain's fierce criticisms of the liberal age have always held a high place in the regard of National-Socialist leaders, including Herr Hitler himself; Schiller is considered to be 'the poet of the national passions'; and Wagner the master of 'heroic music'.[20]

To those beliefs can be added a number of political ambitions, particularly the vision of a Greater Germany, which envisaged a special place for Austria. And although the 'crisis' of the 1930s was mainly about economics, questions of culture and 'national identity' were never far away. In a speech broadcast from Munich in February as part of his campaign against the Dolfuss government, Theodor Habicht (the *Landesinspekteur* for Austria who had been deported from Austria in 1933 after the Nazi party was banned there) outlined the Nazi vision for Austria, with Vienna becoming the art and music capital of a greater German Reich. 'Germany,' he said, 'will raise her trade and tourist embargo as soon as the National Socialists in Austria are given a share in the Government. Austria has nothing to lose and everything to gain in closer unity with Germany.' In his speech, he outlined Hitler's four-year programme for a Nazi Austria when the National Socialists were in the Government. 'Germany would send all her surplus capital into Austria,' he said. 'New hydro-electric developments would be begun immediately. Industries would be started to supply the German market.'[21] Four years before the eventual Anschluss, the attempted coup that July resulted in the murder of Dolfuss and the deaths of 140 Nazis, but it was unsuccessful, becoming the first real failure of the Nazis. Hitler held Habicht responsible for the debacle.

What did Nazi ideology mean for musicians and composers? Nazi Germany's attitude to music was chaotic and often contradictory, and the absurdities of Nazi policy are well known. In a kind of postscript to the events of 1934 written at the very beginning of the following year, *The Times*' Berlin correspondent pointed out the apparently random approaches to such matters by the new regime. 'Like other cultural and spiritual conflicts of these times this conflict by no means discloses a clear-cut alignment of National Socialists against "reactionaries",' he wrote. Even the music critic of the Party organ, the *Völkischer Beobachter*, fell victim to the purge during the affair: 'he, it seems, was not sufficiently wholehearted in his condemnation' of Hindemith and other composers.[22]

As Norman Lebrecht has written in his survey of the music of the twentieth century, the case of Paul Hindemith's opera *Mathis de Maler*, indeed, exposed the 'randomness' of Nazi cultural oppression, the 'notorious' Hindemith case proving that Nazism was 'a ragbag of individual prejudices rather than a coherent ideology':

> Here was a composer who was German by ancestry and attitude, who mined the national heritage for musical inspiration, who worked harder than anyone to bring music back into ordinary German lives – and whose opera was banned in 1934 because the propaganda minister took a personal dislike to his intellectualism and his Jewish friends.[23]

In advance of the staging of the opera scheduled for the end of 1934 at the Berliner Staatsoper, Furtwängler had conducted the premiere performance in March of the symphony of the same name that was drawn from the stage work. Despite Hindemith's long-standing and amicable relationship with the Berlin Philharmonic, however, the symphony received a 'stormy' reception. Misha Aster comments that this was possibly because of 'a clash between the composer's progressive musical language and reactionary Nazi aesthetic tastes'. With its central theme of art and freedom, the subject of *Mathis de Maler* was 'a highly sensitive matter', and politically, 'an act of dissent':

> In July 1934, word arrived definitively that performance of *Mathis der Maler* at the Staatsoper would not be permitted. Angered by yet another affront to this authority, over the following months Furtwängler appealed to his high connections, including Hitler, Göring and Goebbels, in an attempt to see the ban lifted, but to no avail.[24]

The 'abuse and criticism' of Paul Hindemith was growing to such an extent in Berlin that at the end of November, Furtwängler penned a 'spirited defence' of the composer in the *Deutsche Allgemeine Zeitung*. Furtwängler rebuts the assertion 'that Hindemith is of Jewish descent'. Confusing as this is for us (why should the 'assertion' be 'rebutted' at all?), it can be understood only from the perspective of the time. The composer had 'played for years in a Jewish quartet and even dares to go on making chamber music records (presumably with the same quartet) after the National-Socialist revolution' and even to 'trim his sails' to the Nazi 'wind' in *Mathis der Maler*.[25] Furtwängler's resignation on 4 December was not only 'a forceful blow to the regime's prestige', but his departure 'also opened the door for Goebbels's (propaganda) ministry to finally complete the work on the reorganization of the Philharmonic undisturbed'.[26] The resignation of Furtwängler is what *The Times* called the culmination of the repercussion on music on political events in Germany (from the 31 December review article). Furtwängler resigned all his posts at the beginning of December: the vice-presidency of the Reich Chamber of Music, the leadership of the BPO and the chief directorship of the Staatsoper. With Bruno Walter and Otto Klemperer having disappeared from German music at the start of the Nazi regime and anti-Jewish legislation, *The Times* commented that the loss of Furtwängler left a gap which would be doubly hard to close:

> General Göring's recently expressed intention to make of the State Opera a temple of music which would vie with the Scala at Milan will certainly be no easier to fulfil. By an ironical chance the best-known conductor now remaining at the State Opera is a Jew, Herr Leo Blech, who was exempted from the anti-Jewish legislation either in virtue of his many years of service there or because his original appointment was made by the Kaiser.

The Times reminds its readers that earlier in the Nazi regime, Furtwängler had warned Goebbels about the effect his policies would have on German musical life, and in so doing rejecting 'the distinction between Jew and non-Jew, saying that for him the only distinction was that between good and bad artist'. Despite the conductor's apparent reconciliation with the new developments, the affair with Hindemith showed that, behind the scenes, a violent conflict had broken out and that Furtwängler 'meant to stand or fall by Hindemith'. The Nazi defence was that 'for years before the National-Socialist seizure of power (Hindemith) had adopted a deliberately un-German attitude', thereby making his participation in Nazi reconstruction policies intolerable.[27] Further explanation concerning Hindemith was presented by Alfred Rosenberg in the Nazi organ, the *Völkischer Beobachter*, of which he was editor. Furtwängler's offence was to conduct the first performance of *Mathis der Maler*. Hindemith's human, artistic and political associations had now all been removed by the Nazi revolution, and he was out of sympathy with 'the great struggle of our age'.[28] *The Times* devoted an editorial to the 'Nordic Purge' on the same day. Eighteen months of 'regrettable incidents' and the departure willy-nilly of, among others, Klemperer, Bruno Walter and Fritz Busch were followed by the attempted racial purification of the Berlin

Philharmonic, the 'excitement' at the Dresden Opera when it was discovered that the librettist of Richard Strauss's latest opera was Jewish, and now the resignations of Erich Kleiber and Hans Knappertsbusch (of the Bavarian State Opera) was followed, finally, by the Furtwängler affair:

> Whereas Dr Goebbels, as Propaganda Minister, decides what is not to be in German cultural life, Herr Rosenberg has of late months spoken publicly and with authority of what is to be.

As the 'spiritual overseer' of the party, Rosenberg's views were the source of the campaign against Hindemith. *The Times*' tone is clear: dismissing Rosenberg's 'obscure career as drawing master in a Baltic town' as testimony to his, and other Nazis', amateurism. In Rosenberg's 'cultural community the flame of racial mysticism burns in all its purity, tended by ardent amateurs who labour at the task of spreading the "heroic" philosophy of life through the Party and the people', and it is they, it seems, who are now to dictate to the German public what shall be called good music:

> Till lately they had left music alone. Their first effort was characteristic: an obscure composer was given the task of composing new music for *A Midsummer Night's Dream*, Mendelssohn's music being too pretty, too lacking in the awe and mysticism of Nordic Myth – and of course Mendelssohn was a Jew. Their second effort has brought the resignation of one of Europe's greatest conductors, a loss which the vast majority of Germans, whatever their politics, will bitterly regret. But if the Hindemith incident prompts them to ask, as the responsible and thoughtful Protestants and Catholics of Germany are asking every day in increasing numbers, how far along the path of so-called 'cultural revolution' Herr Rosenberg and the leaders of the Nazi Guards and Hitler Youth are to be allowed to go, the incident may still have its redeeming feature.[29]

Alas, it was not to be. The prescience of *The Times*' columnist is noteworthy here. As early as 1934, correspondents and leader-writers were already wise to Nazi ambitions. The ideological battle lines, as defined by questions about music, were already drawn, and can be said to demonstrate that five years before the outbreak of War and just eighteen months or so after Hitler's accession to power, Nazi intentions were clear and that the Party's attitude towards eminent musicians was enough to sound alarm bells. If at the beginning of 1934 Sir Thomas Beecham was urging restraint over changes taking place at the *Philharmonie*, claiming there was nothing to worry about, by the end of the year, it was obvious to British observers that all was not well.

Everyone was taking sides. Richard Strauss made his position clear in a telegram to Goebbels, in which he expressed his 'hearty congratulations' and 'enthusiastic agreement' with a speech by the Propaganda Minister at the first anniversary of the *Reichskulturkamer* in which Goebbels 'vigorously upheld the attitude of the State towards Herr Furtwängler and towards the defence of the composer Hindemith'. Strauss's telegram, *The Times* points out, was subscribed 'in real veneration, Heil Hitler!'[30] Exempt from banning in early Nazi Germany were non-Aryans and those that had been decorated at the front. Fritz Busch, possessor of both these prerequisites, however, had been dismissed from his post at the Dresden State Opera almost as soon as the Nazis came to power and replaced by Paul Adolph. The latter was now also told 'that he had forfeited his claim to this high artistic post', as a result of the affair. This was also the fate of Hans Gal, also a non-Aryan, who was relieved of *his* post at Mainz in early 1933.[31] But, earlier in the year, even Richard Strauss had crossed swords with the regime over the staging of his new opera, *Die Schweigsame Frau*.

> The incorrigible persistence of Jews in the realm of art led to further friction at the Dresden State Opera, involving no less a person than Dr. Richard Strauss. Dr. Strauss has been made much of by the National Socialists as a living justification, in his sphere, of their racial theories; he is eminent, German and non-Jewish, and composers with all these qualifications are not too plentiful.

Arabella, first produced in Dresden in 1933, had been hailed as a great musical event, with nothing 'left undone to celebrate it'. However, the planned staging of Strauss's new *Die Schweigsame Frau* was causing much consternation among Dresden's Nazi authorities because the book on which the opera is based was written by Stephan Zweig, a 'Viennese Jew', reminding readers of its local organ that 'Dr. Goebbels, in the State Playhouse of Dresden, promised to free German art from alien influences'. Although the article in question stopped short of recriminating Richard Strauss on the subject, *The Times* nevertheless mused that 'what will now happen about the production of *Die Schweigsame Frau* none can foretell'.[32] Just a month before, the composer was honoured by the State on his seventieth birthday, with the presentation of the *Alderschild* by President von Hindenburg's Personal Secretary of State, Dr Meissner. Awarded for 'distinctive achievement', the *Alderschild* was 'a large medallion embossed with the Reich eagle and mounted on a stand', and on this occasion inscribed 'to the creator and master of German music' and accompanied by a letter of congratulation from President von Hindenburg.[33] Presumably because he was too ill to attend in person, this was possibly one of the very last civic occasions which bore the name and honour of the president, who died just two months later, in early August.

The death of Hindenburg proved the major turning point in the fate of Germany, or at least Germany's politics. Even as his body was lying in state, and before his final resting place had been determined, the German interior ministry had ordered a plebiscite to be held on 19 August, 'at which the nation [was] to express its sanction to the unification of the Presidency and Chancellorship in Herr Hitler's person', under the same regulations which had governed the November 1933 referendum at which the exit from the Disarmament Conference and the League of Nations was approved (95 per cent of the electorate doing so). But this was all a matter of formality:

> As on that occasion, the nation is required to approve an action already taken. The normal procedure, by past standards, would never have been for President of the Supreme Court, in virtue of his legal rights, to act as President of the Reich pending the election. The Bill uniting the Presidency and Chancellorship in Herr Hitler's person 'as from the moment of the death of President von Hindenburg' revoked this right; and Herr Hitler, in requesting the Minister of the Interior to arrange for the nation to gives its sanction, specifically said that the Bill 'had been resolved by the Cabinet and is constitutionally valid.' A large affirmative vote is to be expected.[34]

At the State Funeral, members of the SS lined the route leading from the Chancery to the Kroll Opera House (by now fulfilling the role of Reichstag). *The Times'* correspondent commented that the Storm Troopers (SA) were again absent, but that the floor of the Reichstag was packed anyway, the gap caused by the recent 'clean-up', still visible at the previous month's meeting, now filled:

> On the table of the House, at the foot of the three-tiered tribune, was a massive white bust of the late President, surrounded by green foliage and arum lilies. The House sat in silence as the Berlin Philharmonic Orchestra, unseen, played Beethoven's *Coriolanus* Overture. The then Führer of the Reich went to the Speaker's tribute . . . and read the oration.[35]

At the Salzburg Festival that year, Richard Strauss's operas were to have been heard there to mark the composer's seventieth birthday. Due to production expense, however, *Die Frau Ohne Schatten* was cancelled; and Strauss withdrew from the festival. Though he was present at the performance of three of his other operas, in practice this meant he would not conduct the planned performance of *Fidelio*. A 'magnificent performance' of *Elektra* was given on 17 August, however. The opera (1909) follows the atonality of Berg and Schoenberg, but

Strauss was never to approach such dissonance again, and in Britain it remained his least accessible work, its 'hectic emotionalism' out of fashion in England. The opera was, for *The Times'* critic, 'morbid in feeling' and it was 'impossible to sympathize' with any of its characters:

> In the last 20 years Strauss has lost much of his popularity in England; he is commonly said to have written himself out. Actually, of his musical output during this period, only *Arabella* has received a fair trial, and that, unfortunately, scarcely represents him at his best. It was in the War that we in England lost touch with his latest music, and we have never regained it. . . . On such slender evidence Strauss's more recent music is supposed to be not worth the hearing.[36]

For the Reich, major music festivals were often a chance for the Nazis to make pronouncements on their view of the place of culture in the new Germany. This usually prompted reaction and claims of philistinism and amateurism. 'Most of those in control of German cultural life have an exaggerated faith in the power of propaganda,' railed *The Times*, after one such pronouncement by the Nazi Propaganda Minister. Opening the 'week of the German book', Goebbels denounced what he called the 'cliques' which, he alleged, once dominated German literary and artistic life, demanding that German authors 'should now tread the paths opened up for them by the tide of the national revolution'. Confusing as it seems to us, the Nazis, however, held Shakespeare in high regard as 'one of the heroes of the organizations concerned with the revival of the German theatre'. An announcement was made that following a recent popular production of *A Midsummer Night's Dream*, members of the 'National-Socialist Culture Community' were to commission a Freiburg musician to compose 'new music' for the play, 'presumably to take the place of the un-Nordic melodies of Mendelssohn, whose works are practically taboo on the Berlin concert platform'.[37]

A 'growing enthusiasm' for the music of Richard Wagner in the new Germany was reported by *The Times* from Bayreuth at the opening of the third Ring cycle of the 1934 festival. Not a single seat in the *Festspielhaus* was empty. Wagner's operas could now be heard all over the world, but what made Bayreuth so different? Though not the 'best in the world', the orchestra there rehearsed more thoroughly than anywhere else; and with only six operas performed over three months, the result was 'a cast that has been drilled to a pitch of perfection that can be found nowhere else and an *ensemble* that cannot be equalled'. That Wagner's prescription is 'religiously carried out' explains the peculiarity of Bayreuth. And in this cycle, some of the singers sang better than at Covent Garden earlier in the year.[38]

And reporting on the first *Reichstheaterwoche*, which took place in Dresden for eight days at the end of May and the beginning of June, *Musical Times* correspondent Nancy Fleetwood was impressed not only by the sheer number of events (including opera, concerts and plays) that were staged but also by how full every performance was. 'This only serves to prove that come what may, Germany is – and the present Government certainly intend that she shall continue to be – a nation of music-lovers and theatre-goers,' she wrote. Fleetwood was also impressed by the presence of Hitler, who together with other prominent members of the Government 'set a good example' by being present at the opening performance in the opera house. As the minister in charge of the Festival, Josef Goebbels remained in Dresden for much of the week, visiting the opera or playhouse every evening:

> Dr. Goebbels made a long and brilliant speech with regard to the future of the German theatre, the chief theme of his speech being that the State intends to undertake everything possible to promote theatrical art, especially German art and artists and more especially German music. Moreover it is to be made possible for every class of the people to visit the opera and theatres regularly; opera, drama, and music are to play an important part in the education of the rising generation, and are no longer to be regarded as luxuries for the favoured few.[39]

By the end of the year this innocent-sounding admiration for the festival would have needed considerable revision, in the light of what the promotion of German art really meant. And, of course, there were already many German refugees in London. But in the meantime, here in *The Musical Times*, we have unbridled enthusiasm for what Goebbels intended. It is incredible to us that commentators in England could write with such unsparing admiration for Nazi efforts in promoting the Arts. But this is 1934, the year of possibilities and of neutral observation (at least in some quarters) of the new regime in Germany. The festival, predictably enough, ended with *Meistersinger*. By December, the reality of Nazi domination of the Arts had much clearer implications for commentators in Britain. In an article published in *The Listener* in December, 'Music Under Laboratory Conditions', we have probably the most important contemporary British comment on the Nazi doctrine of *Entartete Musik*, by distinguished critic M-D. Calvocoressi:

> If I were asked which recent event in the musical world is likely to be of greatest interest to future historians and critics, I should unhesitatingly say: The decision taken by the leaders of Nazi Germany to ban all music of alleged 'anarchical, anti-cultural, and non-Aryan' tendencies – that of Schönberg and his school, of

Krenék, Kurt Weill and countless others – forbidding not only performance, but critical study of it.

At this point the doctrine of *Entartete Musik* had not been solidified with the 1936 *Entartete Kunst* exhibition of banned painting preceding any 'formalities' of trying to publicize the new ideologies applied to music. Calvocoressi writes that this 'constitutes an example unique in history of musical art deflected by coercion instead of being allowed to follow its normal course without interference from outside; and is likely to have very important (although not very wide-spread) consequences'. From the musical (rather than the political or human) point of view, the situation in Germany 'may be summed up in a very few words'. It is worth repeating them all:

> Every artistic trend or style, whether it stands for obedience to tradition or for reaction against tradition, is in most respects a product of evolution; and, up to now, has been allowed to establish itself or die a natural death, influencing or not the ulterior course of the art, according to its vitality and power to appeal. The task of judging its value, of accepting or rejecting it, was left to musicians, critics, and public. Germany, now, is denying certain types of music their normal chance and cutting the whole nation off from them. And so, in one of the biggest music-producing and music-consuming countries of the world, the progress of musical art and culture will continue, for a time, under wholly artificial conditions, while everywhere else it will follow the same course as before.... We may picture musical Germany as a living organism deprived of certain categories of stimuli or nourishment to which the rest of the world still has access.

Calvocoressi doubts that 'coercion in matters of art and culture can ever serve a good purpose'. And yet, even in Britain, the potential for cultural propaganda was understood, with British Council about to begin its programme of musical propaganda with the establishment of its Music Advisory Committee the following year. Calvocoressi remarked that a concert performance of excerpts from Alban Berg's new opera *Lulu* gave rise to a storm of protest in the Nazi press, and it was small wonder that conductor Erich Kleiber should not have been dissuaded from producing them at all. Even Hindemith's music, composed in what the *N. S. Kultur Gemeinde* (Nazi Culture Committee) regarded as the 'lawless' period of the Weimar Republic, was no longer in favour. Earlier in the year, his *Mathis der Maler* symphony had been performed in Berlin and was 'not unfavourably received'. The press even regarded its performance as 'an event of importance from both the political and the musical points of view. There can no longer be any opposition, on grounds of policy, to Hindemith's music, no describing it as destructive of culture'. The symphony was to receive a London performance on 21 December at a BBC Contemporary Concert, and those excerpts from *Lulu* were to be given the following March at a BBC symphony concert. At home, Hindemith and his music were soon outlawed, with Goebbels banning performances of his work from 1936.

> Thus, according to the most radical fraction, so to speak, of the new Germany, the works included in the music section of the Nazi *Index Librorum Prohibitorum*, are to be withheld not only from the listening public, but also from musicians who might wish to study them in private for fear that the works in question might, even so, insidiously exercise a dissolving influence . . .
>
> Such, then, is the state of things at the beginning of the new 'culture' experiment: the conditions created are entirely artificial, and in absolute contrast with those obtaining everywhere else. Considering things from the cold-blooded scientific point of view, one may, while regretting that such an unparalleled condition should have arisen, foretell that the consequences will prove most instructive.[40]

With the reproduction (in professional journals, though not in the daily press) of the rules governing the acceptance of foreign engagements occurring at the time of Furtwängler's resignation (and, indeed, of the appearance of Calvocoressi's article in *The Listener*), Goebbels was reminding him, suggests *The Times*, right at the end of December, of the limitations imposed upon his future. The order forbade German artists from accepting invitations to perform abroad without the express permission of the relevant Culture Chamber, and to disobey it 'entailed expulsion from membership of a chamber, and ineligibility to work in Germany'. The order's 'timely republication', comments *The Times*, 'may explain the difficulties facing such men as Dr Furtwängler, if they do not wish to become exiles. . . . There is still no trustworthy news of Dr Furtwängler's future, other than the cancellation of his concerts in Vienna and London'.[41] January was the traditional month for the Berlin Philharmonic's annual visit to England.

With the threat of such a pronouncement hanging over much of German cultural life, many musicians fled. After 1933 Britain and the United States became refuges for musicians fleeing Nazi Germany. Among the many who fled was Hans Eisler. Coming to London as a refugee in 1934, Eisler was introduced to fellow socialists at a 'concert-Demonstration' held in Morley College at the beginning of the year. Eisler was well known as the famous German revolutionary composer of the 'Song of the Saar'; the words (by Brecht) were printed in December in the pages of the *Daily Worker*:

> Hold on to the Saar, comrades,
> Comrades, hold on to the Saar,
> We'll start a new page in January,
> When we vote to remain as we are.⁴²

He wrote for the documentary film *New Earth* (1934), his work for the cinema providing a useful contrast with a young British composer. In his essay on Eisler's film music, Guido Heldt makes the comparison between Eisler and Benjamin Britten:

> For Eisler as for Britten in their respective biographical situations, film music came in handy. Both had completed their education, both under in the end somewhat unsatisfactory circumstances, which may have triggered the need to ostentatiously distance themselves from these backgrounds. Film music was new for both of them: usable, serviceable music for a modern mass medium ... far removed from the esoteric pursuits of Eisler's teacher Schoenberg or the musical establishment at the Royal College of Music.⁴³

On his arrival in Britain on 21 July 1933, Eisler's pupil Ernst Meyer (1905–88) had already attracted the attention of the security services as a 'suspected communist',⁴⁴ and by September was registered with the British authorities, calling himself a 'musical scientist'. A file was kept on him until he left for East Germany on 22 September 1949, when he became a music professor in Berlin. Meyer had been a member of the German Communist Party and fled Germany on a tip-off from a friend who informed him that the Gestapo was waiting for him at his house. Spending his first months in London seeking out his friend and teacher Eisler, he was eventually recognized as part of a Hampstead-based group of communists with links to the *Kulturbund*. In Britain during the War, he co-founded the Free German League of Culture. Soon after his arrival, Meyer was engaged by the BBC. Beginning on 1 January, a new series of weekly programmes in which a 'great number of works' never broadcast before were planned. The opportunity to 'build up an invaluable catalogue of chamber music timings' was taken at the same time and the series began with the first book of J. S. Bach's Preludes and Fugues.⁴⁵ The series, *Foundations of Music*, included, on 26 February, sixteenth-century instrumental music arranged by Meyer, beginning what has been seen as a fruitful period during his exile in Britain:

> Meyer started composing in his teens, writing songs and chamber music in conventionally Romantic idiom. After a period of musicological studies he

began studying composition with Eisler in 1929 and like him . . . became active in the Workers' Music Movement. Eisler's influence, together with his own rather sudden politicization – 'the hard confrontation with reality', as he put it later – led him away from Romanticism to a style more typical of the period. Meyer's own simple *Kampflieden* ('Fighting Songs') stemmed from the established Eisler type, and this trend continued into the English exile period.

Meyer's *Symphony for Strings* emerges from his years in Britain. Its language, writes Anthony Cross, 'is harshly uncompromising, often highly chromatic and far more radical than in most English music of the period'. Cross considered the symphony to be 'an unknown masterpiece of English music: composed in England for an English orchestra, reflecting the composer's wartime experiences here in both its despair and militant rebelliousness, and perceptibly inspired by English traditions both in the choice of medium and sometimes in the idiom'.[46]

Eisler and Meyer can both be credited with enriching musical life in London from 1934. Like the trio of exiles at Glyndebourne, they brought with them a rich heritage as well as their knowledge and expertise. But there were also cultural implications with the influx of refugees. In the November 1934 issue of *The Musical Times*, ISM president Professor W. Gillies Whittaker argued that this foreign 'invasion' was likely to 'encroach on every aspect of the music profession, from solo performers to composers for theatre and film'.[47] Indeed, as 'Survival wasn't easy in 1933 and 1934,' explains Richard Morrison in his history of the LSO. 'This was the height of the Depression' and 'where money is tight, live entertainment dies'. Unemployment was at a record high with 3½ million Britons out of work. 'There was no artistic or economic reason why a hundred or so orchestral players shouldn't have joined them, especially as this particular bunch of players were widely perceived (after the founding of the BBC Symphony and London Philharmonic Orchestras) to be superfluous to requirements.'[48] But in 1934, what Morrison has called an 'annus horribilis' for the LSO, the orchestra met with the Director General of the BBC, John Reith, who put '£2500 worth of work' their way.[49] More significantly, there was to be another development which almost certainly saved the orchestra from ruin: a trio of three men who had fallen foul of the Nazi regime, and who between them were to enable one of the most remarkable developments in British cultural life in 1934. 'Glyndebourne came as a lifeline to the LSO players,' writes Morrison, with the orchestra for the first season, and several thereafter, 'drawn almost entirely from LSO ranks'.[50] It was, in fact, at the insistence of the Musicians' Union that 'home-grown talent for the orchestra' was used.[51]

There has been much said about John Christie's audacity in building an opera house at his country estate on the Sussex Downs. 'What must have seemed to be a madcap folly in 1934 has become a world-famous guarantee of quality,' writes Michael Kennedy.[52] Designed by Edmund Warre, construction of the theatre began in October 1931 (not unlike those two other masterworks, also first begun in 1931 and revealed three years later: Vaughan Williams's Fourth and Walton's First Symphonies). Knowing little about the practicalities of staging opera, John Christie simply 'knew what he liked' and wanted to please his young soprano wife Audrey Mildmay. 'How about putting on *Parsifal*, suggested the inveterate and uncritical Teutonophile? [Carl] Ebert looked at the tiny theatre and replied sardonically that *Parsifal* would be fine if you put the singers and the orchestra in the auditorium and the audience on the stage.'[53]

In an early review, Eric Blom concurred with this idea. '"Parsival" even if technically possible at a theatre designed for chamber opera, would have the effect of a sermon delivered in a literary *salon* – the better in itself, the worse an error of taste,' he wrote. 'The "Ring" would be a monstrosity, even if one could forget to construe it into an indictment of capitalism.' Blom's contributions as a critic to British musical life were many, and all were to have a political flavour. He continued, 'Glyndebourne, of course, is in the first place a capitalist's hobby and a capitalist's resort, though it has been suggested that it might eventually come to attract visitors at Brighton and Eastbourne to opera in the vernacular.' But he could not complain about the standard and quality of the productions, enthusing that 'there was no provincialism from anywhere, so that one could heartily welcome the international cast all round. Perfect teams were made by artists coming from Germany and Finland, Italy and Czecho-Slovakia, Austria and England'.[54] Of course, Blom's views on *Parsifal* are indicative of his politics. I explore Wagner's final opera in the final chapter of this book.

'Christie's original idea had been to model Glyndebourne on Bayreuth and therefore feature works by Wagner,' writes Erik Levi in his volume on the Nazis and Mozart. 'It is possible that the political situation in Germany, particularly the Nazi appropriation of Bayreuth in the summer of 1933, dampened Christie's enthusiasm for promoting Wagner at this particular juncture. More likely, however, was the gradual realization, largely as a result of Audrey Mildmay's good sense, that the intimate opera house he had built would be far more suited to Mozart than to Wagner.'[55] By Christmas 1933 it had been decided that the first season would begin on 28 May 1934 with six performances of both *Le Nozze de Figaro* and *Cosi fan Tutte*, both to be sung in Italian.[56] Michael Kennedy relates that Thomas Beecham was invited to conduct the performances but did not reply, because he found the whole idea 'preposterous'.[57] The violinist Adolf Busch then suggested his brother Fritz to the Christies. Fritz Busch had been *Generalmusikdirektor* of the Dresden Opera but had recently left because of his opposition to Nazi policies. Though he was not Jewish himself, the Sturmabteilung (SA) staged a demonstration against his tenure, which resulted in his resignation from his post and his departure to Switzerland, together with his violinist brother Adolf. 'Despite various attempts to lure him back to the fold, Fritz Busch steadfastly refused further cooperation with the Nazis and was actively seeking employment elsewhere,' writes Levi.[58] Busch had initially contracted with the Theatre Colón in Buenos Aires for 1934 but a financial crisis freed him and he accepted Christie's invitation in January 1934. On his arrival, Busch realized what ideal conditions Glyndebourne offered, writes Kennedy. 'He needed a first-rate director, a functionary of whose importance Christie was unaware. Busch recruited Carl Ebert from Berlin, another non-Jewish opponent of the Nazis who was anxious to leave Germany.' Carl Ebert had been director of the Städtische Opera in Berlin until early 1933 and had also entered into an agreement with the Teatro Colón. Busch and Ebert had worked together on a Mozart opera at Salzburg.[59] Finally, 'as his "managerial assistant", Busch brought to Glyndebourne Rudolf Bing, an Austrian Jew who had worked with Ebert in Darmstadt until forced to leave Germany for Vienna to resume work as an impresario.'[60] Both Kennedy and Levi, as well as Miranda Seymour have commented on how the émigré 'triumvirate' of Busch, Ebert and Bing brought to Britain a remarkable professionalism that was the direct result of the precarious political situation in Europe.

It is that standard of professionalism that remained a major preoccupation of the experiences of musicians in Britain throughout 1934, and it is to those domestic concerns that we turn next.

Notes

1. Seymour, 2014: 324.
2. Lambert, 1966: 133.
3. Seymour, 2014: 320.
4. 'Visit of Berlin Orchestra: Concert at Queen's Hall', *The Times*, 23 January 1934, p. 10.
5. 'Royal Philharmonic Society: Beethoven Programme', *The Times*, 26 January 1934, p. 10.

6   Aster, 2010: 9–10.
7   'Berlin Philharmonic Orchestra: Dr. Furtwängler's Position', *The Times*, 20 January 1934, p. 8.
8   The Berlin Philharmonic's first post-war visit to England was in November 1928, returning in 1929, 1931 and 1932 – see Levi, 2013: 88.
9   Quoted from the *Sunday Referee*, 28 January 1934, in Lloyd, 2014: 196.
10 Lloyd, 2014: 195–6.
11 Incidentally, in an edition of *The Listener* published in August, Francis Toye explored 'the necessity or the desirability of the cadenza' which by 1934 could be regarded as 'an outworn convention' (*The Listener*, 29 August 1934, Volume XII, Issue 294, p. 365).
12 Translation of Goldberg's statement from Enrique Sánchez Lansch's film *Das Reichsorchester* (2007).
13 See my volume *Culture and Propaganda in World War II*.
14 Volker, 2008: 48.
15 'Nazi Spring Songs: A Feast of Marches', *The Times*, 20 April 1934, p. 13.
16 Edward J. Dent to Herbert Thompson, 4 April 1934, quoted in Foreman, 1987: 172–3.
17 Alfredo Casella (1883–1947) was an Italian composer, pianist and conductor.
18 By the end of the War, this could, indeed, have been the case. With the Nazi preoccupation of *Entartete Musik*, the breadth of broadcasting can be shown to have been considerably narrower than what the BBC was putting out by 1945.
19 I compare Hadamovsky's view on the place of music in the Third Reich with that of British official opinion in *Culture and Propaganda in World War II*.
20 'The Nazi Triad', *The Times*, 7 May 1934, p. 13.
21 'Nazi "Peace Terms"', *The Times*, 23 February 1934, p. 13.
22 'Nazi War with Musicians: Critics Dismissed', *The Times*, 2 January 1935, p. 9.
23 Lebrecht, 1992: 155.
24 Aster, 2010: 23–4.
25 'Nazi Attacks on Herr Hindemith: Dr Furtwängler's Reply', *The Times*, 26 November 1934, p. 11.
26 Aster, 2010: 23–4.
27 'Nazi Aims in Music: Herr Furtwängler Resigns. Race Prejudice and Art', *The Times*, 5 December 1934, p. 13.
28 'Purging German Music: The New Taboos. Herr Rosenberg Calls the Tune', *The Times*, 7 December 1934, p. 13.
29 'The Nordic Purge', *The Times*, 7 December 1934.
30 'Nazi Purge of Music: Richard Strauss Supports Dr Goebbels', *The Times*, 12 December 1934, p. 13.
31 'BBC Radio 3', Donald McLeod's *Composer of the Week*, 7 April 2014.
32 '"Aryan Music": Trouble Over New Strauss Opera; "Jewish" Librettist', *The Times*, 21 July 1934, p. 11.

33 'Dr. Richard Strauss's 70th Birthday: Honour from the German President', *The Times*, 12 June 1934, p. 13.
34 'Hindenburg: Lying-in-state at Nerdeck. Funeral Plans: The Coming Plebiscite', *The Times*, 4 August 1934, p. 10.
35 'This Great German': Hindenburg the Symbol. 'The Past and the Future: Herr Hitler's Tribute', *The Times*, 7 August 1934, p. 10.
36 'Strauss's Operas: The Composer at Salzburg', *The Times*, 25 August 1934, p. 8.
37 'Politics before Art: The New Standards in Germany', *The Times*, 8 November 1934, p. 13. Dozens of attempts at creating new music for the play were made in Germany, with Mendelssohn's music no longer being performed in concert halls. Ironically, émigré Erich Korngold was composing his new music for Hollywood's version of *A Midsummer Night's Dream* at about the same time. The film was made in 1935, using Mendelssohn's music, which was re-orchestrated by Korngold, as well as some of his own linking passages.
38 'Bayreuth Festival': Growing Enthusiasm for Wagner', *The Times*, 23 August 1934, p. 8.
39 'Nancy Fleetwood, "Musical Notes from Abroad: Germany"', *The Musical Times*, Volume 75, Issue 1087, July 1934, p. 655.
40 *The Listener*, Volume XII, Issue 310, 19 December 1934, p. 1024.
41 'Control of German Artists: No Foreign Engagements without Leave', *The Times*, 27 December 1934, p. 9.
42 *Daily Worker*, 24 December 1934, p. 2.
43 Sound Sentiments: Hans Eisler's Film Music in the 1930s, Guido Heldt in *Music as a Bridge*.
44 National Archives: KV2/3502.
45 BBC Internal Memo dated 2 January 1934, BBC WAC, R27/106.
46 'Anthony Cross: The Music of Ernest Hermann Meyer', *Musical Times*, Volume 121, Issue 1654, December 1980, pp. 777–9.
47 'The Foreign Artist Problem', *The Musical Times*, November 1934.
48 Morrison, 2004: 81.
49 Ibid., 83.
50 Ibid.
51 Levi, 2010: 100.
52 Kennedy, 2010: 5.
53 Snowman, 2003: 64–5.
54 Glyndebourne Opera Festival, Eric Blom, *Musical Times*, Volume 75, Issue 1097, July 1934, pp. 651–2.
55 Levi, 2010: 96–7.
56 As a contrast to Glyndebourne, the notable event of the year at Salzburg was, according to *The Times*, a production of *Don Giovanni* in Italian, with Ezio Pinza

playing the title role, and the other main parts also sung by Italian artists. 'The whole performance was on an extraordinarily high level, although the décor was not quite up to the usual Salzburg standard.' *The Times* had only the slightest criticism of the production of *Cosi van Tutti*, which, in contrast to *Don Giovanni*, was sung in German by Austrians, 'but the only fault that the most captious critic could find is the impossibility of translating an Italian libretto into German without losing some of the charm of the original' ('End of Salzburg Festival: Signor Toscanini's Performances', *The Times*, 4 September 1934, p. 10).

57 Kennedy, 2010: 19.
58 Levi, 2010: 97–8.
59 *Die Entführung aus dem Serail*.
60 Kennedy, 2010: 19.

5

Domestic concerns

Lord Londonderry, who was to join the Anglo-German Fellowship – set up to foster relations with Nazi Germany – on its founding the following year presented Hamilton Harty with the gold medal of the Royal Philharmonic Society at a November concert featuring the composer's Violin Concerto, a concert which the composer also conducted. 'In making the presentation Lord Londonderry acclaimed a fellow-Ulsterman, who as composer, conductor, and accompanist, had done something to set the strings of Tara's harp vibrating once more,' ran a piece describing the occasion in *The Times*.[1] Elsewhere in Ireland, nationalist movements were as much a feature of public life as they were in Britain.

Committee members of the BBC's Music Department discussed the success of the recent British Music Festival which had taken place in the New Year. 'It was agreed that it had been a good thing to do politically and possibly musically at the present juncture,' reveal the minutes to that meeting.[2] Praise for the BBC's Festival of British Music in *The Times* also inspired letters of agreement. One correspondent felt that the concerts, broadcast in a series of programmes on the BBC gave 'a sense of National and Imperial solidarity which no series of competing commercial system could possibly afford', and that 'despite strange-coloured shirts and differences of opinion and dialect', Britons were still 'a people yet'.[3] As the only credible patron of music on a wide scale, the BBC clearly understood the political role that it could play, even in the organization of a music festival. And until those 'Strange-Coloured Shirts' (usually black, at least in England) were banned, they were a major feature of public life.

The problem of 'Political Uniforms' was raised by a correspondent to *The Times* in February, who wrote to remind readers that 'Undue influence in the process of choosing a candidate in an election was prevented by the Corrupt and Illegal Practices Prevention Act 1883', section 16 (1), which stipulated that 'No payment of contract for payment shall, for the purpose of promoting or procuring the election of a candidate at any election, be made on account of bands of music, torches, flags, banners, cockades, ribbons, or other marks of distinction'.[4] To the author of this letter, the Act should specify political uniforms of any colour as another 'mark of distinction' and use this as the justification for banning their use as part of 'the new conditions that have unfortunately been imported', that is, the adoption of a coloured shirt as a mark of distinction by political organizations. The phenomenon was not just restricted to Britain. In Ireland, for example, 'Blueshirt' membership 'surged to nearly 50,000 by mid-1934', a case similar to Oswald Mosley's Blackshirts in Britain, but there, rather than ideology, the collapse was due to economics. 'Most of the support came from County Cork and the south-west where cattle farmers had been hard-hit by the trade war that de Valera was waging with Britain. When that dispute was resolved at the end of 1934, Blueshirt numbers collapsed.'[5]

A further case is the plethora of 'shirt' movements in South Africa.

> Their ranks included Manie Wessels's Blackshirts, popular among poor Afrikaners in the Transvaal, and Louis Weichardt's better-known Greyshirts, a Christian National Socialist organisation, never more than 2000 strong, whose logo was a swastika in the colours of the South African flag. Allied fringe groups included the South African Fascists . . . and the Oranjehemde (Orange Shirts), a 'militant shock troop' of young Afrikaners,

writes South African historian Richard Steyn.[6]

The questionability of black – or any other colour – shirts arises in early 1934. Lord Allen of Hurtwood had written to *The Times* on 26 January, mentioning Mosley and men like him, 'who threaten liberty and organize their private armies'.[7] For Lord Allen, the wearing of uniforms was akin to 'organizing private armies under the auspices of political parties', later suggesting that the Swedish precedent be used where the prohibition of the wearing of uniforms 'used to indicate a political opinion' was outlawed.[8]

'While the BUF was notoriously unable to laugh at itself, the movement was easily undermined by humour,' comments Julie Gottlieb. A *News Chronicle* review in February 1934 noticed that the comedian whose song 'indicated that Englishmen have no liking for shirts of any particular colour' received the warmest applause. For the British public, politics requiring 'dressing up' belonged, rather, 'to the realm of comic opera than of public affairs'.[9] Nancy Mitford also famously sent up the movement in her 1934 novel *Wigs on the Green*, the ranks of the 'Social Unionists' representing Mosley's 'Union Jackshirts'. Mosley was unamused. Writes Laura Thompson in her biography of the author, if known at all now, that the book's 'timely parody of Fascism and the British Unionist Party' was 'a subject ripe for mockery':

> Nancy's airy, ironic and civilised soul did not truly grasp the tumultuous passions that had been raised in Europe, and in her own family, by the political situation. She saw it all later, of course. But in 1934 she thought that it could be treated, like everything else, as a joke: this was not political naivety, but it was a failure of imagination (does a Voltaire ever truly understand a Wagner?), a wrongful belief that rationality would triumph over a very certain kind of dark romance.[10]

The privilege of sending up the Blackshirts in a novel was perhaps an expression of an idle existence. But the cause of ordinary workers, rather than the question of 'strange-coloured shirts' or any lofty ambitions regarding the presentation of British music, was the real concern of the Musicians' Union and other bodies representing the workforce. Concerns about 'the menace to music which the BBC monopoly presents' were published in an article in the *Evening Standard* in November by Frank Eames, General Secretary of the ISM, which represented 2,700 musicians.[11] Eames's complaint was that over a three-month period, 415 hours of recorded music had robbed musicians of their livelihoods. The Musicians' Union was careful to dissociate itself from Eames, however, no doubt to ensure its own influence over the BBC where possible. This was typical of the concerns related to the new technologies.[12] And while technological advances posed their own threats, there was also the threat to another kind of music, from a surprising source. Over the past few years 'the Americanization of British music had become an accomplished fact', despite the superiority of the average song written by an English music professional, compared to that of his American counterpart. This was a factor in the employment of British musicians, rather than a sense of xenophobia. So heard a meeting of the Society of British Authors, Composers and Arrangers at Anderson's Hotel, Fleet Street, on 26 October.[13] That the BBC should not be oblivious to its responsibilities towards its audience, as well as to professional musicians was clear to many commentators. In the special broadcasting number published in August, *The Times* was unequivocal about both:

> The task of the BBC is to enlist more and more people in that body of devotees, to reveal the joys of music so persuasively, so alluringly, that one day almost all the world will share in its endless delight. That one day the great majority may know the inspiring, uplifting power of music, which can bear men's spirit to a lovelier realm than the everyday world knows: that is the vision to which broadcasters set their faces steadfastly.

And on the matter of engaging 'foreign' artists:

> Whenever possible, the BBC engages distinguished artists who visit England. Only in the rare event of there being no British artist who can undertake some new or unfamiliar music is someone invited to come especially from abroad. British musicians are given engagements at foreign broadcasting stations, and a great deal of British music finds a place in programmes overseas.[14]

Such arguments had been rumbling on throughout the year. But where matters of music were concerned, there was much else to preoccupy commentators. From the end of February, the death of Elgar dominated. The composer had died the previous day at his home in Worcester at the age of seventy-six, an official announcement appearing in *The Times* on the 24th. As Master of the King's Musick, a position which Elgar had held from 1924, *The Times* duly reported the condolences of the King and Queen in a telegram addressed to his daughter, Carice Irene Blake. *The Times*' leader column provided an opinion piece, and a full obituary was also published, as well as many tributes 'from brother musicians'. Elgar, ran the leader, was recognized everywhere as a spokesman for his country, just as Richard Strauss had been for Germany and Puccini was for Italy. From the 'mystical aspiration' of Elgar's oratorios to 'what was sometimes sneered at as the jingoism' of the Pomp and Circumstance Marches, his music was marked as the product of the Edwardian era, that 'post-Victorian interlude' between the 1899–1902 South African War and the First World War:

> A post-War generation of musicians was inclined to be impatient of just those characteristics of Elgar's music, the sumptuousness of orchestration, the exuberance of melody, the air of general well-being, of contentment with leisure in a spacious world, which declared their period.[15]

After the death of Elgar in February, Sir Henry Walford Davies, inheriting his mantle as the country's senior composer, was appointed Master of the King's Musick on 6 April. 'We join the chorus of congratulations,' wrote a *Musical Times* columnist: 'There is peculiar appropriateness in this honouring of one who, in an unsurpassed degree, has spread the gospel of good music among the King's subjects.'[16] Other no less obscure composers than Rutland Boughton and R. O. Morris also featured in the news during the first week of 1934. The discovery by Walford Davies in the New Year of a manuscript of music written by none other than William Gladstone – a *Kyrie Eleison*, 'of a simple, but beautiful character, privately printed by Novellos, was performed at Eton College Chapel, Walford Davies having completed and edited it'.[17]

Concerts that April included prominent performances of the music of both Delius and Holst. Their deaths only a short while afterwards came as further shocks to the musical world. The BBC Orchestra's concert on Wednesday, 11 April was an all-English programme which featured a performance of Delius's Violin Concerto, with the soloist Albert Sammons, for whom the work was written. 'The final and largest work' was Holst's *Choral Symphony*, which was written for the Leeds Festival of 1925 and premiered there by Albert Coates, receiving its first London performance since that year. For *The Times*, the 'most interesting' event of the week was the Sadler's Wells production on Thursday of a new opera by Lawrance Collingwood, *Macbeth*, which had received a private concert performance at the Queen's Hall some years before.[18] Collingwood (1887–1982), once assistant to Albert Coates at St Petersburg, was a keen recording producer for fifty years. He is credited with conducting the last recording session with Elgar in 1934.

The London Philharmonic's programme for Thursday included Busoni's Violin Concerto and the first performance of Arnold Bax's *The Tale the Pine Trees Knew*. Completed in 1931 (and therefore another new British work which, in a way, had a prolonged three-year gestation), it is close in atmosphere to the Fifth Symphony. Bax referred to both as his 'craggy, Northern works'. Contemporary guides and commentaries on British symphonic music at the time place Bax very highly. A Prom performance of his Third Symphony under Henry Wood in September was 'first-rate', according *The Times*' critic, the epilogue containing, together with the slow movement, 'passages that are unsurpassed in contemporary music for beauty and sound'. The concert also included a performance of Constant Lambert's *Rio Grande* and the first concert performance of Benjamin Dale's 'English Dance', a piece 'sufficiently described by its title' despite what *The Times*' reviewer calls 'an excursion over the border in the matter of Orchestration at one point'.[19]

Arnold Bax was the principal guest at a dinner of the Musicians' Club in London in early November. President Sir Landon Ronald's address concerned the subject of 'modern' music, a common theme in 1934:

> There were differences of opinion to-day, said Sir Landon Ronald, in regard to what was modern music, just as there was about violent argument 50 years ago on what would be the music of the future. To many the name of Arnold Bax was a synonym for modern music. He was certainly a great British composer, and to understand and appreciate any great composer it was necessary to hear his works again and again. It had taken years for the public to realize that Sir Edward Elgar wrote great music. It would probably be some time before the man in the

street would appreciate Bax's works with the same understanding as he had of the works of composers of the past.[20]

Does 'the man in the street' appreciate Bax (1883–1953), who replaced Sir Walford Davies as the Master of the King's Musick from 1942? The *Oxford Dictionary of Music* acknowledges that although he was a prolific composer, Bax's music (including perhaps his most familiar work, *Tintagel*) 'has never established itself in the forefront', a fate so typical of many British composers. A 'brilliant pianist', Bax 'wrote fluently and perceptively for the keyboard'. And although his seven symphonies are 'luxuriantly scored and full of romantic melody', the public apparently finds the 'more concise' tone-poems more palatable, *Tintagel* perhaps the best known. Is this neglect justified? Ninety years ago it would have seemed incredible to music pundits, as we have seen.

Another composer whose music has also sunk into relative obscurity but which received highly favourable reviews in 1934 was Bernard Van Dieren (1887–1936), resident in England in the 1930s. Author and music critic van Dieren, together with Eric Fenby, wrote *The Musical Times*' tribute to Delius in July. The Dutch composer is the author of *Down Among the Dead Men*, written in 1934 and published the following year, the year before his own death in London. *Down Among the Dead Men* contains five 'controversial' essays, including extensive chapters on Busoni and Meyerbeer. (The latter was Wagner's nemesis, so it is significant that van Dieren should provide such an essay just as the pro-Wagnerites in Germany were consolidating power.) The final chapter is a treatise on composition. Victim of the BBC's reluctance to feature any really challenging music, van Dieren finally secured two broadcasts, the first in 1934, of his 'Diaphony' and the second in 1935, of the 'Chinese Symphony' of 1914. Van Dieren had enjoyed a considerable following (the Oxford Dictionary of Music calls it a 'cult' following) in his early days in London from 1909, and Constant Lambert claimed that the opening bars of his ballet *Horoscope* were dictated by van Dieren from beyond the grave. A concert of contemporary music at the end of June was mainly devoted to his music with a performance by the BBC's Orchestra and Edward Clark, with Dennis Noble as soloist. Van Dieren's music, according to *The Times*' review, 'has beautiful moments and very interesting ones' but in the *Diafona per orchestra da Camera e barritono*, a setting of Shakespeare sonnets, the reviewer 'could find nothing to commend' in their 'bald' treatment that night:

> No doubt we are apt to be a little bit touchy about settings of Shakespeare's sonnets. The composer who attempts to put music to 'When to the sessions of

sweet silent thought' is a brave man, but this performance left us feeling that the listener who can endure Mr. van Dieren's settings is a braver.[21]

Testimony to the enduring inspiration provided by music and literature from earlier ages, including the works of Shakespeare, was the announcement in July of the programme for the Leeds Triennial Festival. 'Two new works, both choral, will be performed for the first time: Cyril Scott's "La Belle Dame sans Merci" and Dr George Dyson's "The Blacksmiths", described as a fantasy for chorus, piano-forte, and Orchestra, a setting of a Middle English poem of the fourteenth century,' reported *The Times*.[22] Meanwhile, two contrasting views of music in the Puritan era had been laid out earlier in the year. In June, OUP announced the publication of Percy Scholes's book on music and the Puritans. In it Scholes sets out to prove 'that the Puritans [contrary to popular perception] welcomed music and did not, as alleged, dismiss it from their church services'. Supported by 'a wealth of anecdotal detail', his claims include the discovery of 'Bunyan's flute', a photograph of which is reproduced in the book ('The Puritans and Music in England and New England'), which also 'includes a curiously documented story of the settlement of New England, with contemporary evidence disproving the belief that the early English colonists not only took with them a hatred of music and the dance, but also suppressed any performance of the kind with harsh legislation.[23] Presumably, among those who alleged otherwise included the music editor of *The Times* itself, H. C. Colles. In January he had given two lectures, the first of which constituted 'a historical survey of English Church Music up to the period of Charles II'. His stance on the Puritans is in marked contrast to that of Scholes:

> It might justly be claimed that, but for the decade of the Puritan suppression under Cromwell, Church Music had been cultivated consistently and without break in the English church from its earliest days to the present time.

Colles traces those 'early days' back to Augustine, through to the Saxons who heard those first missionaries, to the Norman Conquest and to the Middle Ages:

> The destruction of choir-books by the Puritans he described as a permanent loss as because of this many of the works of the Tudor composers survived now only in an incomplete form. A deep debt, he said, was owed to modern scholars, such as the editors of 'Tudor Church Music,' who had pieced together the remnants in the Cathedral libraries, executed repairs with infinite patience and skill, and given us back a large proportion of our musical inheritance. This

musical restoration had been as great a work as that of the ancient cathedrals themselves.[24]

That Vaughan Williams as well as others drew on the Tudor church modes shows how much the English music revival of the early twentieth century was the special project of so many, and which thrust Britain into the forefront of new music through the efforts of composers and scholars alike. Lamentably, however, the annual dinner of the London Society of Organists heard that 'Cathedrals were reducing the number of their services, and some churches were disposing of their choirs and introducing "canned" music and pianos, because they could not afford to pay an organist'.[25] Professional organists were thus also under the strain that the rest of the country's musicians were under.

During July, the debate on church music – and music in cathedrals in particular – picked up pace. A distinction between music 'of' the cathedrals began to be used increasingly for music outside the 'Cathedral Tradition' of clerical and lay singing within the order of service. *The Times* could find only six cathedrals in which morning *and* evening prayers were sung daily. 'Five centuries of Church Composition' was evident at Wells: Byrd, Morley, Purcell, Boyce, Sterndale Bennet and Walford Davies among them. But the need for men choristers to work, the boys' education and financial stress were given as excuses for the decline, which had begun during the First World War. Ironically, the decline of 'the longest and finest tradition of English music' could be witnessed just as the artistry was being 'most roused to a sense of responsibility', with the choral foundation never so well directed and organists employed 'of the highest ability'.[26] But was there anything really to be concerned about? A correspondent pointed out later that even a cathedral that dropped its musical service on just four mornings a week would still render 500 anthems a year: hardly evidence of a crumbling tradition. In fact, the standard of music may well improve by 'some slight relaxation of routine', wrote 'Decanus'.[27]

The correspondence continued in defence of the tradition, the breaking of which, at least in one correspondent's view, was 'a matter to be regretted, and the church-going lover of music must perforce be sad that secular music should advance, while the rendering of Church music steadily declines – if not in quality, in the number of performances'.[28] But there was another solution, too. In answer to 'Decanus', another correspondent suggested that 'such relaxation' could be gained 'without injury to the ceaseless offering of choral worship' with six or eight men singing Matins, for example, at St.

Paul's, during the boys' holidays, giving an opportunity for Plain Chant to be heard.[29] The debate about church music continued. Many fine points were made on the letters page of *The Times* well into October. The 'wonderful corpus' of church music which had grown up over the past 400 years owed its origin to what is known as the Cathedral system, wrote clergyman and music scholar Edmund Fellowes (1870–1951). It was essentially English in style and unparalleled on the Continent, and the system was something to which the English could point 'with genuine pride'. The great English *Te Deum*, for example, had been 'built up in uninterrupted succession' by, among others, William Byrd, Edward Gibbons, Henry Purcell and William Boyce, down to Stanford and the 'moderns'. 'Is the English church, at the bidding of Cathedral Chapters, to be robbed of this wonderful heritage?' he asked.[30] Fellowes's expertise on the Tudor tradition was well known. Editor of dozens of volumes of madrigals and lute songs, and twenty volumes of William Byrd's music (as well as a 1936 biography), he was also one of the editors of the ten-volume *Tudor Church Music*, published by OUP in the 1920s. His fear of the disappearance of the *Te Deum* would have been allayed, had he lived to hear it, with the inclusion of William Walton's arrangement for the 1953 coronation.

Meanwhile, the debate continued, with *The Times* devoting even editorial space to the subject, as well as publishing reviews and printing letters. At the end of October, a report on Cathedral Music by the Church Music Society was published by SPCK. Of the fifty cathedral and collegiate churches only three could claim the daily offices of Sung Matins and Evensong. Financial constraints, the education of young choristers, the consideration of the need for working men, as well as attendance were all considerations in witnessing the fast-crumbling tradition, noticed particularly during the previous ten years by the Church Music Society, all very real difficulties faced by the relevant authorities. To do their bit (given the disappointment experienced by visitors to cathedrals where choral services had, to some extent, been abandoned), the BBC announced the beginning of a new series. Presented by Sir Richard Terry, an authority on Tudor and early church music, the 'From Plainsong to Purcell' week, to be broadcast Monday to Friday, would be devoted to plainsong and folk song, as well as 'the early polyphonic music derived from these sources'. The programme, 'Foundations of Music', in a revamped version of its earlier format would run for fifteen consecutive weeks, with successive weeks devoted to Tudor church music, the folk song of the Elizabethans and instrumental and stage music. Among the madrigals to be sung was Thomas Morley's *The Triumphs of Gloriana* written in honour of Queen Elizabeth I.³¹ This revised format, writes David Cardiff, was proposed to present 'the real foundations comprehensively and systematically in due chronological order', rather than presenting the 'standard repertoire' of Bach–Mozart–Haydn, Beethoven–Schubert–Mendelssohn and Schumann–Brahms, which had all been 'done' in a manner that seemed random and 'inconsequential'.³²

In continuing its responsibility for broadcasting programming of a religious nature, 'Greater Flexibility' was the watchword for the BBC in its alterations to its Sunday line-up from October. From the first Sunday of the month at 5 pm, a programme of 'a religious nature, though not a service' would begin with 'biblical plays'. The broadcast of Bach cantatas would cease, as well as the 2.40 p.m. 'talk'. Sundays remained, as a result, largely based on religious programming. To supplement the programmes on Tudor church music, 'Melodies of Christendom' would be broadcast once a month on the regional wavelength, 'with a more even distribution of entertainment value throughout the day'. There were to be other 'less important innovations'.³³

Thus, the church remained central to musical life. Naturally, the 1934 Three Choirs Festival, held that year in Gloucester from 2 September, focused much on the music of the three great composers who had died earlier in the year. At the end of the opening service, a customary afternoon affair, Vaughan Williams was to have conducted Holst's *Te Deum*. In his sermon, the Bishop of Gloucester had 'some trenchant things to say about the tendency to over cleverness in modern art', drawing his illustrations 'chiefly from literature, leaving the musicians to apply the moral to themselves'. The *Te Deum*, for *The Times*, was 'originally direct in its expression of the words, simple in phraseology, yet requiring the utmost alertness and concentration on the part of the singers', and a fitting choice, 'both to commemorate the composer and to give an example of modern church music entirely free of those defects indicated by the bishop's sermon'.³⁴

In the first proper concert of the festival, on the morning of 4 September, a performance of Elgar's *The Kingdom* was given 'in memoriam' to the composer: the nearest to an official recognition of his death. The 'finest interpreter' of his own music, Elgar had always conducted his own works at every Three Choirs Festival. But a 'worthy' presentation of his work by H. W. Sumsion (standing in for Vaughan Williams) was 'no finer tribute' that could be paid to the composer, who would have welcomed some 'ceremonial homage' to his memory. His presence was nevertheless 'sorely missed', especially on rehearsal day, 'when he was always about the cathedral greeting his friends and taking a keen interest in the proceedings'. A performance of Kodaly's *Psalmus Hungaricus* 'provided a forcible contrast' between *The Kingdom* and Vaughan Williams's *Pastoral* symphony. Once again, the unavoidable absence of the composer necessitated a replacement conductor, this time Gordon Jacobs. The inclusion of music by two English greats provided another opportunity for comparisons:

> Elgar and Vaughan Williams may not seem to have much in common in their outward features, but there is a certain community of standpoint, a suavity and assurance which are English.

But the reviewer makes the oft-quoted error about the nature of Vaughan Williams's symphony which he claimed 'muses among the quiet undulations of the English countryside and is content with what it finds there'.[35] The *Pastoral* was up to that point the latest symphonic offering from the composer. Any glib remarks about Vaughan Williams would be consigned to history after the first performance of his Fourth Symphony which was about to be unleashed on the world. The composer said to his second wife Ursula that the *Pastoral*, his Third Symphony, was 'not lambkins frisking'. Rather, it was a depiction of the war-ravaged French landscape. The music is ominous and threatening. In the third movement there is a kind of 'last post' for the dead in the trenches. As we have seen, there was to be as much misunderstanding about the symphony that followed.

All the Three Choirs concerts received a full review in *The Times*, which was not always enthusiastic, it must be said. Apart from a performance of Mendelssohn's Violin Concerto at a concert on 5 September (with Miss Jelly d'Aranyi as soloist), the rest of the programme consisted of British works, most of it 'not the stuff to bring jollity' (a reference to 'Jupiter', the Holst work from *The Planets* placed at the end of the programme), with R. O. Morris's Suite for Violoncello in particular not 'exactly exhilarating':

> We are all in favour of supporting the British composer, but might not the British composer support his supporters with something a little more buoyant and light-hearted? Moreover, there is a danger of becoming too parochial. The Wednesday concert is the opportunity for contrast, and, save for the Violin Concerto, the opportunity was missed.[36]

A performance of Handel's Messiah at the end of a week of 'more rigorous exercises', also given at Hereford the previous year, begged the question whether his music would be restored 'to a place of honour beside Bach's, or will recourse be had to him principally to provide a happy ending? We are still looking for a genuine revival of Handel,' came the answer.³⁷ And a performance towards the end of the week of *The Dream of Gerontius* afforded the opportunity to muse further on Elgar's interpretation of his own works:

> One realized afresh last night that part of the secret of Sir Edward Elgar's interpretation of his own music lay in his freedom as conductor from a too literal obedience to his own meticulous markings in the score. He often minimized their value.

It was known by this stage that Elgar wished this work to be regarded, above all others, as worthy of his memory. The Musicians' Club, London (of which Elgar had also been president), held a memorial dinner for the composer in May, devoting the entire musical programme to the late composer, in the presence of his daughter. During the speeches (which included one by Sir John Reith), Sir Hugh Allen could report that the Royal College of Music was organizing a collection of Elgar's works. In the process, some new discoveries had been made, one of some significance. At the end of the last bar of the original score of *The Dream of Gerontius*, Elgar had written the following:

> This is the best of me. For the rest I ate, I drank, I slept, I loved, I hated, as another. My life was as a vapour, and is not, but this is what I saw and know. This, if anything of mine, is worth your memory.³⁸

For *The Times*' obituary writer, Elgar was 'The Laureate of English Music', naturally enough. Gustav Holst was, simply, 'Composer and Teacher'. An article on Delius goes a little further. It is entitled 'The Search for Perfection' and his obituary, which appeared on 11 June, calls him 'A Dreamer in Music'. The deaths, in quick succession, of these three greats make, for some, 1934 the 'black year' for British music. *The Times* in June acknowledges the sadness of the period:

> Music is greatly impoverished by the deaths of the last few months. Elgar, Holst and Delius are losses not merely to that ill-defined commodity called 'British Music,' but to the art of music itself.³⁹

The question of Delius's nationality was the first observation of *The Times*' obituary writer (as well as the 'blurring' of national identity that characterizes him, given his long-term absence from England):

> As a man, he remained entirely unknown save to a small circle of personal friends. Those friends have been declaring strenuously any time in the last 30 years that Delius was a great English composer, that Germany welcomed his

music years before a note of it was heard in his native land, that he was an outstanding case of the prophet without honour in his own country.

For the *Daily Worker*, Delius 'expressed perfectly the romantic lament of the British bourgeoisie over its lost innocence, and yet managed to preserve a measure of personal dignity'.[40] But Delius's reputation was preserved due largely to the efforts of one man:

> The story of his music in England is closely connected with the career of Thomas Beecham... who made Londoners aware of what may be called Delius's musical personality by playing in turn such things as 'Brigg Fair', 'Paris', 'Over the Hills' and 'Appalachia'.

But Beecham also produced *A Village Romeo and Juliet* at Covent Garden and the first performance of *A Mass of Life*, completing 'his propaganda for Delius in England with the festival of six concerts which he organized and conducted at Queen's Hall in the autumn of 1929'. But Henry Wood also 'did his share' by giving the first performance of the C Minor Piano Concerto at the Proms in 1907 and introducing *Sea Drift* at the Sheffield Festival in 1908. Once again, the Tudors provide a key to the flavour of English 'national music':

> It is in the early choral works that the contrast between Delius's outlook and that of the English people is most strongly felt. They gained the admiration of connoisseurs but little popularity, partly because the composer's choice of subjects for musical setting was antipathetic to the majority of his audiences, and partly because the musical style is the very opposite of everything which English tradition of choral music based on the language has stood for ever since the days of the great Elizabethans.

However, the beauty of the early tome-poems and later concertos, especially that for violin, 'could not fail to make its mark'. Though living in a world of his own, as it were, Delius 'remained intensely sensitive to certain impressions from without', giving his impressions through his music.[41] In Delius's 'search for perfection', the essential fineness of the quality of music distinguishes it from senseless sound. 'The aloofness of Delius's life was a constant witness to this truth, and his music was an unremitting search for the finer distinction of the art of sound.' Delius stands apart for other reasons, too. Never a publicist, he had also refrained from impressing his view as a teacher on others, never holding any public position which made this necessary:

> In that respect Delius's career differed most decisively from those of practically every other musician of English origin. Even Elgar at one time induced to

become a university professor, and the life of his compositions was closely bound up with his own direction of their performances. Holst's memory will long be treasured as that of an inspiring teacher whose enthusiasm for certain types of old music, particularly music of the English tradition, went hand-in-hand with a vivid consciousness of the needs of the present day.[42]

Later in June, no less than three performances of the composer's music took place. *A Village Romeo and Juliet* was given at the theatre of the Royal College of Music under the baton of the composer's most ardent propagandist, Sir Thomas Beecham. The conductor was invited to say a few words to the audience before the performance. Delius, he said, was inheritor of the culture of many nations, and a man of such diverse abilities that he might appear to be a mass of contradictions, but those who know him intimately realized that he possessed a nature essentially simple, which accounted for his outlook on art.[43] Delius remains unique in all music, not just English music. A correspondent in the August 1934 edition of *The Musical Times* aptly summed up the composer's legacy:

> Elgar himself described Delius's music in the *Daily Telegraph*, last year, as being 'always very beautiful'; Philip Heseltine declared in his biography, 'Delius,' that his 'Mass of Life' was worthy to rank with that of Sebastian Bach,' and that 'Great art such as this is not of all time and none' . . . and Sir Thomas Beecham stated during the [Delius] Festival: 'I have conducted the whole of Strauss and Elgar, and found there great beauty as well as ingenuity, but there is something more satisfying still in Delius.

The writer's hope was that as his 'ideal interpreter', Thomas Beecham 'may see his way clear to give us a series of memorial concerts of the Master's music on the line of his previous and immensely successful Festival'.[44] In September the Delius Society (formed in 1932 for the express purpose of recording the composer's music) was to be taken over by Columbia. Beecham was the artistic director of the society, and the first recordings were due for release at the end of November. Some of the works Beecham believed Delius would have sanctioned for priority of appearance were *Paris*, *Eventyr* and the final scenes from *Koanga* and *Hassan*.[45]

The new music season began in October, with the Courtauld-Sargent/ Royal Philharmonic Society marking its 123rd season, and the Fleet Street Choir making its traditional annual pilgrimage to mark its own birthday to Ely Cathedral to honour 'the father of English Music', William Byrd. The first winter series of chamber concerts by the BBC, held at Broadcasting House also began in the last week of October, with the new season of BBC Symphony Orchestra concerts beginning on 14 October. The first, a performance of Delius's *A Mass of Life*, was broadcast live from the Queen's Hall. Introducing the work to listeners, composer and musician Geoffrey Shaw, reported *The Times*, used 'a homely simile' in order to convey some suggestion of the effect of the 'closely packed dissonant harmonies' characteristic of the composer's style:

> A cobblestone pavement, he said, is painful to walk on when the stones are set far apart, when set close together they provide a tolerably smooth surface. The remark was sufficiently pertinent to set the listener thinking about the place of dissonance in a musical texture, and presumably that was all that the lecturer intended it to do.

Once again, *The Times* surprises, for it then proceeds to give an account of the use of discord, from the sixteenth to the nineteenth centuries:

> Modern music has produced a theory that there is no real distinction between concord and discord, but that may be put on one side as a symptom of the agnosticism which has been paralysing the art and thought of our time.

Is anything beyond the triad acceptable as concordant? Scriabin's mystic chord of rising fourths is the author's example (C, F#, Bb, E, A and D) and though a 'point of repose', the author admits that 'most of us failed to think of it as anything more permanent than a specially intriguing example of dissonance'. Delius would have 'deprecated' attempts to 'peer into his harmonic texture' in this way or any other, even believing himself 'to be using the alternations of discord and concord with all the implications of classical tradition'. Employing discord in the so-called 'cobblestone' method, Delius succeeds in making time stand still:

> For the time being the ear is tricked into accepting the combinations of tones for themselves without references to what has just passed or what may be expected to follow.

This accounts for the average listener's inability to memorize the music. But there is fault neither on the part of the listener nor on the part of the composer himself. It is simply 'the necessary corollary of the artist's glimpse of a music beyond the confines of motion within time'.[46] In anticipation of a broadcast from the Queen's Hall of Delius's *A Mass of Life*, Francis Toye discussed Delius and Nietzsche in a highly engaging exploration in *The Listener* of the 'complex, philosophical and dogmatic' sides of both men, as well as their instinctive, 'almost naïve' simplicity. Toye is not afraid. 'The point about Delius is that he and, as I think, he almost alone among contemporary composers, with the possible exception of Sibelius, shows in his music a quality of greatness', one in whose works 'there are scattered little phrases, highly individual, that reveal themselves as products of genius of the highest order'. And, in an echo of Vaughan Williams's words, Toye places Delius within the firmament of other great composers:

> Now, just as one goes to Bach for inevitability and sanity, to Handel for poetry and grandeur, to Mozart for delicacy, so one goes to Delius for those dreams after which any man of imagination hankers at one time or another. I know of no composer who satisfies this better than Delius.

But the composer cannot give everything:

> I cannot imagine myself or anyone else turning to Delius for the kind of thrill that is to be found, for instance, in the best pages of a Verdi opera ... But he gives something which is all his own – and that is as much as we have a right to expect from any artist, and more than we usually get.[47]

As *The Times'* obituary of Delius testifies, both Sir Thomas Beecham and Sir Henry Wood had done much to promote the music of this truly unique composer. Like Beecham, Sir Henry Wood was a towering figure in British music in the 1930s, and *The Times* also recognized what he had done for Delius. But in 1934, Sir Henry was to reveal another side to his personality that provides a contrasting and one of the most entertaining episodes of the year. In his 1938 memoirs, he credits one H. C. Tonking, his private tutor for violin and organ in the 1880s:

> Tonking was a curious fellow and a tremendous worker. He taught me to play Bach's Organ Preludes and Fugues. His phrasing and registration of the 'Great G Minor' and the Toccata and Fugue in D Minor were masterly; and here I may add (in regard to the latter) Klenovsky learned a great deal.[48]

Paul Klenovsky was the pseudonym under which Sir Henry Wood made a famous orchestral transcription of J. S. Bach's Toccata and Fugue in D Minor back in 1929, with the express purpose of confusing his critics, none of whom had ever shown any regard for the transcriptions he had presented under his own name. Sir Henry gave a similar treatment to Jeremiah Clarke's *Trumpet Voluntary* as well as to Chopin's *Marche Funúbre*. Indeed, transcriptions of Bach for orchestra were not rare at the time. In the same year (1929), Respighi's orchestration of the Prelude and Fugue in D Major was premiered in Cincinnati, Schoenberg's transcription of the Prelude and Fugue in E flat Major, 'St. Anne', BWV 552 was performed (and transmitted in a concert broadcast of the BBC Orchestra from

Birmingham on 27 February 1935, conducted by Boult[49]) and Holst's *Fugue a la Gigue* in G, BWV 577 was presented a year later. Even Vaughan Williams favoured some modernization in his arrangement of 'Wir glauben all' einen Gott', BWV 680, which appeared in 1925.

News of Sir Henry's 'jest' reached as far afield as Australia:

> An interesting and remarkable instance of the preference of the average Britisher for anything foreign – or anything which sounds foreign – was contained in a recently published report from London, announcing the confession by Sir Henry Wood, the famous conductor and composer, of a five-year hoax which he practised upon the musical world.
>
> The story goes that following the critical reception in 1929 of several of Sir Henry Wood's compositions, the orchestra at a Queen's Hall concert performed Bach's 'Organ Toccata and Fugue in D Minor', transcribed for full orchestra by 'Paul L. Klenovsky, a young man understood to have lived in Moscow'. This work immediately became a success and was lavishly praised by the critics.
>
> Requests for its repetition poured in, with the result that it has been constantly performed. Replying to the frequently asked question, 'Who is Paul Klenovsky?' Sir Henry Wood wrote in a programme note:
>
> 'It is a great pity that this young man died. His transcription shows the hand of a master in every bar.'

The Australian commentator elaborates on the question of the desirability of anything 'foreign', which serves as a useful commentary from outside the country, and provides another reason for the presence of so many 'foreign' musicians in London, despite the high levels of unemployment:

> This passion for anything foreign – for anything at least believed to be imported – is not by any means confined to matters musical, nor is it limited to Britishers resident in the British Isles. It exists with just as much force in Australia . . . and in addition to music, art, literature, it applies with equal force even to the most mundane things, including almost all the requirements of every-day life.
>
> This strange penchant for things imported, or believed to have been imported, is a curious psychological phenomenon, but so long as it continues to exist, composers, producers, manufacturers and traders, in their own financial interest, have little option but to continue to pander to it.[50]

Sir Henry revealed his 'jest' to a journalist, largely due to the forthcoming publication of the arrangement by OUP which, indeed, was attributed to Bach–Klenovsky. In the five years since the hoax began, it had become a favourite of even the Philadelphia Orchestra. His explanation revealed a deeper truth: 'I brought out one or two pieces under my own name, and it was always a source of soreness to certain members of the public who wrote to me, and certainly on the part of the Press, who were antagonistic to anything of that description,' he said. And, justifying the arrangement of a Bach organ work for orchestra, Sir Henry cited Liszt's piano transcriptions as a precedent. They were a 'perfect revelation,' he said. 'No one ever thought the piano could convey those wonderful colours. It was like an orchestra on the piano – not like a piano playing at all! So I have tried to do the same with this piece.'[51] Sir Henry's own account of the Paul Klenovsky jest appeared in his autobiography:

> After many months of study I eventually finished the transcription to my satisfaction, but I knew I had only to place my name to it to receive the usual storm of abuse. I thereupon decided to have a little joke. Some months previously Glazounoff had visited me and had told me of the death of a promising young pupil of his by the name of Klenovsky. This name took my fancy and I presented the Toccata and Fugue under that name at a Promenade concert of October 5, 1929.
>
> Klenovsky's success was unquestioned. Every season it is asked for and still finds a place in the Promenade programmes. Such was its popularity that in 1932 Hubert Foss, of the Oxford University Press, approached me in an endeavour to ascertain Paul Klenovsky's address – or that of his relatives from which he could obtain permission to publish the work.[52]

Sir Henry was therefore obliged to admit the pseudonym. 'My leg-pull greatly annoyed some but equally amused others, while it gave me enormous satisfaction. Some of my friends of the Press have never quite forgotten it and are ever watchful for further evidences of an attempt to joining the living with the dead.' The *Oxford Bulletin* of 19 September 1934 'embraces all criticisms in one', wrote Sir Henry. Evidently, the disclosure, an 'English musical incident' was, unusually, 'rewarded' in several leaders, including one in *The Times* which was content to go along with the spirit of the hoax. It was well known in England that to possess the highest artistic genius one had to be both foreign and dead, making light of the idea that anything foreign was supposedly superior. Dying young, however, was better still, the gods loving the master more, with even the stalls applauding and sighing for lost harmonies that, despite never having been given by Klenovsky, seemed nevertheless 'to echo yet in the music of the spheres beyond the world'. *The Times* concludes a mock obituary by finding for us a neat parallel closer to the subject of this volume:

> Not only in music but in politics we are assured by some saviours of society that the grandest ideas are revealed only to master minds beyond our

shores. Suppose that some of these gentlemen, recognizing that their sadly native names forbade them to claim primary inspiration, should follow Sir Henry Wood's example and merge their personalities in wholly imaginary characters, bearing appellations taken from the Muscovite, the Latin, or the Teutonic recension of the dictatorial word [Stalin, Mussolini and Hitler]. Could they thus win the popular acceptance that has hitherto been so conspicuously denied them? Before they try, they may perhaps take warning from Sir Henry Wood, who has clearly laid down that even a foreign genius may only claim homage for posthumous work. Our hypothetical dictator should therefore begin by having himself stuffed.[53]

Poor Mosley, the only recognizable politician in Britain fitting this scenario and thus the butt of *The Times*' joke. A review of the Proms concert taking place that very night, however, prompted *The Times*' critic to a more serious consideration of the 'late Russian's' arrangements. 'Two things are essential to the right interpretation of Bach: a sense of line and rhythm,' it ran:

> It was one of those programmes of mixed concertos – Brandenburg No.2 and that quasi-Brandenburg in A Minor for flute, violin and piano, the infectious C Major concerto for three pianos, and the slighter but agreeable concerto for four pianos [BWV 1047, 1044, 1064 & 1065 respectively]. The C Major concerto was taken too fast and too unrhythmically to have infected anyone. The Brandenburg had been tampered with by the notorious Klenovsky before he died, and Bach's lines were smothered with unnecessary and noxious contributions from extraneous wind instruments.[54]

Although *The Times* entered the spirit of the hoax following Wood's revelation, not everyone was amused. Havergal Brian, for instance, wondered if Sir Henry was also testing the knowledge of the public. When Wood wrote as 'La Main Gauche' in the October 1934 edition of *Musical Opinion*, he said he did not fall for it.[55] Brian wrote regularly for *Musical Opinion*. The publication of a new volume on Beethoven in Germany, which claimed that the composer's string quartets and certain piano sonatas were 'but reflections in sound of Shakespeare's love and murder tragedies', would not do for Brian, who, despite acknowledging the thesis's acceptability to British national dignity, remained the sceptic. 'Had the chronology of the case permitted, I believe it might have been proved that Shakespeare's sonnets were but a pale reflection of Beethoven's Sonatas,' he wrote. The book under scrutiny, *Beethoven in Neuer Deutung* (Beethoven in a New Guise) calls most of the late quartets the Shakespeare String Quartets and labels many of the piano sonatas the Shakespeare Sonatas with their associations to Macbeth, The Tempest, Romeo and Juliet and King Lear. Still, Havergal Brian was not moved:

> We have similar people at home: one man, indeed, who so successfully combined music analysis with the political perspicacity that he discovered the Colonial Office, Tariff Reform and General Gordon in the first movement of Elgar's Symphony No.1.[56]

Havergal Brian, whose Violin Concerto in E Minor was written in 1934–5 and whose inspiration had risen in German literature was a Germanophile until the rise of Hitler in 1933. 'Before the end of that year, and before his next work came to light, Brian's faith in Germany was shattered by his disappointment at the rise of the Nazi dictatorship,' writes his biographer. 'He was unaware that this disappointment would alter the nature of his composition, but it is significant that for the next few years his orchestral writing demanded far fewer players, and his literary inspiration was drawn from British sources.'[57]

Incidentally, by the year end, 'Klenovsky' had been consigned firmly to the past. A concert in December which featured some of the same music that had been heard at the Proms in the Bach Transcription concert of 5 September ended with 'Sir Henry Wood's (and not Paul Klenovsky's) arrangement of certain organ pieces by Bach as a suite for small orchestra.'[58] Paul Klenovsky, in *The Times*, at least, was never heard of again. The year 1934 was the fortieth season of Sir Henry's Proms. It was held, as usual, at the Queen's Hall with the BBC Orchestra for a period of eight weeks from 11 August, and it is noteworthy that in those days the programmes were perhaps more rigid, and were admittedly little varied from one year to the next, with many concerts devoted to the German canon, though not exclusively:

> Mondays and Fridays are once more devoted to Wagner and Beethoven respectively, and alternate Wednesdays to Bach and Brahms. British music, it is stated, will be generously represented during the season. On August 23 the music of Frederick Delius will occupy the main part of the evening's programme, and on September 27 the programme will consist of works by Vaughan Williams.[59]

It was at this concert that the world was to hear for the very first time his celebrated *Fantasia on Greensleeves*. The Proms season – short by modern standards – opened on 11 August. There was much new music to look forward to. The three winning overtures in the recent *Daily Telegraph* competition were to be worked into the programme of 30 August. Only one had not been heard before – Frank Tapp's *Metropolis*. The winner, the *Festival Overture* by Cyril Scott, had been heard already in May, and Arnold Cooke's Concert Overture No.1 was to be heard in London for the first time. Vaughan Williams's *Running Set* (a 'Quodlibet of dance tunes') was also to be heard for the first time, on 27 September, with the entire first half of the concert devoted to Vaughan Williams's music. E. J. Moeran's suite *Farrago* was given on 6 September (heard before only in a studio) and more Bach arrangements were planned, including Respighi's transcription of the Prelude and Fugue in D on 29 September and, on the opening night, arrangements for strings of two Bach Preludes by Pick-Mangiagalli.[60]

Whether written by Sir Henry Wood, Busoni or even 'the late Klenovsky', the continued presence of Bach arrangements on the concert platform bothered purists. 'Why are "Prom" audiences still overfed with orchestral versions of the most hackneyed of Bach's organ music when there are still finer and hardly less attractive works that might be given as organ solos,' asked a columnist in *The Listener* shortly after the Proms season had ended. When staging performances of music, Harvey Grace argued, it was often the case that rather than playing the best music, organizers programmed music of the best composers, 'which is often quite another matter'. Grace was not alone, however. Ernest Newman had also recently complained about 'the performance on Bach evenings of some concertos that did not exemplify the greater side of Bach'. Harvey Grace's article 'The Choral Fantasia and Some Reflections' compares the Beethoven Choral Fantasia (the 'composer's first crude conception of an idea') and the Choral symphony ('the splendour of the final form') following a performance of both works at the 5 October Prom. Grace considers the Fantasia 'a waste of labour and time' and 'some of the worst music Beethoven ever wrote'. Extraordinary words in an age when Bach and Beethoven were Gods. Who would dare to publish this? 'Scarcely a good word, surely, can be said for the long, sprawling and trivial instrumental section of the Fantasia' and the sole interest of the choral finale, its connection to the Ninth Symphony.

Grace's piece is also a review of the Proms as a whole, with the Beethoven concert the penultimate in the series. He laments the 'thousand-and-first' performances of so many compositions when by way of example, Bartok's Op.3 Orchestral Suite, written over thirty years previously had enjoyed only its second London performance at the proms on 1 October after a gap of fourteen years. This was also Constant Lambert's example, discussed in his 'Sunday Review' column on 7 October. Composers such as Rossini were at the time considered second rate but, as Sir Thomas Beecham had shown, could provide many a 'delightful essay' and this surely pointed to the unfamiliar works of many Continental composers. But what of British music?

> The present flourishing state of British music owes so much to the group to which Parry and Stanford belonged that gratitude alone ought to ensure the occasional performance of as much of their music as possible.

However out of fashion British music of the late nineteenth century was, Grace asks whether it was 'too much to expect the ordinary commercial concert-giver to be independent of fashion'. He wanted to know whether the BBC could afford to disregard those influences, confessing that in so many ways, he was 'occasionally surprised and disappointed' at the BBC's 'limited outlook'. The question was one of repertoire, he argued, and though 'not being overlooked at Broadcasting House', it was also being asked by many musicians:

> It must not be forgotten that even the word 'repertory' no longer means what it did when it referred to the supply of music for a mere few dozen concerts a year attended by an aggregate of about 20,000 people. Both concerts and hearers are now multiplied beyond computation, whereas the repertory stands too nearly at the old pre-wireless mark.[61]

However, at the end of the fortieth Proms season, meanwhile, *The Times* doubted 'whether any have been so consistently well attended as this one', with the standard of playing 'maintained on a higher level to the very end than in some past years'.[62] The season was special in another way, too, thanks to the technological advances that were rapidly taking place at the time and a source of wonderment for many. Broadcast to Britain and the Empire, that season's Last Night was also relayed by many foreign stations, including Brussels, and several across France, giving 'yet another fillip to our imagination, jaded as it is by the marvels of broadcasting':

> To think of the 'Fantasy on British Sea-Songs' rippling out over the waters of the Rhône and the Vienne; of the thunderous applause that follows it rolling out over Languedoc and Alsace and Brabant; of Sir Henry Wood making his bow to the wide Cannebière and the Mediterranean harbour of Marseilles – that seems to us in some ways even more amazing than a broadcast to Parramatta or Chittagong.[63]

Even if the fortieth season of the Proms had been the most successful – and well attended – not everyone was happy with the behaviour of the audience (even allowing for the usual rowdiness at the Last Night). One correspondent to the *Radio Times* put into words what he considered to be a decline in standards of etiquette and, indeed, of intelligence among Promenaders:

> The rowdy and indiscriminate applause which the Prom audiences indulge in shows that they have a low level of musical intelligence. These rowdy demonstrations may be appropriate for ballad singers in public-houses, but they are surely out of place in the Queen's Hall. For example, when Myra Hess

played Beethoven's C Minor Pianoforte Concerto recently, the conclusion of the slow movement was greeted with a burst of applause. Surely the way to show appreciation of the rare spiritual beauty of this Beethoven movement is by silence, not by a silly noise.[64]

To our ears this seems unforgivably snobbish (though some might lament that the argument was, alas, lost long ago), but it must be remembered that the new world of mass communication and the unprecedented reach of music and its popularization provoked the kind of enthusiasm that would have been alien to seasoned concert-goers of the pre-broadcast era. Ever the larger-than-life personality, Sir Thomas Beecham admitted using the phrase 'Stop Talking' and even 'Shut Up, You' to members of the audience at Covent Garden earlier in the year. Not only was he irritated with latecomers and, 'occupants of the stalls who continued loud conversations', but he was also exasperated with members of the gallery who interrupted music with applause. He explained his irritation in a statement:

> After all these years of musical education – colleges, academies, concerts by the thousand – that an audience should dream of applauding when you have begun the *Leonora* Overture No.3, which is obviously a part of the whole business of opera, is – well, it is an incredible piece of barbarism. If it occurs again I shall stop and address the house. Yes, I shall do that. I shall ask if they are savages or the fine flower of the audience of the greatest city of the world.[65]

Music was becoming more accessible, and more and more people were attending performances. Perhaps someone needed to educate opera-goers, but also forgive them for their 'barbaric' lapse in manners. M. Montagu-Nathan, of the London Musical Club, showed his support for Beecham's 'welcome rebuke' in a letter to *The Times* a day or so later. However, Beecham's 'cue' was unlikely to deal with the cause, which 'lies in the practice of performing in theatres non-relevant music either before the rise of the first curtain or during the *entr'actes*'. At Covent Garden, certain parts of the audience 'mistakenly rank the prelude of an opera with the overture to an ordinary play', a practice no longer familiar.[66] Another aspect of 'Music in Decline'? The subject became increasingly topical during the year following the publication of Constant Lambert's book. Correspondent (and, later, regular contributor) W. R. Anderson wrote to *The Musical Times* in October on the subject, what he called the 'manifest decline (whether permanent or temporary) in musical values and in public regard for our art'. His particular concern was the decline in music in the provinces, particularly in the municipal orchestras which at the time were still part of the cultural landscape in towns such as Bournemouth, where the Winter Gardens were built for the purposes of staging concerts in 1911. However, writes Anderson, 'Since the war, the psychology of the people has entirely changed, and has produced a new type of entertainment.' The conclusion, if not the reasoning, to Anderson was very clear: 'Orchestral entertainments have gone.'

While able to gather evidence for this decline, he had no intention of gathering it into a general survey of the state of music, suggesting that a companion volume to Lambert's study of the decline in musical composition might be required to understand the meaning of the decline in the performance of 'serious' music. Perhaps, as he suggests, it had something to do with the people themselves, quoting an *Observer* survey in which its readers were invited to apply five adjectives to describe themselves. The paper saw that 'People are evidently afraid of being called "clever", and [that] it is only a handful who would like to see themselves described as "wise" or "cultured", or even "intelligent".'[67] Perhaps it was a matter of comfort that the increasing taste for jazz and a preference for the light entertainment associated with British seaside towns that made any admission of appreciating 'serious' music a growing rarity among ordinary people. It might be hard to imagine now, but the Municipal Orchestra was a feature of British seaside life right up until the Second World War, with resident orchestras performing at Hastings and Margate, both of which were casualties of the War, with Bournemouth surviving as the Wessex Orchestra during the War, transforming into the Bournemouth Symphony Orchestra later. The Bournemouth Orchestra was discussed at length in the September 1934 issue of *The Musical Times*.

That publication's own review of Lambert's study appeared in June 1934. Its advice to readers was not to look for Lambert's conclusions 'which may be not easy to agree with', but to enjoy its 'fascinating prose' and 'the vigorous knowledge it possesses of so much besides music'. Indeed, the challenge of the book was not to allow disagreement to lead into what the author terms 'a psychological cul-de-sac'. Such is the breadth of the writing – which covers 'the other arts and life too', and on material of 'which most musicians – and not all others – are ignorant', that its conclusions may be a matter for debate; far more important things are all there in abundance: 'brilliant wit, intense vision, full-blooded knowledge of what is and not just what ought (or ought not) to be, a fine love of music, and a capacity for writing first-hand prose'. As a survey of the preceding thirty years in music, 'few better expositions' of Schoenberg, Stravinsky, Debussy or Hindemith exist for the reviewer, who knew of 'none that more clearly sum up jazz, the cinema, and our own funny ways of life as 'modern' people'.[68]

A useful caveat to Lambert's study, and aimed at the Australian radio audience, academic Keith Barry's *Music and the Listener, A Guide to Musical Understanding* was published in the same year in Melbourne. Though written for the concert-goer as well as the 'listener-in', it was surely the burgeoning radio audience that was the main beneficiary. 'No one who owns a wireless set can afford to ignore this informative and fascinating little book,' boasts the dust jacket, and the final chapter on 'practical hints for listeners' recognizes that as gramophones 'came in', to be followed shortly thereafter by radio, thousands of drawing-room pianos were at the same time standing neglected – consequent surely on the new ways of engaging with music in the home. Nevertheless, Dr Barry's intention was to provide the radio audience with the necessary knowledge to at least listen rather than merely hear, and appreciate what was broadcast, recognizing the all-pervasiveness of music in the modern world:

> Since the invention of recorded and broadcast music it is impossible to escape from sounds, melodious or otherwise. They wake us in the morning, chase us down the streets of our cities, entertain us while we eat, and help us to pass our evening hours. We are hearing music all day and half the night.[69]

In his foreword, ABC chairman Charles Lloyd Jones too warns against complacency about the new broadcast medium, 'this magician – this prophet – this informer – who has stepped into our homes in the material form of a "radio". Its message goes straight to many thousands of listeners and more than fifty per cent of that message is the message of music.'[70] Two comments deserve special attention, the first the final paragraph in a chapter entitled 'The Truth about Chamber Music':

> Before we leave the subject of chamber music, let us admit quite frankly that one cannot be converted to it in a single night, or by hearing a single work. It is the type of music that calls for thought, attention and quietness. It is not the sort of music to put on to form a background to a bridge evening, or to fill the gaps in conversation at a cocktail party. On the other hand it is of all music essentially suited for the quiet of the armchair and the hush of the evening hour. That being the case, one suggests that it may eventually become the most popular form of broadcast music.[71]

The second is on British music, about which it was 'refreshing to be able to say' that recently 'British composers have come very rapidly to the front, and are now undoubtedly numbered with the world's best', though 'Australia is as yet too young to have found very much soul capable of being expressed in musical terms' and even America 'has yet failed to produce any musician of world-wide importance'.[72]

Written as a broad introduction to the music listener, its emphasis on the still-young medium of broadcasting was intended to provide the reader with a basis on which to appreciate the ever-increasing access to music, most of which will have been new to him or her. The Austro-German canon – as is to be expected – features prominently. Barry does not diverge from the standard line presented throughout the 1930s by organizations like the BBC, that the baton of symphonic writing was passed from 'papa' Haydn (the 'Father of Symphony') to Mozart, to Beethoven, Schubert, Schumann, Brahms ('next to Beethoven, the most profound symphony writer') and to Tchaikovsky. According to Barry, 'Probably the last of the great symphonists is Elgar, that great British musician, who is still alive and whose two symphonies rank high. There are many other modernists writing symphonies whose place is not yet fixed in the musical ladder. Amongst them is Sibelius, that very distinguished Finnish composer, whose symphonies are often performed in Europe.'[73] Barry's musical stance is identical to that of the average British educationist of the time, so while his views may not have been, even for the time, particularly broad, his perception of the English musical renaissance provides a useful contemporaneous perspective

> It is refreshing to able to say that in this twentieth century British composers have come very rapidly to the front, and are now undoubtedly numbered with the world's best.

For Barry, Elgar was the outstanding name among British musicians of the previous fifty years with Delius, Parry, Holst, Bantock and Vaughan Williams all having shown in their work 'unmistakable signs of ability.'[74]

This was not an unsupported view at the time. That great music critic, essayist and playwright George Bernard Shaw commented upon music over a period spanning more than fifty years, particularly in his early career. By the 1930s he was writing less on the subject but occasionally took up the subject when compelled to, always expressing unstinting support for English music. In particular, Shaw came to Elgar's defence in a letter to the *Manchester Guardian*, signed by eighteen composers and music lovers including Shaw, Walton, Peter Warlock (Philip Heseltine) and John Ireland, to express their disagreement with Edward J. Dent's contribution to the new edition of *the Handbuch der Musikgeschichter* published by Adler in Germany in which Dent singularly failed to appreciate Elgar's music, calling the omission a 'gross misrepresentation of the composers' position in the esteem of his fellow countrymen'. To the letter, Shaw added his own postscript: 'Professor Dent should not . . . have belittled his country by belittling the only great English composer who is not dwarfed by the German genius.'[75]

In October, *The Times* provided its own readers with an explanation of the dominance of Germany from the end of the seventeenth century by way of an overview of the work of ISM president W. Gillies Whittaker of Glasgow University, whose work on Purcell was presented in the pages of *The Musical Times* in October. 'We are all now ready to realize that the harmonic methods of the Restoration composers represented a standard and not an excrescence.' Restoration composers 'inherited certain ideas as a result of the late efflorescence of vocal polyphony in the Jacobean era and the development of the fantasia at the same time which had transferred vocal methods to instruments. Their insularity kept them closer to their past than their Continental contemporaries were, and their enterprise drove them to originate something further.' But the greatest of them, Purcell, achieved the publication of only one set of twelve sonatas for strings and harpsichord, however, and it was only through the efforts of his widow that another ten survived (these receiving analysis in *The Musical Times* article) following the composer's early death, other composers leaving their work in manuscript only or in 'a printed obscurity from which they have not yet been rescued'.

> Professor Whitaker recalls that when the International String Quartet played some of them on the Continent there were musicians among the audience who declared that 'no composer of that period could have written such music' and were ready to pronounce them 'fake'.

The crux of the matter lay in the 'native language of English music', which had been driven underground by the arrival of the Italian-Germanic language of the Continent proclaimed by the compelling genius of Handel:

> It is scarcely known now except as a dead language. There was a well-informed German musician to whom an Englishman, thinking to show his culture, expressed his reverence for Bach. The reply was 'You English are always fussing about Bach. Why don't you know your Purcell better?'[76]

Indeed, as the *Oxford Dictionary of Music* points out, Purcell's rehabilitation began only on the bicentenary of his death in 1895, and with the work of the Purcell Society, composers such as Holst and Vaughan Williams and, later especially Britten, whose *Young Person's Guide to the Orchestra* which is subtitled *Variations and Fugue on a Theme of Purcell*.

Another significant article in *The Times* the following month reported on a series of essays published in the *Wiener Zeitung*. The first, by Professor Egon Wellesz, discussed music in England. *The Times* covers this for two very specific reasons: 'It is so unlike what usually appears in the Continental Press about

English music, and also so unlike what many English people think about their art.' *The Times* conveniently sums up the 'misprisal' [*sic*]: the results of 'the misfortune that early in the nineteenth century, when continental concert life had its beginning, England had no contemporary composers to contribute to its repertory'. Although Wellesz recognizes, through his visits to Britain, the quality of England's great composers, her 'splendid orchestra' and the 'noble work for musical appreciation the BBC is doing', his interest is in why, despite all this, 'musical Europe' still considers English music 'with considerable prejudice'. It is based in a different outlook towards music, the result of 'a long historical development' through which Britain has made a significant contribution to the world's music. Rooted in the voice, British music is pursued 'among all of the community', unlike the continent where the standard of performance may be high but because it exists only in the concert-room it is absent from the universities, the 'small country towns' and from cathedrals and country homes. In England, on the other hand, choruses from the *Messiah* can be heard at the pithead.[77]

Of all the composers working hard to determine a truly English style of composition, it is Gustav Holst who, for *The Times*, 'exemplified the new creative spirit in English music, making a clean break with the nineteenth-century German tradition'.[78] Holst's sudden death on 25 May was 'a serious blow to British music and musicians and to innumerable devoted friends', began the tribute to him in *The Times* the following day. Making a clean break with the nineteenth-century German tradition, the composer had built up 'his strongly individual style' with English folk song, the Tudor composers and Purcell. For *The Times*, Holst's work would stand high not only in Britain but also elsewhere if genuineness was a 'criterion of art'. Everywhere in Europe and America, his work had obtained recognition in his lifetime, and it 'showed decisively the new creative spirit that was stirring in English music at the turn of the Century'.[79] The BBC Orchestra's performance of the *Choral Symphony* just a few weeks before had, indeed, begun with Purcell's Coronation Anthem, *My Heart is Inditing of a Good Matter*. Holst's ashes were placed in Chichester Cathedral on 24 June, in front of the Thomas Weelkes memorial. Weelkes, the Elizabethan madrigalist, was much admired by Holst. At the ceremony, Vaughan Williams conducted his *Kyrie Eleison* from his own Mass, which he had dedicated to Holst. The Holst Whitsuntide Choir (to whom the Mass was also dedicated) also sang Holst's own music to the Cornish poem 'Tomorrow Shall be my Dancing Day' and the Cathedral Choir joined them for a performance of Holst's anthem, 'Turn Back, O Man'.[80]

One of Holst's final works, his *Lyric Movement* (1934) for viola and orchestra was dedicated to Lionel Tertis, and it is Tertis who provides another link between the two composers and friends. Vaughan Williams's own works for viola have a special place in his output because he was a violist himself. In the *Tallis Fantasia* (1912) there is a solo viola section, and the score of *Flos Campi*, written for wordless chorus and orchestra, also includes a viola solo. 'It is in *Flos Campi* that we first are exposed to the relationship between Lionel Tertis and Ralph Vaughan Williams, a relationship that would culminate in the 1934 *Suite* and would last for many years to come,' observes violist Bernard Kane.[81] Commissioned by and dedicated to Lionel Tertis and premiered by the London Philharmonic under Malcolm Sargent with Tertis as soloist at the Queen's Hall on 12 November, the *Suite for Viola and Small Orchestra* consists of eight individual pieces that look back to the English folk song of Vaughan Williams's earlier idiom.[82] For *The Times*, the work was 'very much Mr Tertis' own', as well as that of his instrument ('it would be unthinkable transferred to violin or violincello'), and yet, 'also the composer's own in every detail of its design and phraseology'. Tertis was no insignificant figure in the importance of British music at the time, and this new work by Vaughan Williams was to receive two performances on consecutive nights. In the first, for *The Times*, in 'turning the viola into a virtuoso's instrument', he had succeeded in even reconciling English composers to 'instrumental virtuosity'. This contemplative work is, for Heffer, one that is greatly underrated, 'both for its intrinsic beauty and its thoughtfulness',[83] qualities immediately recognized at its first performance:

> The whole is a most engaging series of miniatures, and throughout, though the character of the viola seems the chief motive, the delicate colouring of the orchestral background contributes essential and subtle beauties. It is music to which one must listen for every jot and tittle of its expression.[84]

While the viola may have held a special place in Vaughan Williams's heart, he was no stranger to composing music for the other instruments of the orchestra. In his exploration of Vaughan Williams's works for wind, Jon Mitchell comments that 'It is not by chance Vaughan Williams's biographers have used 1934 as a watershed in defining his compositional output'.[85] The early death of his friend and collaborator Gustav Holst came to him as a major blow. His own ailments prevented him from taking part in a major event that summer when he was to conduct his music for the first of three Pageants. As a manifestation of the cultural preoccupations of the Left, the staging of a Pageant was a familiar expression during the 1930s, and beyond. Mitchell has provided extensive analysis of the *Abinger Pageant* of 1934 as well as two other Pageants, *England's Pleasant Land* of 1938, and the 1939 *Festival of Music for the People*, for which he wrote just one number, the 'Flourish' for wind band. 'Politics were at the centre of Vaughan Williams's decision to write *Flourish for Wind Band*,' writes Mitchell. 'During the 1920s and 1930s there were the beginnings of a "Red Scare" in Europe and the United States that came to fruition during the Cold War period that followed World War II. Freedom of speech and expression were at stake and there were many different views on the issue.'[86] Famous for his wartime support of Alan Bush's right to remain a conscientious objector (while 'strongly opposing his views), Vaughan Williams shared with Bush the experience of composing music for that peculiarly typical expression of the times. Bush also worked on three such events during the 1930s. *Pageant of Labour* (1934) was followed by *Pageant of Cooperation*, staged at Wembley in 1938, and he also contributed to the *Festival of Music for the People* in 1939.

> *The Abinger Pageant* opened with a woodman, in the role of narrator, driving sheep out of the arena so that the pageant could proceed. He is an important figure and the only performer who has a speaking part. He tells the story of Abinger in six episodes with a prologue and epilogue. Vaughan Williams was responsible for all the music though he was laid up with a poisoned foot and unable to take the later rehearsals or conduct on the day.
>
> Vaughan Williams had written descriptive music for the various episodes (for example the Roman invasion of Britain). He used mostly traditional music such as Latin plainsong, hymns, folk songs and dances. One of the episodes tells of pilgrims visiting Abinger on their way to Canterbury. For the last scene Vaughan Williams composed the anthem *O How Amiable* – published in 1940 and dedicated to Fanny Farrer, Secretary of Leith Hill Musical Festival – that ends with 'O God our help in ages past'.[87]

The Abinger Pageant's underlying message about preserving the countryside, one of Stanley Baldwin's favourite causes, is an enduring theme that continues to remain relevant generations later. A clear parallel exists between the pageants of the 1930s and what has now become a worldwide cultural phenomenon. A clear left-leaning theme was present at the opening ceremony of the 2012 London Olympics, staged by Danny Boyle, with an opening scene of bucolic bliss (complete with forty sheep, as well as horses, cows, goats, chickens, ducks, geese and sheep dogs, and accompanied by 'Nimrod' from Edward Elgar's *Enigma Variations*), leading to an expression of the industrial blight on England's landscape. Conservative MP Aidan Burley remarked at the time that the ceremony was 'The most leftie opening ceremony I have ever seen – more than Beijing, the capital of a communist state!'[88] Historian Tim Stanley, writing for the *Telegraph*, pondered what the ceremony told the world about Britain:

> A country that can still put on a show, that has many identities, that is culturally rich, that has a battered landscape, that lost a lot when the factories were first built, that has patches of God still found lying about, that is intensely proud of what it got right (free healthcare, women's votes), but not too comfortable about what it got wrong (empire was never mentioned). It is a mess. A jolly wonderful mess. We're good at those.[89]

So, while we no longer stage events similar to the pageants of the 1930s, their legacy reappeared in a kind of politically motivated supporting role for a major global event that said much – from one perspective – about how Britain perceives itself. Ironically, Vaughan Williams's cultural concerns are often associated with or even subsumed under the obsessions of the Right with what has been called the 'fascist undercurrent' associated with folklore,[90] but his lifetime support of Labour causes and sympathy with the preoccupations of the Left often confuse. We may even find contributors to the right-wing press agreeing with those whose opinions or attitudes with which, like Vaughan Williams, we find ourselves in sympathy. Take, for example, the Klenovsky case. Writing in The *Blackshirt* of 21 December 1934, one Selwyn Watson regarded William Walton as 'the most important young man in British music today',[91] and Jean Sibelius 'probably the greatest living composer'. On the other hand, of one Paul Klenovsky, the great orchestrator who had just 'died' in Moscow, it was claimed by the Soviets that 'only the Slavonic mind' could conceive such a brilliant orchestration of a Bach organ work because 'It takes the Russians to orchestrate as colourfully as that'. Much to the delight of this BUF member and *Blackshirt* columnist, now that Sir Henry Wood's famous 'jest' was exposed, such arrogance – and prejudice against Henry Wood ('who could not orchestrate') – could also be exposed for what it was:

> It is not suggested that any British music should be given indiscriminate and vociferous welcome. But when a nation loses so much sense of pride in its artistic creations as we have done, when in fact a composition is looked at askance purely because of its origin, then nothing short of a national revival, an awakening of the national consciousness, can rescue the national art from slow expiration.

And, like Vaughan Williams, Watson evokes an earlier era as an age when British music led the world:

> For those who still think a musical inferiority is something indigenous to the British character, let them remember that in the Elizabethan era – the Golden

Age of Britain – we were the supreme and acknowledged leaders of the art of music. The men who defeated the Armada prided themselves on their singing of madrigals: and although we of Fascism are of necessity concerned at present with the more challenging sounds of martial music, let us reflect that with the dream of a Greater Britain[92] – a dream so surely materialising – we can well expect British music against to be paramount and indomitable.[93]

Among the very first activities of the British Council's Music Advisory Committee, formed just a few months later, was organizing the performance of Elizabethan madrigals. It is difficult to acknowledge that in 1934, fascism was an acceptable – if controversial – home for some thinkers, who shared some ideas with those for whom fascism was abhorrent, and that some of their ideas were even shared by British official opinion, and the activities of government bodies. It is the contrast between two ends of the political spectrum that I turn to in the final chapter of this book.

Notes

1 'Royal Philharmonic Society; Presentation to Sir H. Harty', *The Times*, 23 November 1934, p. 12.
2 BBC WAC R27/221/1 – Minutes of the Meeting on 1 February 1934.
3 'Music and the BBC: Encouraging British Composers, Letters to the Editor', *The Times*, 2 February 1934, p. 13.
4 'Political Uniforms: "Marks of Distinction", Letters Page, Joseph Baber of Lincoln's Inn, WC2', *The Times*, 28 February 1934, p. 15.
5 Quoted from other sources in Reynolds, 2013: 279.
6 Steyn, 2020: 77–8.
7 'Private Armies, Challenges to Political Liberty, Letters', *The Times*, 26 January, p. 8.
8 'Political Uniforms, Discretionary Power of Prohibition: A Swedish Precedent, Letters to the Editor', *The Times*, 24 February 1934, p. 13.
9 'A New Phase of Fascism', *British Free Press*, 2 February 1934, quoted in Gottlieb, 2004: 98.
10 Thompson, 2003: 120.
11 BBC WAC R8/107/1.
12 Alongside the *Evening Standard* article, incidentally, was the broadcast listings for that night: 'Stravinsky or the Minstrels: The BBC Offer You Your Choice.'
13 'U.S. Song-Writers for British Film: London Protest Meeting', *The Times*, 27 October 1934, p. 10.

14 'Music Grave and Gay; Preponderance in Broadcast Programmes, Preference for British Performers', *The Times'* Broadcasting Number, p. xx.
15 'Sir Edward Elgar', *The Times*, 24 February 1934, p. 13.
16 *The Musical Times*, Volume 75, Issue 1095, May 1934, p. 405.
17 'Mr Gladstone as Composer of Music', *The Times*, 3 January 1934, p. 8.
18 'Music This Week: A New English Opera', *The Times*, 9 April 1934, p. 10.
19 'Promenade Concerts: Bax's Third Symphony', *The Times*, 26 September 1934, p. 10.
20 'Sir Landon Ronald on Modern Music: Tribute to Mr Arnold Bax', *The Times*, 7 November 1934, p. 14.
21 'Contemporary Music: BBC Concert', *The Times*, 2 July 1934, p. 14.
22 '"Leeds Music Festival": Two New Choral Works', *The Times*, 10 July 1934, p. 14.
23 'Books to Come: The Puritans and Music', *The Times*, 12 June 1934, p. 19.
24 'Survey of English Church Music: Destruction of Tudor Choir-Books', *The Times*, 16 January 1934, p. 15.
25 '"Canned" Music in Churches: Organists and Curtained Services', *The Times*, 8 May 1934, p. 10.
26 'Cathedral Music: A Crumbling Tradition', *The Times*, 7 July 1934, p. 34.
27 'Cathedral Music: To the Editor', of *The Times*, 10 July 1934, p. 12.
28 'English Church Music: To the Editor', of *The Times*, 12 July 1934, p. 10.
29 'Cathedral Music: To the Editor', of *The Times*, 14 July 1934, p. 7.
30 'Edmund H. Fellowes, William H. Harris, Choral Worship in Cathedrals', to *The Times*, 25 September 1934, p. 10.
31 'Foundations of Music: New Series to be Broadcast', *The Times*, 15 September 1934, p. 8.
32 Cardiff, 1991: 197.
33 'Programmes of the BBC: Changes Next Month. "Greater Flexibility" on Sundays', *The Times*, 21 September 1934, p. 14.
34 'Three Choirs Festival; Opening Service at Gloucester: Simple Impressiveness', *The Times*, 3 September 1934, p. 10.
35 'Three Choirs Festival: "The Kingdom"', *The Times*, 5 September 1934, p. 10.
36 'Three Choirs Festival: Vaughan Williams' "Magnificat"', *The Times*, 7 September 1934, p. 10.
37 'Three Choirs Festival: Elgar and Handel', *The Times*, 8 September 1934, p. 10. This is hard to imagine. But 1942/3 afforded a revival of some sort at the two hundredth anniversary of the first performance of the Messiah, as I have shown in my book on music in wartime Britain. To live audiences and listeners alike, Handel was still the stuff of local choral societies. By now his place is surely assured in the English canon
38 'In Memory of Sir Edward Elgar: Special Programme at Musicians' Club', *The Times*, 18 May 1934, p. 16.
39 'Frederick Delius: The Search for Perfection', *The Times*, 16 June 1934, p. 10.

40 The Wireless Notes column in the *Daily Worker*, 8 November 1934, p. 4.
41 'Obituary: Frederick Delius: A Dreamer in Music', *The Times*, 11 June 1934, p. 11.
42 'Frederick Delius: The Search for Perfection', *The Times*, 16 June 1934, p. 10.
43 '"A Village Romeo and Juliet": Delius's Opera at the R. C. M.', *The Times*, 28 June 1934, p. 12.
44 The Music of Delius, Letter, *The Musical Times*, Volume 75, Issue 1098, August 1934, pp. 737–8.
45 'The Delius Society: Forthcoming Gramophone Records', *The Times*, 15 September 1934, p. 8.
46 'Discord: As Delius Uses It', *The Times*, 27 October 1934, p. 10.
47 *The Listener*, Volume XII, Issue 302, 24 October 1934, p. 680.
48 Wood, 1938: 43. Henry Wood's friendship with Tonking ended after the latter's dismissal from Westminster Chapel as organist. He took merriment in exchanging the soft and loud craw-knobs on the instrument' the newly incumbent organist thus baling out what was supposed to be a 'quiet voluntary'. '"What a filthy trick!" I said in disgust, and left there and then.'
49 Doctor, 1999: 308.
50 'The Foreign Label', in the *Western Argus*, Tuesday 9 October 1934, p. 2.
51 'Paul Klenovsky', A Musical Hoax by Sir Henry Wood, *The Times*, 4 September 1934, p. 10.
52 Wood, 1938: 431.
53 'The Late Paul Klenovsky', *The Times*, 5 September 1934, p. 13.
54 'Promenade Concert, The Interpretation of Bach', *The Times*, 6 September 1934, p. 10.
55 'On the Other Hand', *Musical Opinion*, October 1934, p. 16.
56 *Musical Opinion*, November 1934, quoted by havergalbrian.org.
57 Nettel, 1976: 182.
58 'Royal Philharmonic Society, A Bach Programme', *The Times*, 7 December 1934, p. 12.
59 'The Promenade Concerts: 40th Season Opening Next Month', *The Times*, 13 July 1934, p. 12.
60 'Promenade Concerts: First Performances', *The Times*, 30 July 1934, p. 10.
61 *The Listener*, Volume XX, Issue 301, 17 October 1934, p. 661.
62 'End of the "Proms": A Successful Season', *The Times*, 8 October 1934, p. 12.
63 'Both Sides of the Microphone: Queen's Hall to Cambridge', *Radio Times*, Volume 45, Issue 576, 12 October 1934, p. 89.
64 Rowdy Demonstrations (Letter from S. Robinson of Felling-on-Tyne), What the Other Listener Thinks, *Radio Times*, 12 October 1934, p. 96.
65 'Bad Manners at the Opera; Sir Thomas Beecham's Protest', *The Times*, 2 May 1934, p. 12.
66 'Bad Manners at the Opera', *The Times*, 4 May 1934, p. 15.

67 *The Musical Times*, Letters Page, W. R. Anderson, Volume 75, Issue 1100, October 1934, p. 934.
68 'Review of Music, Ho! A Study of Music in Decline, by "H. J. F.", *The Musical Times*, Volume 75, Issue 1096, June 1934, pp. 514–15.
69 Barry, 1934: 12.
70 Ibid., 9.
71 Ibid., 71–2.
72 Ibid., 111–12.
73 Ibid., 62.
74 Ibid., 112.
75 Letter to the *Manchester Guardian* published on 6 February 1931, quoted in Lawrence (ed.), 1981: 732.
76 'Purcell's Style: A Native Language in Music', *The Times*, 13 October 1934, p. 10.
77 'Music in England, As Others See It', *The Times*, 17 November 1934, p. 10.
78 'Gustav Holst', *The Times*, 26 May 1934, p. 12.
79 'Mr. Gustav Holst: Composer and Teacher', *The Times*, 26 May 1934, p. 7.
80 'In Memory of Holst', *The Times*, 25 June 1934, p. 11.
81 *Journal of the Ralph Vaughan Williams Society*, Issue #44, February 2009, pp. 15–24.
82 Heffer, 2000: 84.
83 Ibid.
84 'Courtauld-Sargent Concerts: Vaughan Williams' Suite', *The Times*, 13 November 1934, p. 12.
85 Mitchell, 2008: 73.
86 Ibid., 88.
87 Ralph Vaughan Williams and the two Surrey Pageants: *The Abinger Pageant* (1934) and *England's Pleasant Land* (1938), Renee Stewart, *Journal of the Ralph Vaughan Williams Society,* Issue #53, February 2012, pp. 22–3.
88 *Media reaction to London 2012 Olympic Opening Ceremony*, 28 July 2012, http://www.bbc.com/news/uk-19025686, (accessed online 25 June 2015).
89 Ibid.
90 Hughes, 2001:177.
91 Walton's 1st Symphony had just been performed – without its final movement – for the first time on 3 December.
92 A reference to the title of Oswald Mosley's 1932 book, which had just been reprinted.
93 Selwyn Watson, 'The Future of Music: No Easy Road for the Composer', *The Blackshirt*, Issue 81, 21 December 1934, p. 5.

6

National music

The Elgar Memorial Concert on 24 March, which had featured a performance of *The Dream of Gerontius*, was held for the benefit of the Musicians' Benevolent Fund, of which Elgar had been president. *The Times* printed a statement concerning a new appeal for 'musicians in distress' on 6 April. It highlights the real situation for many:

> To-day, approximately half the musical profession of Great Britain are out of employment. A large number of musicians are sick and ill, and the plight of the music-makers in our country is tragic, as thousands of them are destitute.[1]

An appeal by Lord Blanesburgh broadcast the following Sunday evening raised £3600, a huge success compared to other appeals of the time, which were routinely presented on the Sunday night slot.[2] Apart from raising funds for 'musicians in distress', what was to be done? For some, the presence of 'foreign' artists posed a further threat to the livelihoods of ordinary musicians but, as we have seen, it was also a matter of standards and commitment to quality that convinced institutions like the BBC to go on recruiting artists from the Continent. Suggestions for reducing the level of unemployment among musicians came from both ends of the political spectrum. Certain practical programmes were also put into place. For example, in January Henry Wood conducted the Unemployed Men's Orchestra at Manchester's Free Trade Hall, and in London in the first week of December, the London Musicians' Orchestra – its members also recruited from the ranks of the unemployed – performed in a concert conducted by Theodor Otscharkoff, with Nancy Broadbent as soloist. The conventional programme of 'established classics' (Beethoven's *Coriolan* Overture, and *Eroica* Symphony, plus Saint-Saëns' first Cello Concerto) was justified artistically by the inclusion of an 'effective but unfamiliar' work. According to *The Times*, Frank Merrick's *Celtic Suite* was the orchestra's chief justification and distinctive contribution to music in London that week and though 'no great matter', it was well written and 'lighter in the hand and agreeable for a moment of relaxation in an otherwise serious programme'.[3]

Throughout the 1930s, there was a strict policy in place that determined whether foreign musicians would be permitted to enter the country. As Erick Levi has suggested, the impetus for a cabinet proposal by the Ministry of Labour to restrict opportunities for foreign musicians in January 1932 almost certainly came from the ISM, which held that it was 'nothing short of scandalous' that well-played musicians should be allowed to take funds out of the country.[4] Arnold Bax, Cyril Scott and Julius Harrison supported this 'anti-foreigner' campaign, which lasted for several months, but despite the extremely heated arguments that resulted from the ISM's 'insular' attitude, it maintained a hard stance throughout the decade, though allowing some leeway for 'merit'.[5] In early 1935, various methods of reducing unemployment among musicians were presented at the ISM's annual conference. With the BBC the largest employer of musicians, it was clearly responsible for ensuring that musicians could be gainfully employed, argued one speaker. Among the various statistics presented at the conference, it was said that 400 hours of gramophone music was broadcast in the space of three months. The first solution to the problem of unemployment was therefore that the BBC should abolish the broadcasting of gramophone records and allot the time to British artists. Not only that, but the BBC should also modify the regional policy whereby one programme was relayed several times over several hours, and rather than using amateur musicians, the BBC should use professional musicians only. The problem of 'foreign artists' continued to be a major aspect of the arguments presented. In the first 11 months of 1934, 104 vocalists and 612 instrumentalists from abroad received permits to work (with just 2 refusals) and the value of the fee total was somewhere in the region of £50,000 for German artists. Just 10 shillings could be taken from Germany, claimed former ISM President Harry Plunket Green, who criticised 'snobs' who 'wanted foreign names to bring out at their parties at the expense of British artists'.[6] Charitable events were one thing, but a number of practical measures were also proposed by political parties, including those on the Right, with an emphasis, naturally enough, on military or marching music:

> Amid its multifarious activities, and in the midst of its very active and energetic organisation, the appeal of music has not been overlooked by the British Union of Fascists. On all important occasions the Headquarters' Military Band renders well executed and inspiring music.
>
> The band was recruited from the Musicians' Group of the Fascist Union of British Workers, formed to protect the interests of British professional musicians. The unemployment among British people in the musical world, compared with

the comparative affluence of alien members clearly demonstrates the need for some protecting organisation whose policy will be 'Britain First'.

The following are a few of the objectives of the Musicians' Group of the Fascist Union of British Workers:-

1. To insist upon the registration of all professional musicians, who will be employed at professional rates.
2. To register members of military bands as professional.
3. To negotiate with cinema proprietors to incorporate orchestral music to offset the blow to the music profession consequent upon the introduction of the 'talkie'.
4. To assist the unemployed musicians.
5. To organize an Institute of Professional Musicians to effectively defend and represent the profession.
6. To ensure that for every foreigner employed in Britain, one Britisher will be employed abroad.

The conductor of the Blackshirt Military Band was Me. J. W. Mansfield, well known in music circles as composer of many famous marches, including 'Red Cloak' and 'Sovereign's Escort,' both of which were written for the King's birthday and played by the Massed Guards Band on the occasion of Trooping the Colours. He, as were all the members of the band, was an ex-Serviceman and served in the Irish Guards.

The band was to play a programme of music at the forthcoming 7 June meeting at Olympia to be given 'prior to the Leader's entrance'.[7] As an expression of fascism's 'regenerative projects', Graham Macklin shows how music was far more than mere entertainment for members of the BUF. Rather, music was used to 'underpin party mobilisation strategies, to anchor choreographed set pieces' at BUF rallies and to 'reinforce' emotion, especially using 'fascist songs'.[8]

The Olympia meeting, eagerly anticipated by BUF members, was destined, of course, to be the turning point for the Movement. Following a successful gathering at the Albert Hall in April, there were great hopes for an even larger meeting. In the German election of 1928, the Nazis managed only 2.6 per cent of the vote and yet, within five years were to gain power: a consequence of the economic situation. Similarly, the BUF in 1934 fully expected to head a government within a year, and in April they were full of hope:

> At a mass rally at the Albert Hall in April 1934, Mosley addressed an audience of ten thousand supporters. The evening began with an orchestra and choir playing the 'Horst Wessel' song, set to English words. According to the *Manchester*

Guardian: 'Just before eight the spotlights were turned to the long gangway leading through the arena to the platform and a procession of twelve standard bearers marched in carrying alternately Union Jacks and fascist banners. The standard bearers grouped themselves round the organ, the spotlights swung back to the main entrance, and there stood the Man of Destiny. Slowly he paced across the hall, chest out, handsome head flung back, while his followers, every man on his feet, cheered and cried 'Hail Mosley! Hail Mosley! Hail Mosley'!'[9]

The meeting was held on 22 April 1934, and gave William Joyce, the BUF's head of propaganda who took on the sobriquet Lord Haw-Haw during the war, the chance to experiment with propaganda techniques, using music, banners and standards, processions, lighting, and spotlights and chanting.[10]

Six weeks later the anticipated larger event, the infamous Olympia rally on 7 June with 15,000 in attendance, was marred by violence. An orchestra began by playing the Nazi anthem the *Horst-Wessel-Lied* and the Italian fascist hymn *Giovinezza*. The effect was something akin to a latter-day pop concert, complete with warm-up bands, the crowd waiting in anticipation and, of course, the dramatic entrance of the star.[11] As the leader entered with his party flag, the audience rose to 'Mosley!', an anthem composed for the occasion.

As Mosley waited for the fanfares of trumpets and cheering to die down before beginning his speech, violence broke out in the crowd. Medical evidence from the sixty or so protesters who were taken to hospital showed that Mosley's Blackshirt guard had come prepared with knuckledusters and razors. In a civil yet pointed correspondence in the *Daily Mail*, Lord Rothermere firmly withdrew his support.[12]

The June rally was a disaster for Mosley and his followers. Apart from the *Daily Mail* – which had only in January run a now-notorious piece 'Hurrah for the Blackshirts!' – withdrawing its support, members also left in droves. If 1934 saw the height of the BUF's popularity and support (membership having reached at least 40,000), it dwindled thenceforth and it never recovered from the ignominy of the June event. The BUF's decline can also be seen as a product of the English disregard for pomposity or violence. But that month the BUF was still keen to highlight what was being done elsewhere to alleviate the plight of unemployed musicians, particularly in Germany. John Porte, ISM member and *Blackshirt* columnist, had recently witnessed a concert 'of unusual and rather pathetic interest' at Morley College, Westminster. Composed of unemployed professional musicians, the orchestra played some fine music, 'for indeed they were fine musicians with nothing to do'. Some of them had been displaced by the advent of the 'talkies' and until recently would have played their instruments in the cinema for a living. Others had been displaced by mere economic considerations. 'Feeling a little more English and patriotic than usual', Porte 'could not help thinking of some other musical performances in London given with success by foreign musicians, both residents and visitors', his mind turning to Germany in his search for a solution to the problem:

> At about this time I had read a speech by Dr. Richard Strauss in Berlin. He was expressing his delight in the new life which was opening up for German musicians in Germany. Posts had been vacated by alien musicians and German unemployed orchestral players were once more able to earn a living in their own country. Incidentally, Strauss saw no signs of inferior standards arising because music in Germany was being performed by native musicians. I thought then that it was rather a pity that we in England have always been shy of holding similar views. However, that is an old topic which we need not go into here.

Presumably, by 'alien' Strauss meant 'Jewish', and 'the new life' meant life under the Nazi regime. Others in the BUF were more direct. In June a 'supporter' wrote to *The Blackshirt* about those he called 'alien' musicians. 'The number of aliens engaged in theatres, hotels, restaurants, and the "Talkie" industry is enormous,' he wrote. 'Practically the whole of this industry is closed to British musicians. The alien hordes prosper whilst British men and women starve, primarily because the management are mostly alien.' He ends his letter thus: 'The alien must go. Justice demands it.'[13]

On the other hand, offering no opinion one way or the other, Porte was 'merely stating facts', even though those 'with what are called advanced views on the type of Government the country should have will naturally draw a moral from the contrast I have just shown'. Evoking the position of the ISM concerning foreign musicians seeking a livelihood in Britain ('We are not without an active professional musical organisation in our country'), the author expresses reservations about the 'infiltration of Jewish refugee musicians', with the ISM recognizing their plight but also cognizant of the needs of local musicians. If 'our first duty in these difficult days is to our own people', there was, indeed, a contrast to be found in Germany:

> In Berlin, Dr. Strauss has been congratulating himself that the problem has been solved. In London we have got as far as pleading with our Government.[14]

If that were true, then there were other contrasts to be found in Germany that surely exposed the absurdity of the politics behind Strauss's speech. In October, the president of the *Reichsmusikkamer* decreed that its members were henceforth forbidden from adopting foreign or foreign-sounding names for the purposes of publicity or other reasons. It seems as though they felt a similar problem existed as in Britain. 'The tendency of many Germans to esteem only what is foreign at the expense of what is German, must be combated with all possible means. German musicians must be to the front of this struggle.'[15]

The German Propaganda Ministry was at the forefront of the 'struggle'. Some other kind of government body might do the same in Britain and, to this end, calls for a fine arts ministry were repeated throughout the 1930s. 'Feste' suggested one in the columns of *The Musical Times* in March 1934, an inevitability in view of the fact that 'unmusical' France had one. A London correspondent (and BUF member) responded in the May issue that such a ministry was 'long overdue'. However, Henry Welsh also felt that unless there was a reshuffling of Whitehall personnel, or while the present government was in power, there would be 'no action taking the place of talk' until a 'clean sweep' was made: 'Truth to tell, the political parties are played out. Working [on] 19th-Century lines, they have again and again proved themselves utterly incompetent to meet the facts of a new age.' Even musicians could benefit from taking an interest in the affairs of the country and needed to look to no other than the person of Sir Oswald Mosley. Quoting *Fascist Week* he declared that under fascism a ministry of fine arts would be one of the first bodies to be created:

> It will be the first task of Fascism in the cultural plane to elevate the public taste by releasing the national culture from the tyranny of commercial standards. Gone is the old aristocracy, which in the 18th century – to their honour! – patronised such men as Dryden, Pope and Samuel Johnson. Fascism must take over this duty of patronage, and with as generous a hand.[16]

Henry Welsh's letter in the May issue of *The Musical Times* (itself a response to 'Feste' in the March issue) provoked a full response from a Manchester correspondent, published in the June issue. J. H. Elliott did not know 'whether to laugh or weep' at Welsh's promise of a ministry of fine arts under a BUF government, which would belabour 'the Philistines . . . into building for us one of the finest opera houses in the world' here in Britain. 'What real value,' he asks indignantly, 'could a cultural institution have if it were forced on an unwilling public?' By this point the BUF had attracted much negativity after the disastrous rally at Olympia where party thugs dealt summarily with communist hecklers in the audience. The public, appalled at the violence, quickly turned its back on the BUF and members deserted the party in droves. 'And are we musical people really anxious to become the pampered pets of a state policy designed for a minority and founded on brute force?' Making a thinly disguised reference to Germany and Italy, Elliott pointed out that if Welsh were to follow the rise of fascism elsewhere, making his observations 'with the same care that he applies to matters musical, he would have seen that the path to power was strewn with broken promises – not to mention broken heads'. And while he agreed that an artist who takes no interest in the affairs of his country is a poor citizen, and does not even dispute the 'good intentions' of Mosley, he is reminded of the saying that the road to hell is paved with them.

> 'I will go as far as to say that the theories of Sir Oswald Mosley himself seem to me admirable. Theory and practice, however, are notoriously separated. If the British Union of Fascists consisted of Oswald Mosleys, all might be well. It does not. It contains numbers of blackshirted young gentlemen who, lacking the realism of their leader, fall back on provocation to violence, ranting rhetoric, parrot slogans, and the superstitious allegiance to shirts, symbols, and salutes that passes for patriotic sentiment among the muddle-headed.'[17]

The editor of *The Musical Times* eventually put a stop to the correspondence though he owned that 'no musical journal ought to ignore the question of possible political influence on the art and profession,' but not before two further letters were published giving opposing viewpoints. The first, from 'an enthusiastic follower of Sir Oswald Mosley', claims that

> 'Fascism in Britain would confer on the musical profession the right to elect its own representatives to voice its demands in the legislative assembly. Purely musical questions it would settle of its own accord, to the satisfaction of the interests of the profession. Thus, the question of State control of music does not arise, but the State makes the path along which music will progress.'

The opposite point of view was presented by a Cincinnati reader in the same issue, who was amused as the earlier correspondent's answer was published in June, which 'was most encouraging', though he was 'still in doubt as to whether *The Musical Times* [was] competing with the *Saturday Review* or *Punch*. Doubtless the editor accepted Mr Welsh's letter in good faith. An answer from him ought to prove highly entertaining.'[18] The Cincinnati reader, in the event, had the last word.

The precarious position of ordinary musicians (the subject of the present letter) was to be highlighted in view of the difficulties encountered by them at the outbreak of war a few years later, the LPO's struggle for survival depicted in *Battle for Music* (1943). The success of the orchestra's regeneration – under the auspices of its own members – 'exposed a weakness and a danger', according to a wartime account of the LPO's experience. The orchestra became, 'like the Vienna Philharmonic, a *Kunstrepublik*, an artistic republic which maintained its integrity in spite of the praise of its admirers and the sneers of its denigrators'.[19] As a consequence the LPO was able to continue 'almost unaffected by external conditions', but it did highlight a 'fundamental weakness' in British musical life and organization: 'for isolation, as Fascism has proved, must lead to competition and antagonism, and the keynote of musical advance is cooperation on nothing less than a national basis.'

Twenty-five years before a ministry of fine arts would have received support 'but the dangers of external control in this and other spheres have become only too apparent, while the virtues and strength of organised bodies lead us to believe that here lies the future type of organization'. And as the experience of the LPO in the War proved, 'it is not too much to suppose (therefore) that the whole musical planning of the country may safely be left to the musicians themselves, to those who know from their own personal and practical experience what are the problems and how they can best be solved'. Myra Hess's achievements in this regard during the War are also testament to the truth of this:

> I do not consider that a Ministry of Fine Arts is likely to prove the most satisfactory form of administration and control. Its name alone betrays it. It connotes a Minister, a gentleman moved by political exigencies, liable to be changed and replaced at any time for reasons not always connected with his abilities, a possible victim of cliques and cabals, and a rallying-point for the artistic intrigues and jealousies which have marred the history of subsidised music in France and Germany. Secondly, 'of Fine Arts,' I contend that this term, obsolete except in its application to the precious wares of the collector, has little significance for us.[20]

On the contrary, music in Britain 'can, and will, be enjoyed by a growing mass of people . . . provided that we offer them the best within our power to give'. This was precisely the attitude adopted by the BBC and was, indeed, the impetus behind the eventual creation of the Arts Council, which did not materialize until after the War, after much debate about its role and structure. 'That such a council would be without several of the most undesirable qualities of a Ministry [of fine arts] is quite true; that it would also be without most of the eminently desirable qualities of a national body . . . is no less true.'[21]

The idea of a ministry of fine arts comes from an article in the March issue which imagines a debate in the future on the 'present conditions of solo singing' in Britain in 1942. It discusses the relationship between the concert hall, the BBC and institutions of government, as well as the technicalities of broadcasting, and presents a 'Pink Paper', setting forth 'the attitude that a wise State should take' towards mechanized music or, more specifically, 'electrical musical instruments'. Here we see an anxiety expressed in 1934 regarding the effect of the increasing technologization of music and the imagined outcome, particularly on the livelihood of musicians, of the rapid development of recorded music. This debate continued throughout the 1930s, particularly at the outbreak of War. The question of a fine arts ministry was to remain at the outbreak of war when A. P. Herbert, independent MP for Oxford University, asked in the House of Commons what the likelihood of establishing a fine arts ministry was, when the continuation of the arts was under threat.

The debate about a fine arts ministry reappeared soon after the War. Among those calling for an official body to represent the arts was Victor Hely-Hutchinson, whose role in establishing policy at the BBC during the War was one of his key contributions. 'Victor felt strongly that if music was to take its proper place in British culture in the future it would need a central controlling body irrespective of the BBC,' wrote Donald Brook:

> He wanted State support for music, not State control, and could see no reason why this should exert a restrictive effect if it was thoroughly understood that the musician's value to the community lay in his own individuality, which must be free to develop.
>
> To the critics of State support of music, he pointed out that University Professors were entirely free from restrictive influence, and therefore if a University music faculty could work satisfactorily under this system, there was no reason why a Ministry of Fine Arts should not do likewise.[22]

The call for a fine arts ministry was realized only in 1946, with the advent of the Arts Council, which was formed out of the institutions set up to encourage the arts during the War. The Arts Council was established with the not inconsiderable contribution of Ralph Vaughan Williams whose own ideas of nationalism in music were laid out in 1934. With the establishment of the Arts Council immediately after the conflict, the mitigation of such concerns (musicians' livelihoods) began, but in 1934 concerned parties were already sufficiently worried about the prospects of musicians and music in an increasingly mechanized world. The 'Ministry of Arts' even suggests to a BBC facing a dearth of singers that 'an occasional fifteen minutes of silence would be no bad thing' should there be gaps in its programming.

Although to our eyes – in an age of almost unlimited choice – the idea of tolerating a gap of a quarter of an hour in the broadcast on a single channel is hard to comprehend, the imagined scenario sketched out by the author is not without relevance to the all-pervading *digitization* of sound that is apparent today. Take the writer's concern, for example, that 'the persistent portamento that is an inevitable effect of musical sounds produced by means of the thermionic valve' has always been rightly regarded, 'as a serious fault in a human performer'. And its 'legalisation, so to speak, by a scientific device would add to the already too numerous means by which the public taste is vitiated'. Evidently, the probable results of such a prospect were too deplorable to contemplate: 'the public use of electrical instruments must be restricted to scientific lectures at which they may be employed for demonstration purposes. Which, as all the world knows, was accordingly enacted' (presumably by the envisaged ministry of arts). This may all sound rather Lilliputian to twenty-first-century ears, but it is thinking like this that was eventually to pave the way for bodies such as the Arts Council:

> The point that seems to stick from reading this typescript is the immense potentiality for good of a Ministry of Fine Arts. That such a Ministry will come is pretty certain.

With France having a long-standing Ministry of Fine Arts and Hitler having recently established a 'musical directorate' under Wilhelm Furtwängler, the author states that 'An Arts Ministry of some sort will come in this country, and we shall see as a result that music, hitherto dependent on a mixture of patronage, commercialism, and mere luck, can be a vital part of the nation's life, supported and directed by the nation itself through an administrative body representing both profession and public.'[23]

Here, through this letter and the subsequent reaction to it, do we see music and politics in 1934 Britain in a nutshell: the increasing mechanization of music and its reproduction; the political elements; the BUF; Walton and his new symphony; its 'heroic materialism'; and how every opinion, from all quarters including those that are now frowned upon, had some contribution to make to what was to come. As we have seen, the BUF enjoyed widespread support including from the *Daily Mail*, until the disastrous Olympia rally in June. The sympathies of the middle classes were withdrawn soon after, not least, surely, those of the readers of *The Musical Times*.

Calls for a fine arts ministry were heard as early as January 1934. Addressing the annual conference of the ISM on the subject of opera, Sir Thomas Beecham compared the attitude of the state towards music both in Britain and on the

Continent. Despite receiving guests from foreign countries, Britain sent few musicians in return, especially for opera. Beecham said that the problem was a financial one:

> Every great visiting musical institution abroad was highly subsidised. Every enlightened State in the world, Germany, Italy under Mussolini, and even Russia regarded art, and particularly musical art, as an object of special consideration and protection.[24]

And despite the quality of British musical colleges and the strength of its choral tradition, Britain differed 'essentially and profoundly' from other countries 'in our refusal to create that official centre and representation of art which had existed in Continental countries for 100 and 200 years'.[25] Discussing the wisdom of establishing a fine arts ministry, Beecham recognized that while the BBC aspired to be the centre of culture in Britain, he doubted 'that the functions of a Ministry of Fine Arts such as existed in Continental countries were compatible with those of a great Broadcasting institution', advising musicians who wanted an independent fine arts ministry 'to begin and to continue to agitate for it'. In reply, George Dyson compared the current state of British opera with that in 1840 Germany where Wagner was up against a tradition of what 'was still a very strong fashionable opinion' in favour of Italian opera. 'Public opinion in this country,' he continued, 'was growing on this subject just as it was growing in Germany 100 years ago,' and he hoped that while Wagner and the best Italian opera should remain, 'we should also want to have our British works performed', as the country was 'awakening to the importance' of home-gown music.

Beecham's relationship with H. C. Colles, music critic of *The Times*, was never a happy one. Following the ISM address, Colles had written to Geoffrey Toye, criticizing Beecham's views. In response, Beecham felt that 'perhaps it would be better' if he put in writing what he wanted to say to Colles. Being 'the last person to object to honest criticism', even liking it, he believed that much of the criticism directed towards him by Colles in the pages of *The Times* 'is either unfair or unenlightened'. Rather than a comment on his views about a fine arts ministry, and concerned largely with the standard of performance in opera, Beecham's long letter defends his record of performances at Covent Garden, what he calls a 'concert tradition', which he intended to 'impose' on 'the inefficient second-raters' from the Continent that appear there:

> This is not a personal matter; it is one of principle, and the principle involved is of the highest seriousness for the future of opera in London. I charge The Times as being not only the utterer of prejudice and inaccuracy but as the defender of

reaction and incompetence. This is a grave business, and if it continues there is going to be open war between us.[26]

For the BUF it was the spirit of commerce that did not care for music or any of the arts and for whom the only valid test was 'Does it Pay?', which was to blame. It responded to Sir Thomas Beecham's complaint: red rag to a bull for an organization among which one of the bugbears in the arts was international opera:

> Music is a luxury for a country when so many want bread-and-butter, but if Britain were properly organised, if the colossal waste of the present system were cut, there would be bread-and-butter, and all the other necessities of life, in plenty, as well as plenty of money for opera and all the other arts.[27]

Charges that the BUF was actually 'anti-cultural' (an accusation now usually – and justifiably – levelled at the Nazis) were refuted. For regular columnist in the BUF press, E. D. Randall, this 'curious conception' 'engendered in the shadowy minds of vague, white-fingered intellectuals at cocktail gatherings in some recess of Bloomsbury, and trumpeted forth by legions of well-fed bourgeois intelligentsia, is in reality as misshapen as their art and as puerile as their utterances', and the elevation of 'false and graceless conceptions' by artists and intellectuals whose 'unlovely' work was harsh, dry and uninspired, and their culture 'shapeless and inanimate'. The 'cult of ugliness and distortion in art, music and literature' was the product of 'neurotic post-war minds, sickened by long incarceration in dim cities' and their achievements 'the blind groping of the imprisoned soul'.[28] John Porte, signing himself as a member of the ISM, offered, instead, an example of the kind of music which did meet with party approval, namely Edward German's *Merrie England*, its suitability about which he went to great lengths to explain. *Fascist Week* and *The Blackshirt* were not just party organs, however.[29] The right of reply was exercised in a letter in the former in opposition to Porte, written in a more conciliatory tone. Though the correspondent had not heard *Merrie England*, he had no doubt that if it were worthy, it could be produced at Covent Garden. (In fact, a 1934 production from the Princes Theatre was broadcast in 1934.) The correspondent wondered sarcastically whether 'Hey Robin, jolly, jolly Robin' was as beautiful as some of the arias in *La Traviata*:

> As a Blackshirt, and a very ardent Blackshirt, I feel very strongly on this subject, as I think articles of the type I've mentioned are not going to do our great Movement any good. We must never give people the chance to say 'Fascism will lower the standard of art in the country', so let us do all we can to encourage our

own musicians, while at the same time we have the best, but only the best, of the foreign element over for us to enjoy, learn from, and compete against.[30]

Despite regular rantings on the perils of international opera, John Porte had claimed that he had never been 'down' on it, and complained that one could not say anything that was 'incapable of misconstruction'. Neither could he deny that opera included some of the world's greatest music, or that if it were no longer performed, it would mean 'we became barbarians, knowing nothing of the musical treasures which are the common property of all peoples'.[31] For him, the point was that the best seats in the house would be filled with genuine opera enthusiasts, instead of 'by Society folk and international financiers'. In the future he envisaged a British national opera, and, indeed, a Scottish and a Welsh opera, possessing 'a national flavour' which reflected 'the spirit of our own people'. Cardiff, Edinburgh and Glasgow would be centres of national opera, as would London, Manchester and Birmingham:

> With these points established there will bud and flower our own national talents. Give our men the encouragement and they will supply the goods. Why did the greatest British composer, Elgar, write no opera? Well, one very good reason is that he would have been lucky to have ever heard it produced in a worthy manner – at the Grand Season at Covent Garden. Perhaps it was as well that he spared himself the humiliation of writing an opera which would not have been considered good enough to rank with the array of imported 'stars' in the capital of his native country.[32]

One wonders for how long the correspondent, from Ardleigh, Essex, remained 'a very ardent Blackshirt' with those views. He was not alone, however. Another correspondent took 'great pleasure' that someone was 'at last protesting at the attitude put forward in *The Blackshirt* with regard to world music and artists'. Elgar did not write opera simply because 'he did not feel himself fitted for the task,' she wrote:

> Supposing we did have foreign opera in English what would happen? It would fail: Because the greater part of the British public would not be interested and the musical public would not patronise it because they would hate to hear lovely music ruined. That is why the Metropolitan Opera Company failed and the Vic-Wells Opera Company is having such a struggle to make both ends meet.
>   Let us have British music and opera with British artists, but never exclude the foreigners' music or artists, for we shall lose half the beauty of the world and half our national stories, for is not Wagner's greatest work our own epic story? Why then exclude it because it was written in Germany by a German?

> What I suggest is best music and artists for Britain at better prices, but don't let us be so narrow as to attempt to confine our thoughts of art in appreciation of one country's efforts.[33]

Although she was in tune with the emerging policies at the BBC, whose mantra was 'the best music of the best composers performed by the best artists, no matter its origin', the success of English National Opera in later years debunks her argument about opera in English. Rather predictably, Porte's example of a great precedent for National Opera was a German one. Wagner's *Meistersinger*, which reflects the spirit of the German people was 'known to all Germans, whether musical or not'. Loved as much in Britain, 'almost as much as the Germans do', there was an equally lovable opera that reflected the 'Old English spirit', that could represent 'the start for real national opera in a future national England', wrote Porte. 'It is entitled "Merrie England" by Sir Edward German, who although, I believe, Welsh, has certainly made his spiritual home in English music.'[34] One cannot help being rather amused at such enthusiasm. Porte admitted to growing impatient for 'its time to draw near':

> At present we have to fall back on an excellent little set of gramophone records of the work, conveniently abridged to suit popular pockets. The Waltz song is as good as any that I, as a solemnly and fully trained musical expert, can discover, only I must point out that it is written in a good English idiom and has no trace of the Viennese-cum-Johann Strauss tang about it, so under present conditions it is not likely to be honoured on State occasions.

Despite 'the wasted existence of a fine national musical work', Porte considered the work 'an outcast among the garish high lights of international opera in Britain'. But there was a 'brighter side' to its life:

> How many provincial and suburban choral societies have given performances of the work? And how many military bands and light orchestras play a selection from it? Fortunately the answer is Legion, and thus 'Merrie England' is kept alive, waiting for its day, in spite of 'international' opera.

Here we can detect the smell of anti-Semitism where, for the familiar jibes 'international' opera and 'international financiers', we read 'Jewish'. A regular contributor of articles on music, Porte believed that the opera 'should be known to every Englishman, woman, boy and girl', and looked forward to the day when *The Yeomen of England* and *The English Rose* took their rightful place. They were 'more than we deserve; but we will keep them until the national spirit awakens in our country'. But Porte shares a view with someone eminently more respectable.

E. J. Moeran rated Edward German very highly. Following the BBC's festival of British music, German having been omitted from the programmes, he wrote to the *Telegraph* to complain. Besides wanting to have heard 'something by Finzi, Rubbra and Elizabeth Maconchy' (among others), 'A serious omission from the programmes was the name of Edward German. He is interesting historically, apart from the value of his music. In the 1890s, when others were purveying second-hand Brahms, German was producing symphonies and suites with a distinctly English flavour and original character.'[35] Could this also be seen as an objection to the BBC as the arbiter of taste? Primarily a composer of operetta, German is at least recognized today for completing Arthur Sullivan's *The Emerald Isle*, which had been left unfinished on the composer's death, 'as well as composing works such as *A Princess of Kensington* and *Merrie England*, with its immediately popular songs *The English Rose, O Peaceful England* and *The Yeomen of England*'.[36] Earlier in February, John Porte had been keen to distinguish what a state opera, or a state orchestra might look like in Britain, as opposed to what he called 'bourgeoisie' and Communist countries. 'It is hard to get into the heads of musical people that getting the best out of an art is not to be done by this or that fancy method, but by seeking for the best results along the most natural lines,' he wrote.

> Music is an integral part of the social life, not [of] a few, but of a nation. It should be allowed to grow and flourish on the natural soil of its country. People who know no better still try to tell us that the natural home of music is in Germany, or in Italy or in Vienna, which is on a level with saying that the natural home of potatoes is in France. It is astonishing when one thinks of the Elizabethan age, when England was almost, if not the leading musical nation in the world.
>
> We have for long had the greatest living composer, Elgar, yet owing to our muddled musical mentalities and the turning over of musical affairs to an international fetish this great man had to bear with obstruction, neglect, and rebuffs which would have broken the heart of almost anyone but an Englishman.[37]

The key, writes Porte, is to 'release' music. One of the benefits of a fascist state would be the rescue of the great heritage of folk singing and dancing, and amateur choral societies. 'Release our natural genius in all directions and music in this country would flourish as it did in the Elizabethan era,' he claimed.[38] Indeed, wrote another contributor to *Fascist Week*, 'The coming of Fascism to Britain has led inevitably to the demand for music which is both British and Fascist.'

> To utilise English melodies would be to supply but one half of the demand, whereas to gather up wholesale and turn to our own purpose the Fascist music of Italy and Germany would not only be shirking the task but would perpetuate

the hitherto sedulously fostered belief that the British people are *ipso facto* musically inferior to other European races.[39]

Two songs had thus passed the selection process at Fascist HQ: 'Mosley!' by Selwyn Watson with words by E. D. Randall, 'which crystallise the Fascist sentiment [making] the song both a salute to the Leader and a call to action', and J. F. Welsh's 'Britain, Awake!' expressing 'the solidity and the basically sterling qualities of the spiritual foundation of the Fascist Movement'. And yet, surely, the main musical contribution in this genre was a translation of the *Horst-Wessel* song! Both Welsh and Randall had already contributed their views on music and fascism in the pages of the BUF organs, as we have seen. Here, the writer wanted to point out specifically how the BUF was avoiding 'what in some circles' was regarded as 'the ideal Fascist song', but the BUF did not use 'Land of Hope and Glory' because 'it sums up in music the self-satisfaction of a certain era that is past – it is the Albert Memorial in sound', and that 'it stands for ideals we regard as obsolete'. As for the future, 'more music is coming in' – a reference to the continual incoming stream of 'manuscripts, marches, full songs or just a melody line' submitted to the BUF's offices. There were high hopes for the project, even as a result, 'that the fight to build the Greater Britain is giving rise to a new national music'. So what was the ideal fascist song? It was militaristic but not imperialistic, patriotic but not jingoistic. 'The story of song is the history of the world.' This bold statement opens a front-page article in *The Blackshirt* on the history of the revolutionary song:

> The 'Lilibulero', the song which made the revolution of 1688 bloodless but glorious, bringing over the whole country against the tyranny of James II; the 'Marseillaise' of the French Revolution, to the strains of which, soldiers of France swept the enemy from their country; and 'John Brown's Body' which gave courage to the Northern troops in the worst days of the American Civil War are a few of the classic examples of the revolutionary songs of the past.
>
> In the present era we have the stirring 'Giovinezza' of Fascist Italy and the stately 'Hörst Wessel' of Nazi Germany . . . Indeed in the latter country some fifty marching songs have been composed throughout the period of struggle of the NSDAP.[40]

The author of this piece, the BUF's musical director J. E. Graham, spent three weeks in August travelling 'the length and breadth of the country' to promote the songs of the movement. Offering his services to any branch, he promised to assist to the utmost of his ability. Reporting back after his journey, Graham related that 'everyone was eager to learn the songs', noting that 'the shyness which is supposed to be a British characteristic was forgotten in their desire to be able to join in the singing which will be a feature of all future meetings'.[41] It was important for BUF members to learn the songs, ran an editorial, 'so that at all Blackshirt gatherings we can display unity and enthusiasm, giving vent to our emotions, and rouse the laggards within our ranks by the power and passion of our music'. But time was running out. *The Blackshirt's* editorial column had already carried an appeal from the 'Leader' that members of the BUF should learn at once the fascist songs which have been written and accepted as official songs of the Movement, in time for the Albert Hall meeting. Inviting members to rehearsals at national headquarters, he said arrangements would be made 'for all London Branches to bring their members at least twice before the date of the meeting'.[42]

The same issue of *The Blackshirt* carried a notice of the appeal for funds by MPs to set up a day nursery in Lambeth for the Lady Cynthia Mosley memorial. His connection to 'Cimmie' had caused William Walton much hand-wringing in January the previous year. That Walton was in any way involved with the BUF might seem surprising. But it was, in fact, his friendship with Osbert Sitwell and Cimmie, Oswald Mosley's first wife, that entangled him in an association with the Party. It had been nearly a year since her death on 16 May 1933 arising from complications following the birth of her son Michael. In January 1933, Walton still felt committed to writing a 'hymn' for the movement, because Cimmie had asked him personally:

> Meanwhile I'm in a stinking rage with Bertie about that there Fascist 'ymn. As Cimmie wrote me I could hardly refuse but made the stipulation that I must have the words first (Onward, Oswald, Onward) but if Bertie ever writes them I'll kick his bl--- ar---. I hear that at a Fascist meeting in Grosvenor House Tom announced the fact of our writing this song. Anyhow it is the only possible thing that could 'make' the party.[43]

In this letter 'Tom' is Sir Oswald Mosley and 'Bertie', Osbert Sitwell. 'Dear' Cimmie died shortly afterwards, Walton's conscience allowing him to take a step back with her sad passing. Never a convinced fascist in the short period between the creation of the BUF in October 1932 and her death the following May, Cimmie (no doubt stressing the rebirth) nevertheless contributed some ideas, including designs for a fascist flag. She also discussed with her husband the idea of using Sousa's march *The Stars and Stripes Forever* in a fascist anthem with words by Osbert Sitwell. Later, she asked William Walton to write music for the

BUF. Walton's involvement, stemming from his friendship with the Sitwells in the late 1920s, was difficult for him. Cimmie's death in 1933 had freed him from his commitment to write an anthem to some degree, but he had made a promise to her. Besides, in 1933 he was having difficulties of his own, his relationship with Imma proving to be a source of pain, pain that would find expression in his new symphony, particularly in the Adagio.

Graham Macklin has described the palingenetic aspirations of members of the BUF, the hope that through a process of cultural regeneration, a 'national community' would arise, music playing a part in reversing the perceived decline and decadence prevalent at the time. Music was to be 'an integral part of the fascist experience',[44] though it was not until 1934 that it began to emerge as a rudimentary form of a specific policy. As we have seen, the creation of a ministry of fine arts is the most explicit idea formulated/supported. The rudiments of this musical upliftment began by commissioning marches and anthems. One idea was to appropriate *Land of Hope and Glory*, many grassroots fascists considering it as the ideal fascist song, but this was rejected for its 'obsolete' ideals: 'the Albert Memorial in Sound'.[45] Oswald Mosley took a personal interest, with the development of Sousa's *Stars and Stripes Forever* one idea for an anthem.[46] Osbert Sitwell was to write the words, and it is this connection that links Walton's involvement (he was still resident at their London home). Willie had promised Cynthia Mosley a new anthem as an alternative. Although nothing came of either idea, Walton was still fretting about his promise a year after Cynthia's untimely death.

Another British composer, despite a similar reluctance but committed through family ties, did succumb, however. Gerald (Lord) Berners (a Mitford family friend) was also persuaded to contribute. Merely because she asked him to while on holiday in Italy in early 1934, Diana Guinness (who later became Mosely's second wife) suggested to Lord Berners that he write 'twelve bars of a fascist march'.[47] It was published in the *Daily Express* and used at a 1934 rally in Oxford which Nancy Mitford had reluctantly attended. Although he contributed the 'dreary little tune', he was at pains to warn Mosley 'to tone down his remarks about Jews and homosexuals'[48] – the anthem was *Come All Young England*, with words again by E. D. Randall. Lord Berners, whose music was much admired by Stravinsky, ultimately rejected the fascist musical aesthetic.[49] A member of the BUF policy department, Randall was also 'the poet of fascism in Britain' who eventually wrote lyrics for most BUF anthems. A former communist, his use of the word 'comrades' in a lyric was not 'universally popular', but he justified its use in the *Blackshirt* by remarking how even the crimson of the Nazi banner was used in the Swastika, as well as the songs and slogans usually associated with the Left.[50]

During 1934, the BUF also developed its own fifty-strong symphony orchestra, which it hoped would counter the 'canned' and mechanically reproduced music of the modern age, as well as representing the movement in music. The conductors included Edward Carwardine and A. M. Gifford.[51] Carwardine, who was until 1928 first violinist at the LSO eventually became conductor of the short-lived Light Symphony Orchestra. A broadcast recital of gramophone recordings from Edinburgh in January 1934 included Carwardine conducting Eric Coates' *Miniature Suite*.

Besides the orchestra and even a 'Fascist Hot Number Dance Band', there were also several fascist choirs. To begin with, the Blackshirt choir was formed in 1934 for the purposes of recording, but by early 1935 several choirs had been established, and later still fascist bands were formed, partly in response to the perception that the Musicians' Union had let them down at a time when work was scarce. Whatever the logistics and aspirations of the movement's musical director J. E. Graham, the aesthetic and elevating qualities of music, much expressed by the likes of Diana Mosley, were also a part of the fascist ideal. One of the party's members, who was in charge of propaganda in the south, was noted for his love of 'good music', which for *Action* exemplified 'the dictum that the able propagandist must have in him something of the artist, some of the fine perception which delights in a balanced achievement'.[52] In the BUF, music was not mere entertainment, and although it aspired to loftier things, it succeeded in at least one respect: its militarization of music, and the effect was 'to draw easy parallels with continental fascist parties', particularly in the use of the tunes of *Giovinezza* and the *Horst-Wessel-Lied*, 'the marching anthems of Fascist Italy and Nazi Germany, respectively'.[53]

By May 1934 *The Blackshirt* was congratulating itself on the success of the music element at the April meeting at the Albert Hall, boasting that so far 'the Music Section of the BUF has cost the Movement nothing, indeed, the Movement has no money for this purpose', and it was looking forward to the publication of the first songs and marches as well as a release of gramophone records. It was also actively encouraging member instrumentalists to make themselves known.[54] The songs were, indeed, legion by that time. 'Mosley! Leader of thousands!', 'Up Fascists!', 'Shout for Mosley', 'Comrades! Raise the Martial Chorus' (sung to the tune of *Men of Harlech*), 'Onward Blackshirts' (to the tune of the Italian hymn, *Giovinezza*), 'The Blackshirts Parade', 'Britain Awake!', 'Land of Our Birth', 'Song of Union' and 'Come and Join the Blackshirts' were all rather predictable (and, surely, would have horrified the likes of William Walton). The English version of the *Horst-Wessel-Lied* was simply called 'Marching Song':

> Comrades: the voices of the dead battalions
>   Of those who fell that Britain might be great,
>   Join in our song, for they still march in spirit with us
>   And urge us on to gain the Fascist State!
>   We're of their blood, and spirit of their spirit,
>   Sprung from that soil for whose dear sake they bled;
>   'Gainst vested powers, Red Front, and massed ranks of Reaction
>   We lead the fight for freedom and for bread!
>   The streets are still; the final struggle's ended;
>   Flushed with the fight we proudly hail the dawn!
>   See, over all the streets the Fascist banners waving – Triumphant standard of
> a race reborn!

The power and the presence of that music – its endurance – is vividly demonstrated in Nicholas Mosley's account of the battle for Monte Cassino in May 1944. By then disgraced, his father, though recently released from Holloway prison after 3½ years' imprisonment, had become his confidante and mentor. They exchanged many letters. Those written by Nicholas survived, including several which describe the privations as well as the absurdity of war:

> The other day I heard two riflemen in my platoon bellowing at the tops of their voices the tune of the *'Horst Wessel'* with all the old words in English including the line – 'We'll fight for Mosley!' I was covered with confusion and have not yet dared to ask them where they learned the words. They are very probably old members of the B.U., being extraordinarily pleasant and sensible men.[55]

Later, Nicholas Mosley found himself fending off newly liberated crowds of ecstatic Italians, begging him for cigarettes and cash and humouring him by telling him how much they admired the English and hated Mussolini. To put them off he told them he was a fanatical admirer and 100 per cent fascist:

> One little boy broke into the lusty strains of *Giovinezza* until he was hustled away by an outraged policeman.[56]

In September, members could also enjoy one of the regular Wagner evenings held, using gramophone records:

> For over three hours we had sat enthralled at a Wagner concert. First we had heard the Tannhäuser Overture, then the bridal procession of Elsa, the solemn

grandeur of the Funeral March form Götterdämmerung, Tristan longing for his Isolde, and, finally, the unforgettable closing scene from 'The Twilight of the Gods'.

The echo of the rising ferocity of the brasses, the shrill, eerie wail of the flutes and the screams of the violins mounting up and up, and the quickening thunder of the insistent drums, as the vast orchestra swept madly on to the last grand climax, still deafened us.

For contributor Henry Gibbs, it was a relief to escape and 'get back into the mundane stream of every-day life,' but for him music also had 'its seamy side, as the article in the adjacent column shows'. He is referring to a report which was written as a companion to the observations of the Wagner concert on the plight of British musicians for whom 'no Government assistance' was forthcoming:

Near Trafalgar Square we found a violinist in the gutter, playing 'The Londonderry Air', and giving the best rendition either of us had ever heard. A few pennies lay in the cap on the kerb, the man was blue with cold, [and] his clothes were shabby.

My companion became suddenly quiet and sad. 'What a contrast,' he said later, 'that orchestra and that man. Both gave us beauty and dreams and hopes nobody else ever can. Think of all the hundreds of those men we hear in the streets.'

Blaming the rise of amateur bands and the advent of the 'Talkies' for the plight of thousands of professional musicians, the author cites several examples of obviously trained, competent musicians eking out a living where they could. Music had become 'a sphere of violent contrasts'. The author doubts whether a lack of organization and a nation-wide poverty existed in any other profession, with 'the pressing problems confronting our musicians' blindly ignored by the Chancellor of the Exchequer, because 'the land of song and sweet music, which charmeth away all fears, is not a profitable notion these days'.[57]

A couple of weeks later, another columnist added more to the debate. 'Music in the Gutter,' wrote George Baker, 'gave a realistic and true picture of the tragedy underlying some of the music we hear in London's beggar-infested streets.' A 'racket' of agents' fees, rehearsal costs, advertising fees and meagre income for aspiring musicians only add to the misery. Even the BBC had begun to restrict auditions (while engaging foreign artists) and the tragedy of the musicians' lot was not confined to the streets: one case, among many, deserved mention, that of a pianist, 'whose magnificent playing and classical profile were the talk of London' a few years before:

> It was widely advertised that he was receiving a fee of £1000 for each concert. The fact was that he, or rather his wealthy wife, paid the management £200 for the 'privilege of a London appearance'.[58]

The BUF's response, it must be acknowledged, showed that it was also serious about practical measures that could be taken to alleviate the plight of unemployed musicians. By the end of November, the 50-strong 'BUF Symphony Orchestra' were able to give an 'excellent' concert in the clubroom at national headquarters in which, *The Blackshirt* enthused, 'The quality of the entertainment was a definite justification of the argument that British talent, now neglected and disregarded in an age of imported performers and "canned" production, is of sufficient merit to provide really meritorious entertainment'. The concert was staged 'to bring home the realisation' that much of the beauty of such music was lost in mechanical reproduction. 'Live' music was the best quality available, given the rather primitive nature of the day's reproduction technology. Rather ironically, it was the *William Tell* Overture, Jarnefelt's 'Praeludium' and the Overture to *Tannhäuser* that 'were perhaps the most appreciated', but 'Lady Mosley expressed the feeling of the large audience when, thanking the musicians, she expressed her pleasure at seeing that rare phenomena, an orchestra of all-British Performers'. Further concerts were planned and possibly rather predictably, it was rumoured that there was to be 'an exclusively Wagner evening'. Conductor Major Carwardine and his colleagues, continued the review, 'must be heartily congratulated on their *representation of the Movement in music*' (emphasis mine).[59]

Fascism in Britain was 'Seeking a Newer World', railed yet another *Blackshirt* contributor, Edwin Cornforth. It aspired not to be just a political movement, but 'it must be an intellectual movement as well'. While 'the forces of Democracy' could corral 'a large army of writers, economists, lecturers, scientists, publicists – even musicians, composers, painters, sculptors and architects' – they were merely 'hangers-on at the skirts of Democratic thought and Democratic art', serving to 'reinforce the apparent solidity and certainty of Democratic ideas in the eyes of a too easily guiled public'. And while it was 'well understood' that communism 'despite its crudity' possessed a certain philosophy, 'the original economic and social teachings of Karl Marx are hideously expressed in that hacked and disfigured block of stone which [Jacob] Epstein calls "Night", and in the inane dirge of Hindemith's music'. Presented in July, this was a blatant attack on democracy itself, a new trend that emerged after the Olympia meeting which, like much of the material that followed in the BUF's publications, as if, flush from the thrill of the rallies, there is a new belligerence in the voices of its propagandists complete with all the fanaticism of Nazi ideology:

> The student of modern literature, music, painting, sculpture, architecture etc., sees only too clearly that the spirit of Democracy has devitalised even Art. For the spirit of patriotism and adventure is indispensable to a virile and aspiring Art.
>
> [O]ur philosophy, as it grows, must reach down to the roots of Science, Art and every branch of human intellectual activity. Our thinkers must interpret the Universe in a new and more inspiring manner.
>
> Thus shall be created a splendid Aristocracy of Talent, the flower of youth of our land, who will be really equal to the task of grappling with the problems of the modern world. Before this onslaught the Tower of Lies which men call Democracy must finally and forever fall.[60]

Cornforth continued in a similar vein in November. He attacked what he called Bloomsburyitis in 'The Twilight of British Culture', an article that perhaps constitutes the most explicit manifesto yet of what the BUF thought about music:

> To speak of 'Modern' music, for instance, as 'intellectually advanced,' is absurd. If it is advanced, why is it imitative – like a monkey? Running through much 'modern' music one hears discord, noises like machinery, choruses shrieking inanely. Why? Because, replies the Modernist, this is an age of discord, of machinery, of a 'confusion of tongues!' Could anything be more elementary? These composers know very well that, in choosing to 'express' the noisy and discordant features of modern life, they are selecting the easiest subject of all to render into music. Not content with this, they choose the most superficial method of expression, the aurally imitative! Such music can have no genuine intellectual appeal, and is advanced only on the technical side, it being not a little difficult to torture instruments into making noises like steam-engines and so forth. The old masters undertook the infinitely more difficult task of expressing abstract experiences of the human mind, universal in their appeal to all ages, as great art must be. Schubert expressed moonlight and romance; Chopin melancholy beauty and tragedy; Beethoven great passion. The grovelling materialism of Liberal-Democratic culture has deprived most modern composers of the inspiration necessary to emulate the achievement of the past. Their music is deficient in that maturity and richness which alone indicates the cultivated intellect.

So here he ends again with the arch-enemy – democracy. That the left-wing and Soviet composers wanted to depict the mechanical age in music was quite deliberate. But the BUF had no name – yet – for the music it disliked so much. The Nazi-coined phrase 'Entartete Musik' would have befitted Cornforth's description. Citing architecture, too, as subject to the ravages of modernism, Cornforth bewails the modernists' desire to express 'the Spirit of the Age', as he puts it. And although the Greeks set the example in literature, the Iliad standing unrivalled as a work of literary art, 'we have no need to go to the Greeks,' he wrote. 'Fascists regard the reign of Elizabeth with admiration.'

> 'There is a Song of England,' it is truly said, 'that wanders in the wind.' To express the British racial Spirit will be the mission of Fascist art. Through this means will the jaded modern Englishman feel, throbbing down the ages, the thrill that Drake and Raleigh, and the great Elizabethans knew, and the spirit of high adventure will come to him to face the problems of the present age.[61]

Once again it is fascinating to note that during the War, Vaughan Williams and others did just that – they drew on the Elizabethan era, though Vaughan Williams was at, or leant towards, the other end of the political spectrum! So while Cornforth was setting out what was, effectively, a 'manifesto' of the BUF's stance on music, we can turn to what Heffer calls Vaughan Williams's 'personal manifesto'[62] as laid out in the *National Music* lectures. 'In the wake of the Fascism of the inter-war years,' writes Alain Frogley, 'we tend to associate expressions of nationalism as full-blooded as those of [Cecil] Sharp and Vaughan Williams with right-wing ideology. In fact, throughout Europe nationalism took on different political hues according to local conditions.' It did in Britain, too:

> In England, ruralist nationalism was attractive all across the political spectrum, and even imperialism was by no means exclusively the preserve of the Right. Although Elgar was a Tory, Vaughan Williams and Cecil Sharp, along with Gustav Holst, were socialists. Part of the reason for which English socialists could express such ideas with a clear conscience was that, for all the home country's faults, it was more democratic than most of its European competitors, including Germany (the main oppressor in things musical), and Englishness and socialism were seen to be linked by powerful historical bonds. These went back to the Puritan revolution of the seventeenth century, when the reformers, taking the Old Testament as their model, developed the idea that the English were a chosen people in world history, and made England the first overtly nationalistic country in Europe.[63]

Frogley acknowledges that although Vaughan Williams was by no means 'a jingoistic patriot', it has been difficult 'to escape the impression that he was swayed to some degree by the further heightening of nationalistic sentiment around this time'.[64] In her biography Ursula Vaughan Williams writes that it 'was certainly true for Ralph' that he believed what Gustav Holst had once said: that 'the artist is born again and starts again with every fresh work'. Vaughan Williams wanted to record Holst's view on aristocracy in art, that 'art is not for all but only for the chosen few – but the only way to find the few is to bring art to everyone'.[65]

According to Michael Kennedy, speaking in Tony Palmer's film *O Thou Transcendent*, Vaughan Williams's 'nationalism' was a mystical association of music with the nation in which he combines Tudor polyphony, folk song and church music, mixing it all up and making it English through and through. It is unnecessary to retell all Vaughan Williams's ideas here. What is important is that in the first part of *National Music*, entitled 'Should Music be National?', he concurs with the objection to the standard view about music from abroad, that is can't be both native to us, and at the same time be necessarily better when imported. 'It began in England,' he writes, 'in the early eighteenth century when the political power got into the hands of the entirely uncultured landed gentry and the practice of art was considered unworthy of a gentleman, from which it followed that you had to hire a "damned foreigner" to do it for you if you wanted it.'[66] Vaughan Williams's work is mainly concerned with the evolution of folk song which, he writes, 'is not a cause of national music, it is a manifestation of it'.[67] But his final thought surprises for its audacity and prophetic quality. For Vaughan Williams, Wagner's *Meistersinger* (which concerns the emergence and preservation of musical standards among the people) represents the spirit of a nation more than any work of art, where there 'is no playing with local colour, but the raising to its highest power all that is best in the national consciousness of his own country'. For Vaughan Williams, this was 'universal art in truth, universal because it is so intensely national',[68] a viewpoint almost identical to that of John Porte of the BUF.

Vaughan Williams also weighs into the problem of 'foreign' musicians, noticing that 'the national spirit' in music has occasionally shown itself in a 'keep out the foreigner' movement, and observing that 'the protest usually comes from professional musicians and is purely economic [rather than artistic] in origin. They demand protection as members of other professions do so as to secure their means of livelihood.'[69] As usual, as with many other sensitive issues, Vaughan Williams's wisdom prevails. Music is no mere commodity, rather 'It has its spiritual value as well. It shares in preserving the identity of the soul of the individual and of the nation,' and though 'the business of finding a nation's soul' was long and slow, 'a great many prophets must be slain in the course of it. Perhaps when we have slain enough prophets future generations will begin to build their tombs.'[70]

Vaughan Williams's *National Music* was not merely the record of his 1932 US lecture series. It was, he claimed, the formal writing of things he had been saying for years. It remains a relevant and enlightening history of music and neatly showcases the composer's belief that while Covent Garden and the Queen's Hall were the 'crest of the wave', behind that wave was 'the driving force' of music that was going on at home, in schools and in the local choral societies.[71] And it was not the 'distinguished names which appear in the front page of the newspapers' which gave him hope for the future of music, though he could acknowledge 'a certain number of composers who have achieved fame'. Elgar and Parry represented the older generation, Holst and Bax the 'middle age', and Walton and Lambert the 'quite young'. The English folk-song revival of the turn of the century had freed him and other composers to find the musical idiom they were cultivating unconsciously in themselves, freeing them from the weight of 'foreign influences', and uncovering from them 'something which had been hidden by foreign matter'.[72] Without the folk-song movement, Vaughan Williams believed that the 'young and vital school' of Walton, Bliss and Lambert 'would not have come into being'.[73]

For Vaughan Williams, the folk song was the key in defining national music, and in particular the relationship between melody (pitch) and rhythm (duration) based on a very simple understanding of folk art, born out of the natural experience of the ballad singer. Because it is so rooted in the rhythm of ordinary life and of the pitch of speech, music takes on the characteristics of the locality in which it is formed, hence the broader national characteristics found within it. 'Melody can exist apart from rhythm just as rhythm can exist apart from melody,' he wrote.[74] For that member of the 'young and vital school', Constant Lambert, in folk song was to be found 'the most natural and powerful form of national and racial expression in music',[75] with the 'differentiation' between composers as much to do with 'national reasons' as anything else:

> It is true that the outstanding feature in *Le Sacre* is its rhythmic experiment, an element which on the whole is lacking in the French school, mainly for national reasons. The French folk song has almost as little rhythmic interest and variety as the German, and the rhythmic tradition of French music lies more in the

popular music of a later day, square-cut marches, can-cans, and gallops, material that is obviously unsuited to the fin-de-siècle aestheticism of Debussy's more mannered works. The French as a race have a remarkably poor sense of rhythm as compared with the Russians, and it is only to be expected that the rhythmic element should play a greater part in Stravinsky's make-up than in Debussy's.[76]

For Lambert, the difference between Debussy and Stravinsky was merely that 'Barbaric impressionism has taken the place of super-civilized impressionism – that is all',[77] and that *The Rite of Spring* had enjoyed 'immense prestige' only because 'it is barbaric music for the super-civilized, an aphrodisiac for the jaded and surfeited'.[78] Ironically, despite its stormy reception, when *The Rite of Spring* was first performed, the work was considered 'the outstanding reaction against the invertebrate qualities of the Impressionist school', observes Lambert, even if 'the influence of Debussy's technical methods is even more marked, though the self-consciously barbaric colour of the ballet may make this influence a little hard to recognise at first'.[79] Lambert's withering attack on Stravinsky reaches fever pitch at this point and provides for us the title of this volume. Although a French or Italian composer might feel 'some embarrassment' about 'jazzing up the classics', he wrote, 'Stravinsky is like a child delighted with a book of eighteenth-century engravings, yet not so impressed that it has any twinges of conscience about reddening the noses, or adding moustaches and beards in thick black pencil'. In fact, in Stravinsky's adaptation of the expressive and formal content of eighteenth-century style 'the expressive element is treated in a mechanical way, and purely conventional formulae of construction are given pride of place. Like a savage standing in delighted awe before those two symbols of an alien civilization, the top hat and the *pot de chambre*, he is apt to confuse their functions'.[80]

For another contemporary view, we can turn to Cyril Scott and his volume on the 'secret influence of music throughout the ages', first published in 1933 and reprinted in May 1934. He adds a further dimension, if a somewhat esoteric one, to the debate in a chapter entitled 'The Ultra-Discordant and Their Effects'. Scott believed that intense and continued passionate emotions, especially 'mob-emotions', could 'create a variety of thought-forms in the lower of the unseen planes, and that these thought-forms endure for a number of years, until destroyed by some specific agency'.[81] Such 'thought-forms' have manifested throughout time, he notes – witness the cruelties of the Middle Ages and the excesses of the French Revolution. Music might have an 'educative' role in society, but it also has a 'destructive' one:

> The specific type of music essential to the destruction of these undesirable obsessing thought-forms only began to come into existence around 1906 – it is the music of the ultra-discordant type. For it is an occult musical fact that discord (used in its moral sense) can alone be destroyed *by* discord, the reason for this being that the vibrations of intrinsically beautiful music are too rarefied to touch the comparatively coarse vibrations of all that pertains to a much lower plane.
>
> Thus the work of destroying them [i.e., the negative thought-forms] was to a certain extent allotted to Stravinsky, but more particularly to Schoenberg and one or two of his followers to whom some wags have referred to as 'the excrutiationists' or 'the boys of the sour chords'![82]

Ultra-discordant music was also responsible for breaking down the 'conventionality' that continued to exist as the legacy of Handel. But it has also had an undesirable effect – on music, and on composers – because although no longer needed, it had become fashionable to write it, 'and even to label all non-ultra-discordant contemporary music as "romantic" – a catchword which has become one of abuse'. Scott also believed that jazz, 'which was definitely "put through" by the dark forces', was responsible for 'a very marked decline in sexual morals', as well as an increasing 'love of sensationalism' provoking the increased appetite for 'crook dramas', 'sensational fiction' and even the prize fight. This is not to say that the disdainful attitude to sex – manifested in Christianity, care of St. Paul – is any more helpful. With the opportunity for gratification so prevalent, the lesson is one of control, and the reason why the 'higher powers' permitted its diffusion is that 'Jazz-music has tended to make that lesson rather more difficult, and consequently the learning of it all the more conducive to spiritual evolution'.[83] In our less prudent era we find such views somewhat eccentric, to say the least. But in 1934, even respected figures such as Constant Lambert could be controversial, by today's standards. Lambert acknowledged, rather prickly for us, that 'most jazz is written and performed by cosmopolitan Jews'.[84] Controversial? Yes. The year 1934 was a time when such views could be printed without attracting general disapproval. But if we set aside the obvious and stop and listen to what Lambert is saying musically, we can accept his right to mention an uncomfortable notion. He could also be witty, even in his inflammatory language:

> The most irritating quality about the Vo-dodeo-vo, poo-poop-a-boop school of jazz is its hysterical emphasis on the fact that the singer is a jazz baby going crazy about jazz rhythm. If jazz were really so gay one feels that there would not be so much need to mention the fact in every bar of the piece. Folk songs do not

inform us that it's great to be singing in six-eight time, or that you won't get your dairy-maid until you have mastered the Dorian mode.⁸⁵

No, you probably wouldn't. But jazz (and its later manifestations in the more general worlds of pop and disco) does somehow lead directly to getting laid. Then Lambert turns to another subject that makes the modern reader even more uncomfortable, 'the nostalgia of the Negro who wants to go home has given place to the infinitely more weary nostalgia of the cosmopolitan Jew who has no home to go to'. Indeed, he believed that because 'at least ninety percent' of jazz tunes were written by Jews, this accounted for their 'curiously sagging quality', with the 'almost masochistic melancholy of the average foxtrot' typical of Jewish art. This 'masochistic element', a 'stronghold in the Jewish temperament', he believed, was 'becoming more and more a part of general consciousness'.⁸⁶

But Lambert was not all one-sided, however, and could demonstrate his ability to give credit where it was due in recognizing that the scoring and execution of jazz had reached 'a far higher level than that of any previous form of dance music, and in Duke Ellington's compositions jazz [had] produced the most distinguished popular music since Johann Strauss'.⁸⁷ So much for Lambert's views on jazz. It's true that some of his views would not have seemed out of place in *The Blackshirt*. Take, for example, an article commenting on the preservation of villages and the horror of 'ribbon development' (issues not unfamiliar to twenty-first-century commentators) as well as the demise of music:

> The traditional English music is now seldom heard outside the churches, but it would also come into its own again, and international jazz give way to the music which was good enough for the men who fought the battles which made England feared and respected throughout the world. The main thing is to insist that 'Britain First' shall apply not merely to pork and razor blades, but also to the things of the spirit, which nerved our forefathers to heroic efforts and which alone can save our race from decay.⁸⁸

Worse was the charge that jazz was actually 'undermining national stability'. With thousands of British musicians unemployed, 'bands that bleat Negro melodies in our dance-halls contain large numbers of foreigners', with most of their tunes imported from New York and of the lowest 'savage type' of musical form. 'Indeed, it would not be an exaggeration to say that present-day jazz is to music what pornography is to the pictorial arts'.⁸⁹

Contributor George Baker was writing again towards the end of December on art and fascism. The recent ban of jazz music in Germany was 'only a small evidence of a nation-wide cleansing process in the Arts,' he wrote. Under the banner of 'freedom of intellect' a general revolution in all the arts was witnessed after the Great War:

> In music the new school, which threw all the old rules of harmony, counterpoint, rhythm, etc., on the rubbish heap, produced 'compositions' without rhyme or reason, in which music became no more than ear-splitting noise.[90]

There was no doubt in Baker's mind regarding who had turned art into enterprise ('The importance was transferred from the stage to the box office'), especially in the theatre and cinema . . . where 'thrills' are favoured over 'artistic beauty', and 'if we go through the art of those who write, publish, advertise and produce this dope, in any country, we find that the most successful and influential among them are Jews.' The argument against jazz was not that it was 'Negro' or Jewish *per se*. As far as its opponents were concerned, jazz was cynically commercial, anti-intellectual and very negative (especially the Blues), and could 'undermine' society. These people felt that jazz 'should be stopped'. But how could you stop what people loved and enjoyed? By December, the subject of music had become even more prominent in the pages of *The Blackshirt*, with jazz and modern serious music now expressly associated with 'Jewry'. On 7 December, following its recent ban in Germany, a columnist laments the advent of jazz as afflicting British youth with 'a form of St. Vitus dance, a neurosis' that imbues jazz with a spirit of negation and cynicism, a spirit 'not likely' to lead to courage, intrepidity or vitality. 'For that reason, at least, Hitler's ban is justified.'[91] The author explains at some length the connection between jazz and 'Hebrew sentiment', a view that sits uncomfortably with Lambert's observation of that 'curiously sagging quality – so typical of Jewish art'.

To modern readers, even *The Times*' choice of words jars. A competition held at the Crystal Palace featuring 'jazz bands from all over the country took place on Saturday, 21 April. 'Misleadingly named', because they had 'nothing in common with dance orchestras', the jazz band in this sense was 'a body of 50 to 80 performers, costumed alike and equipped with a musical instrument called a jazz horn or kazoo, through which they hum wordless tunes in harmony', with points awarded 'for dress, music, display and so forth'. The movement, 'simple and humorous and democratic, and not a bit arty', was born of the industrial depression and flourished in the 'industrial North and Wales'. Going by names such as the Aberfan Coons, the Abertridwr Chocolate Coons, the Colenso Star Band, and the Cacrau Rajahs, they were, of course 'minstrel' ('or as some would have it, carnival') bands in which their members 'strutted like stage darkeys'.[92]

Graham Macklin has also thoroughly analysed the BUF's obsession with 'foreign' influences on music, on the decline of British music and the insidious influence of Jewish 'middle-men' on the industry, as well as their views on jazz. For the BUF, jazz was 'a cipher for national decline', its sound the stuff of 'negro-Semitic nightmares'.[93] It is impossible to say what the general public thought about the musical aspirations of the BUF, its idealism and desire for cultural renewal. One suspects that most couldn't care less. During the War, Rank released its bicentenary tribute to G. F. Handel (*The Great Mr. Handel*). This supposedly 'elevating' film was a flop. Why? Because in the week of its release in 1942, rather than being uplifted and educated by this deliberately didactic and 'worthy' film, the cinema-going public preferred to go a bit further down the road from Leicester Square to queue up for *Me and My Gal*. Perhaps the 'negro-Semitic' nightmare had come true?

Of course, one can find controversy everywhere in the 1930s. Sir Hamilton Harty revealed *his* views on 'foreign' music in a letter to Joseph Holbrooke in which he congratulated Holbrooke on a performance of one of his symphonic poems:

> The success of the 'Raven' the other night gave me much satisfaction and pleasure – because, in studying the work, I came to like and admire it immensely. There is beautiful and impressive music in that work, and, as I told the orchestra it is so infinitely superior to the foreign *muck* with which we are deluged nowadays.[94]

Leaving aside the controversial aspects of contemporary views on jazz, then, the overriding theme of Constant Lambert's *Music, Ho!* was, as he wrote in his own preface, of modern music in relation to the other arts and to the social and mechanical background of modern life.[95] He provides a useful analysis of the purely political song in which 'the most obvious example of the connection between nationalism and music is, of course, the somewhat bastard one, the patriotic or revolutionary song, where the presence of actual words is apt to confuse any estimate of the evocative power of the music qua music'. It was important, therefore to 'try carefully to distinguish between those tunes that are moving in themselves and those that are only moving through political and verbal associations'. Lambert contrasts *Le Marseillaise*, 'a work in which national or political feeling is paramount', with 'the best written' of British national songs, *Rule, Britannia*, which he can imagine being played by a ship's band or being hummed on the quarter-deck by some 'dilettante admiral', but hardly 'sung by sailors as they go into battle'. No, in England at least, there was something missing:

> It would be childish, for instance, to pretend that the growth of the Communist Party in England has been in any way influenced (save perhaps negatively) by

the music of *The Red Flag*; but in the case of a song like the *Marseillaise*, the most far reaching of popular songs, the effect is clearly dependent for its major appeal on the music itself and it is significant that the tune if not actually popular in technical origin is popular in general allure and non-classical in construction.[96]

Apart from *The Internationale*, of course, *The Red Flag* continues to remain the single most recognizable song of the Left. Originally sung to the tune of an old Jacobite song White Cockade, it is more well known in the tune of *O Tanenbaum*, the custom begun by Adolphe Smith Headingly. The words of *The Red Flag* were written in 1889 by Jim Connel, an Irish journalist. There are many verses, each followed by the familiar chorus:

> Then raise the scarlet standard high,
> Within its shade we'll live and die.
> Though cowards flinch and traitors sneer,
> We'll keep the red flag flying here.

The Red Flag even made an appearance at the funeral of one Welsh activist in August, 'with a large gathering of mourners singing outside the house of the deceased,' writes Thomas Linehan. Modelled on Russian funeral observances, such observances fulfilled a social dimension. 'In the ritual expressions of collective mourning or dedication, such as the intoning of revolutionary hymns in the crematorium, they affirmed the social affinity between those left behind collectively to continue the struggle.'[97]

The Communist Party of Great Britain's 'Artists' International Association', for the visual arts, was formed in 1934 but it did not formally establish an attitude or stance to music until the formation in 1947 of the National Cultural Committee with the Music Group's newsletter 'Music & Life' not appearing for the first time until 1956.[98] Earlier, in 1920, party discourse on music had 'intended to instil an appreciation of the "classics" in working-class musical taste,' writes Linehan. 'There were frequent expressions of appreciation in communist writing for composers who hailed from the traditional canon, with reference made to the "poignant beauty" of Tchaikovsky's Violin Concerto in D Major or the "beautiful and intricate trellis-work of sound" that enlivened Bach's organ works.'[99] But it wasn't until 1936 that the Workers' Music Association (WMA) was established. The WMA was 'the period's principal forum for bringing music and the working class into closer relation', bringing together musical societies such as choral groups and orchestras, as well as promoting social songs, putting on courses for the instruction of workers' choirs, composers and conductors, and aiming 'to democratise performance skills and musical taste more generally'.[100] Its first president was Alan Bush.

Between 1929 and 1931, Bush had studied philosophy (with musicology as his second subject) at the Friedrich-Wilhelm University in Berlin 'to discover more about the world and more about politics', but left Berlin without completing his doctorate, citing the rise of fascism as the reason for abandoning his university course. According to Derek Watson, Berlin not only helped him establish a network of contacts (many of whom he was able to help in London after they had fled), but his studies there also 'profoundly influenced him and to a large extent shaped his future career', his political and musical bonds with Hans Eisler and Ernst Meyer creating post-war opportunities for Bush in the German Democratic Republic and the wider socialist bloc which then formed Eastern Europe:

> [H]e was attracted to Eisler's idea that music should be universally accessible, that it should be central to the struggle of the working class against oppression, that the menace of fascism must be actively resisted and that music has an essential part to play in propaganda for and unification of that struggle.[101]

Appointed musical advisor to the London Labour Choral Union (LLCU) in 1929, Alan Bush remained until its collapse in 1940. The LLCU 'had a significant unifying effect on the socialist movement of the 1930s when it was to involve refugee musicians from Germany', writes Derek Watson. 'Its membership consisted of local choirs from all over London who came together for large events such as the Pageant of Labour of 1934'.[102] Bush's credentials also included *Songs of the Doomed*, written in 1929 and *Song of the Hunger Marchers*, with words by Randall Swingler with whom Bush collaborated until 1950. A unison song for mixed chorus and piano accompaniment, *Song of the Hunger Marchers* was written in 1934 and included in Victor Gollancz's *The Left Song Book*, which was published in 1938 and edited by Bush and Swingler. Also publisher of *The Musical Companion*, left-wing millionaire Victor Gollancz, a serious music lover, was happy to go on printing its 1934 first edition for a full twenty years before commissioning a second edition, such was the success of its reach. First published in November 1934, this 'compendium for all lovers of music' included contributions from many authorities, Edward J. Dent, Julius Harrison, W. R. Anderson, and Eric Blom among them. Other songbooks of the Left were already available. News of a selection of 'Proletarian Song Books' from the Proletarian Press of Glasgow appeared in the *Daily Worker* on 24 October. 'They are excellently got up and the school edition contains practically every revolutionary song which has been written since the "Marseillaise"', it boasted. Meanwhile, the 'Red Singer', soon to be available at the Workers' Bookshop in London, contained the latest songs, music and parodies, some of which were good enough to have been 'sent to the W. T. M. [Workers' Theatre Movement] Music Section'.[103]

Conscious of the threat war posed even to the composer, in *Music, Ho!*, Lambert had asserted that artists simply couldn't be neutral, especially in wartime:

> An artist must either take part in action or withdraw from it entirely. He cannot glorify it from outside. One can sympathise with the artist who enters with gusto into warfare and also with the artist who is a conscientious objector. But the artist who puts not himself but his art at the service of warfare, the composer who writes battle hymns, and the novelist who indulges in bellicose propaganda – those are the figures who should rightly incur the dangers of the trenches and the rigours of solitary confinement.[104]

Lambert could sympathize with the 'conchie' then, as could other figures like Vaughan Williams, who famously defended Alan Bush during the War. The relationship between Alan Bush and Vaughan Williams was complicated. In July 1939, Alan Bush thanked Vaughan Williams warmly for agreeing to be guarantor of a £100 overdraft for the WMA. Bush was keen to answer some of Vaughan Williams's concerns and explained that the organization's support was not conditional to any political view, but simply to all workers in the field, those 'who contribute to the material wealth or spiritual culture of humanity'. The WMA, he wrote, did not aim to advertise any brand of political opinion by means of music, but to express through music 'the issues most deeply and widely agitating human consciousness'.[105] Vaughan Williams had reminded Bush that he did not care about mixing propaganda and art and that, in fact, he held 'all political opinions to be good or bad according to the nature of the people who hold them'.[106]

Vaughan Williams strongly disagreed with Alan Bush's political opinions. But in March 1941, the BBC banned Bush's music on account of them. Infuriated, Vaughan Williams wrote to the Director-General withdrawing his offer of a choral song (*England, My England*) on the grounds that by banning Bush's music, the BBC was guilty of the 'victimization of private opinion'.[107] The BBC's defence, issued in a public statement, was that 'no one is invited to the microphone who has taken part in public agitation against the national war effort'.[108]

Michael Tippett, who joined the Communist Party in 1935, was another prominent objector. He too was cut from a similar cloth to Alan Bush, taking part in the *Pageant of Labour* at the Crystal Palace in a centenary celebration of the Tolpuddle Martyrs in October. The 1934 pageant was 'the first significant use of the form by the Left in Britain'. Mounted by the London Trades Council's

Central Women's Organization Committee, its aim was to attract women and young people to the communist movement. Michael Tippett assisted Alan Bush with the music.[109] Earlier in the summer, he ran the musical activities at a week-long miners' work camp near Boosbeck, Yorkshire, as he had done the previous year, when he staged a shortened version of John Gay's *The Beggar's Opera*. In 1934 he wrote music for *Robin Hood*, a 'folk opera', staged at the same camp. Tippett completed his first published String Quartet in 1934, a work that has been recognized as one in which he found his own voice.

Summer camps for mine workers and other local groups show that the Left in Britain were as extensive as the BUF in their reach. The Left's organ of propaganda, the *Daily Worker*, took as much trouble in reporting musical matters as had *The Blackshirt* and *Fascist Week*. In June, it was sure that 'Those who heard the Red Army song "13th Cavalry" rendered by the Lewisham Group (Workers' Theatre Movement) at a recent show, will learn with regret of the death of its composer, Alexander Davidenko'. Davidenko, who was born in Odessa in 1899 and died in Moscow (somewhat ironically) on 1 May 1934 was a writer of anthems and the like to Lenin. A favourite of the *Daily Worker's* music correspondent, he was 'an outstanding master of mass-song and choral work', who would be remembered 'as a pioneer of the new spirit in workers' culture'. The high hope for this composer was that 'his music will yet achieve the popularity among the masses of this country that it has won in the Soviet Union, as an inspiration to the toilers in the struggle for freedom and life'.[110]

Another Soviet 'cavalry song' is mentioned in a *Daily Worker* review of Rutland Boughton's new volume, *The Reality of Music*, which perhaps succeeded in presenting the most formalized view from the Left of the relationship between music and politics. The reviewer was impressed that Boughton quotes in full the Soviet *Red Cavalry*, among the most popular of Soviet war songs, 'as an instance of a song actuated by motives of freedom alone'. Boughton's 'important book', published in May 1934 was, for the *Daily Worker*, possibly 'the first attempt in English at a Marxian historical interpretation of music'. The review is not uncritical, though the book was 'obviously a labour of love for the author, and to the student an important introduction to the Marxist study of music'. Showing how 'music was intimately bound up with the communal life of the people, songs of work, of war, love and death', the volume traces music from the earliest times:

> Boughton's is the book to see you get into the local library, as a good introductory study, and as an offset to the abundance of theoretical musical rubbish with which public libraries are loaded.[111]

A contrast to those other major 1934 publications on the subject of music – Lambert's *Music, Ho!*, and Vaughan Williams's essay *National Music* – *The Reality of Music* is a tough critique of the status of music and, specifically, of three kinds of music identified by the author: 'light music, good and bad; music which has passed the test of time, and [which] contains elements of depth as well as lightness; and antimusic, noises carefully or carelessly based on the inversion of natural musical law'.[112] It is, by and large, a book about politics, and about where music fits into everyday reality. 'A real music for life means a real music for sex,' he writes.[113] Music and Labour, and Sex and War, and Death all get their own chapter. Boughton wants to consider life as it was expressed in primitive musical forms, in folk song, and music's place in Christian civilization.

But, beware, because in 1934, 'at the breakdown of civilization', there is one figure who 'shows himself to be the typically decadent composer'. Stravinsky provides Boughton with many examples of music in the modern age. None of his contempt for the composer is more palpable than in this:

> As he destroys music as an art, and restores the religious conceptions of the savage, he proclaims the sexual instinct, in Petrouchka, as the mere irritation of non-seminative puppets whose life-strings are pulled by a money-making showman.[114]

Although a work of 'great distinction',[115] for Boughton *Le Sacré du Printemps* has 'many features in common with a primitive Voodoo sacrifice',[116] a view he shares with Lambert. 'As Stravinsky has become a European figure he represents something pertaining to the whole of Christian civilization.'[117] Referring to the first performances of *Le Sacré*, Boughton writes that 'Experienced musicians have their fingers to their noses on such occasions. It is only very young, inexperienced and ignorant folk who are dared or cowed into looking knowing and solemn, and afterwards to shout their hollow applause and write drivel in the press about it all.'[118] Boughton finds in this a particular cause for the crisis of confidence evident abroad:

> As Stravinsky's stuff is the special result of the kind of civilization rampant in Russia before the war and now spreading through Europe, so all modernist musical imposturing is one of the results of the breakdown of Christian civilization.[119]

As for music and War, Boughton is no less incensed. Referring to the Anglo-Boer War of 1899–1902, he writes that 'It was left to a leading British composer [Edward Elgar] to celebrate the defeat of his enemies (in 1900) by setting to music a poem of Henley which says "Blow, you bugles of England, blow, Though you break the hearts of her beaten foe"'. In wars stimulated by misplaced patriotism, flag-waving and the ambition of financiers, writes Boughton, 'the possibility of ignoble emotion can be gauged by the previous quotation from Henley which celebrated a war of which every British person is now ashamed, because its real causes have since been laid bare in the written lives of Rhodes, Jameson, Milner, and the rest'.[120] And in the modern age, music written on the siege of war 'has neither depth nor consistent appeal to what is fine and lasting in human nature'. Fair enough. However, 'It is the more significant, therefore, that in these days commercial interests in music-making are able to revive the musical rubbish of the Great War. That is being done chiefly through the cinemas which have supplanted the music-halls in public favour, and through the British Broadcasting Corporation'.[121] Boughton stands back in his assessment of Elgar's contribution to war music. At the beginning of the First World War, Elgar's 'imperialist outlook simply fell away from him', writes Boughton:

> Before the war he even idealized British imperialism. During the war his chief utterances were on behalf of oppressed peoples, the Belgians and Poles. For the homeland itself his three choruses called 'The Spirit of England' tell all he allowed us to know of his feelings in association with words.[122]

Rutland Boughton adds his own annotations here to Lawrence Binyon's words from the first of the set, 'The Fourth of August':

For us the glorious dead have striven;	[They have indeed, say the capitalists.]
They battled that we might be free.	[Are we?]
We to their living cause are given;	[The dole!]
We arm for men that are to be.	[That they shall 'be' as short a time as future wars admit.]

England, once regarded as 'among the nations noblest chartered' could no longer claim the sentiments expressed in *The Spirit of England*, after Versailles and 'our subsequent treatment of soldiers and their families, [which] proved us to have been wrong'.[123] And besides, Elgar's great wartime music, was not expressed in any of these choruses, writes Boughton. Rather, his noblest genius can be found in his chamber music of the period – 'the sort of music a man makes when he most completely retires from the world of action'.[124]

Boughton's final chapter (temptingly entitled Music = Mathematics + Mystery) leads him to consider a work which, for him, epitomizes all that is problematic in modern British composition. Ignoring 'the tripe of the drawing-rooms, ballrooms, and cinemas', Boughton uses the example of a work 'which has been hailed as (and under more favourable conditions might have been) a work of immediate and lasting importance'. Boughton chooses *Belshazzar's Feast*, not merely for Walton's acknowledged genius in composing the work, 'but because it might so easily have been a living musical example of the Doomsday which is so real – the Doomsday which is threatening us now, sending our statesmen scuttling about like ants in a disturbed ant-hill. Just as they did in the days immediately before the Great War.' Boughton continues by asking if there is 'no means of effecting union between such men as Walton and the musical need of our time'. For him, Walton falls short. 'His is the sort of divisionary music which leaves the conviction that, after all, he has nothing to say that is relevant to the subject.'[125] Can we agree with Boughton on his assessment? Surely not: we listen to the music of *Belshazzar's Feast* and forget such accusations. Moreover, it is one of the major British works that, during the Second World War, the British Council selected for its recording programme. Its release in 1943 tempted Yehudi Menuhin to imagine Hitler hearing it and recognizing in it the spirit of a noble (though war-like) cause, and the will to victory.[126]

Boughton, like so many of his time, predicts a war, in a sobering précis of his beliefs about music and the modern world. Possibly cynical, certainly thought-provoking, it is worth repeating it in full, since Boughton's book has never been republished, his music largely ignored and his name almost completely forgotten. And it is not devoid of present-day relevance. Great music, Boughton finds, is possible only when the noblest of human thoughts are the inspiration behind its composition. Without this 'will to freedom' found in human nature, everything else is worthless:

> The Great War could only be waged by pretending to all the peoples concerned that their freedoms were at stake. So a moderate degree of musical inspiration was possible when the destructive mood of hate did not entirely dam the force of inspiration. But the comparatively poor musical result of the war in all countries is a sign that everywhere the spring of patriotism was turbid, because opposed to the deeper spring of common human nature.
>
> To-day the financiers, politicians, and priests are at their old work. The inevitable opposition between a dying capitalist civilization and the incipient communism of Soviet Russia is being rendered to the public in false terms . . . Members of the capitalist class whose lives are a continuous rebuke to Christianity work themselves up into fevers of mock-religious frenzy as they declaim against the natural will of the communists to keep their people free from superstition. Sooner or later war will result from the hatred fostered by

these religious ones. Creative art and creative music will arise where the fight is of a defensive nature.[127]

Rutland Boughton's *Bethlehem* had been the first musical event of the year. It is apt that this survey of music in 1934 should include the prescient words of this long-neglected and forgotten composer.

Though Vaughan Williams and Boughton did not see eye to eye, by 1952 there seems to have been a thawing in their relationship. In June that year, following the first performance of the work which had occupied him for many years, his *Pilgrim's Progress*, Vaughan Williams wrote to Boughton with the news that a certain Mr. Dunsman had sent him his review of the opera:

> I am sorry he should see in it any particularising to certain political views in my work. Of course everyone has the right to apply the generalisations of music to their particular views, but I do not like to be pinned down to 'meaning' anything in particular, like Bernard Shaw's ridiculous degradation of Wagner's 'Ring' into political propaganda.

We can hear an echo here of his irritation regarding the interpretation of his Fourth Symphony. Vaughan Williams continues (and here we can glean the crux of Mr. Dunsman's 'notice'):

> All right-minded people are in theory communists insofar as they believe that everything ought to be done for the common good, but when Socialism in practice means the unholy mess which the late government made of things and when Communism in practice means tyranny, double dealing and insincerity by Russia, one cannot join with its present manifestation.[128]

The Pilgrim's Progress had no doubt received a political interpretation from this correspondent. The reference to Shaw is to his famous essay *The Perfect Wagnerite*, which first appeared in 1898. 'Shaw's brilliant, important, and vastly amusing analysis of the Ring is a pleasure to read. He deconstructs the tetralogy as an allegory of class struggle, using Marx's theories when they are convenient but dispensing with them just as fast when they get in the way,' writes William Berger.[129] During this period, Vaughan Williams 'entered into heated correspondence with Rutland Boughton on the subject' of the gap between rich and poor, and, in particular of 'peace campaigns'. Vaughan Williams 'regarded such movements as being imposed by the Kremlin and in refuting Boughton's arguments he gave a clear account of his political history as a labour voter on all occasions except one'[130] (this was after the War, because he was 'disgusted' by the Labour party's 'mean tricks' in forcing one).

Boughton had replied that, of course, Shaw set out to be ridiculous, but that Vaughan Williams's official position made it harder for him to live up to the liberalism of his nature and his past. 'Even Elgar dared not come out into the open when he discovered the corruption of the official world,' wrote Boughton, 'but at least he ceased to serve it.'[131] This provoked a row with Vaughan Williams, who wrote on 9 July 1952, 'This really is too bad!' and then setting out his political views: First pointing out that as an O. M. (Order of Merit), he was not, in fact, under any official obligation (and would never accept any honours and appointments that would involve any), he ended by writing, 'I believe in freedom and that is why I will not be bullied by Nazis, Fascists and Russians.'[132] Earlier he had accepted the University of Hamburg's first Shakespeare prize in 1937 only after much hesitation, because 'it implied no political propaganda'. He did admit, however, that German honours were 'not what they used to be'.[133]

Ever the conciliator, on the same day, he also wrote to Herbert Howells about his upcoming eightieth birthday celebrations, to be hosted by the ISM. He was at pains for both Boughton and Alan Bush (with whom he had also recently rowed) representing the WMA of which he was president to be invited. What Rutland Boughton represented 'I do not quite know', he quipped.[134]

By the 1950s, some reconciliation and reflection were perhaps possible. For example, despite being a socialist, Vaughan Williams shared some sympathies with those on the far right. He defended Alan Bush (but disagreed with his politics), sparred with Rutland Boughton, but agreed with him on Shaw's views on the *Ring*, which aligned him in opposition to Oswald Mosley. And while Vaughan Williams and Boughton found Shaw's 1898 interpretation of the *Ring* in *The Perfect Wagnerite* 'ridiculous' political propaganda, Mosley took it much more seriously. Mosley recognized that Wagner had seen further than both Shaw and Nietzsche. Although there is little contemporaneous indication of the Mosleys' preference for Wagner (apart from the knowledge that they were able to listen to recordings during the latter part of their joint incarceration at Holloway prison), later in the 1950s Mosley wrote about Wagner, and in particular about the *Ring* cycle in *Wagner and Shaw: A Synthesis*, which was published in his journal *The European*. Nicholas Mosely writes that his father's *Synthesis* was one of the best of his non-political essays, and that for Mosley, '"Parsifal" was not only Wagner's vision of a Christian knight who was superior to Siegfried; he was also a prototype of Nietzsche's third metamorphosis of the Child – though neither Shaw nor, indeed, Nietzsche saw this.'[135] For Nietzsche, *Parsifal* heralded a parting of ways. Unable to tolerate the compassion element, in 1876 he began work in a new direction. *Human, All Too Human* was a 'change of voice' in him: 'Wagner, after the *Ring*, turned toward the mystical ritual of *Parsifal* – a staging of the Schopenhauerian ethic of self-abnegation, with elements culled from the great world religions, Nietzsche veered more or less in the opposite direction,' writes Alex Ross in his recent volume *Wagnerism*.[136] For Nietzsche, the 'knowing through compassion' theme of the opera was 'a badge of weakness',[137] a view shared by prominent Nazis later.

Jungian analysts have also seen in *Parsifal* a metaphor for a masculine archetype, notably Robert Harris, whose *He: Understanding Male Psychology* first appeared in the 1970s, and James Hollis, who has remarked that 'modern men recapitulate the timeless lineaments of an ancient myth, that of the wounded Fisher King'.[138] In T. S. Eliot, *Parsifal* is evoked as a myth for the waste land of spiritual death, apparent in the meaninglessness of the 'capitalist nightmare' of a London rush-hour, and a myth that underscores the plight of the post-agrarian man following the catastrophe of the industrial revolution. It is a question of male identity, rootedness, meaning and place:

> When fathers and sons stopped working together in the fields, in the small trades, when the family left the land and migrated to the cities where the jobs were, when father left home and went to the factory and the office, the son was left behind ... the chain of causes and effect [reaching] back to the beginning of industrial and urban man.[139]

That camaraderie and the sense of belonging was found again, ironically, in the trenches of the First World War. But by then, the structure of Western society had all but collapsed. After that conflict, politicians – notably Sir Oswald Mosley – tried to pick up the pieces. The devastation, economic turmoil, confrontation finally led to the outbreak of another war. What was to be done with the masses of unemployed, and the resulting hardship? A blending of political responses with the psychological significance of Parsifal, especially in its Jungian interpretation, lays the foundation for understanding the ideological position taken by those on the Right. If the Marxists thought that the working classes were the tools of the ruling classes and at their disposal, then the Right in sharing this belief, sought to rejuvenate them and rescue them from their plight. But theirs was a creed of individuation, rather than one of the collective.

Here we see a further development from a Marxist interpretation of the *Ring* by George Bernard Shaw to a Jungian analysis of *Parsifal*. Early detractors did not, however, have the benefit of modern Jungian accounts, and there is certainly a divide in responses to *Parsifal* down the years. Despite Shaw's recognition of 'the wonderful workmanship of the Parsifal period',[140] one such detractor wrote in 1913 that 'the plot would disgrace Wagner's memory if we did not know it to be the work of his tired-out old age', and that though, technically, Wagner had 'retained his hand', to compare 'this decrepit stuff with the music of the Valkyrie would be preposterous'. John Runciman regarded *Parsifal* as the last 'sad quaverings of a beloved friend':

> Wagner had written so magnificently about the ecstatic state of Palestrina and such of the other church composers as he knew, that he must, absolutely must, have realised that his *Parsifal* stuff was essentially untrue.[141]

It was the plot of *Parsifal* that puzzled most, the story in danger of being dismissed 'as a farrago of nonsense', explains Roger Scruton in his final work, as we will see. Graham Macklin has covered the place afforded Wagner in his survey of music and fascism in *Patterns of Prejudice*. For example, the career of the great Wagnerite Reginald Goodall (1901–90) comes under particular scrutiny, Macklin noting that it serves as a reminder that Wagner 'looms large' in the history of fascism.[142] But as Alex Ross has recently shown in his monumental volume on Wagnerism, the composer 'looms large' for many other 'isms' too. 'To blame Wagner for the horrors committed in his wake is an inadequate response to historical complexity: it lets the rest of civilization off the hook,' he writes.[143]

'The place of music in the fascist spectacle was confirmed at the BUF's "Great Rally" in March 1936,'[144] continues Macklin. In 1938 'Greater Britain Records' produced a recording of Mosley's speeches and some fascist songs, the idea for it to be used at small gatherings of the faithful. Such endeavours were part of the greater project to reinforce cultural rejuvenation. As Macklin remarks,

> more than simply providing a forum for cultural and biographical essentialism, music also became a powerful integrative force both politically and ideologically as a means through which to accentuate the 'positive', regenerative aspects of the fascist creed as much as it was used to highlight the 'negative', corrosive and degenerative effects of Jewish 'cultural Bolshevism' on British society. It also served to reflect the fascists' own beliefs as to what constituted 'high' and 'low' culture.

Indeed, all culture for the BUF was a 'key battleground in the struggle for the soul of the nation'.[145]

This 'struggle for the soul' extended, not unsurprisingly, into the realms of the church, particularly among the lower clergy of the Church of England, as Thomas Linehan has pointed out. However, unlike Nazi ideology, British fascism attempted to 'wed' Christianity and Nietzschean doctrine, and 'BUF clerics did not see fascism as a substitute religion for their own Christian beliefs. Instead, fascism was the articulation of their Christian faith through political means.' But it can also be seen that the British fascists, particularly in the light of evidence of the attacks on churches in Spain, believed that fascism underpinned their Christian belief. 'It was also official BUF policy to uphold the principle of religious belief and worship, thought to be under threat from secular liberalism as much as communism.' This is in direct contrast to Nazi doctrine, which largely attempted to supplant Christianity. Fascist clerics interpreted the efforts to bring a spiritual dimension to politics was, for them, at one with Christian precepts:

> Mosleyite fascism, along with most varieties of the fascist species, was soaked in palingenetic myth. It claimed that it was seeking to bring about a spiritual awakening in man in order to rescue 'him' from the torrent of decadence that supposedly assailed him in the modern era.[146]

The quasi-Christian aspects of at least two of Wagner's operas can also be seen through the lens of palingenetic myth. The Grail myth, present both in *Lohengrin* and especially in *Parsifal* (Lohengrin, one of the knights of the Holy Grail, is Parsifal's son) belongs to this layer of esoteric belief, its regenerative theme of redemption puzzling many since its first performance in 1882. One *Action* columnist, despite admitting that he did not understand anything about music, was 'enthralled' by *Parsifal*. If not a music lover, then, why *Parsifal*?

In their personal stories, The Mosleys' latter period of incarceration under Regulation 18B was alleviated by the right to a gramophone on which they could listen to recordings of Wagner. On examining Mosley's specific beliefs, Thomas Linehan has shown that the reconciliation between Christian doctrine (principles of service, self-abnegation and personal sacrifice – themes found in *Parsifal*) and Nietzschean ideas of 'virile struggle' and the 'superman' found expression in fascism. Mosleyite fascism, together with its Christian underpinning and its aspirations towards highbrow musical culture met at Wagner. *Parsifal's* overriding message of *durch Mitleid Wissend*, 'knowing through compassion,' writes Alex Ross, 'diverged from a Nazi culture that all but outlawed sentimental weakness', representing a marked difference to Mosleyite fascism. In Germany, *Parsifal* was ultimately rejected: 'Goebbels, Rosenberg, and Himmler all thought that it should be removed from the repertory because its quasi-Christian message was irreconcilable with Nazi ideology', writes Alex Ross. Once again, attitudes are far more nuanced than we might like to admit:

> Hitler thought this criticism foolish, although he had no use for the opera's churchly trappings. He told the Wagner grandsons to think about designing a 'timeless Grail temple' – a setting that 'takes us into the mystical, thus into the indefinable and intangible.' Wieland Wagner was nonplussed to hear Hitler

saying that he wanted 'to have *Parsifal* performed so to speak *against* his own party!!!!'[147]

Diana Mosley corroborates this. In *A Life of Contrasts*, she writes how in 1936 having heard, for the first time, the opera at the Bayreuth festival, she confessed to Hitler that of all Wagner's operas she liked *Parsifal* least of all. His reply, she writes, was 'That is because you are young. You will find as you get older that you love Parsifal more and more,' a prediction, she admits, that came true.[148] This is borne out by Roger Scruton, whose last book *Wagner's Parsifal: The Music of Redemption* reflects on his own life through the lens of Wagner's last opera. Why *Parsifal*? This 'Music of Redemption' contains within it not only a drama or a pseudo-Christian parable about the 'never-to-be-repeated act of sacrifice' but also the story of Everyman:

> Such, perhaps, was Wolfram von Eschenbach's original intention. His story describes a quest – a journey in search of a treasure once glimpsed, and thus lost through stupidity or ignorance. This trope survives in Wagner's version, but the quest is for something *inner*, for a triumph over weakness and temptation, as the hero shifts his attention from Self to Other, in an attempt to rectify the world.[149]

In this respect, the opera bears some relation to the palingenetic aspirations of the Right and is also, therefore, a political allegory as well as a Jungian quest. It is both a narrative of the personal and a calling, in Scruton's words, 'not to explore the world, but to rescue it'.[150] The palingenetic core of the Fascists in the 1930s sought renewal, regeneration and even redemption. Wagner alone saw beyond, argued Mosley in *Wagner and Shaw: A Synthesis*, to a new form, shadowy, as yet obscure, visible in outline only, but still to a higher form: the mysterious shape of Parsifal, the man who fulfils life's creative purpose by renouncing the fullness of the present life to serve the future life, the final hero symbolizing the generation of higher men which is ready to give all that all may be won.

This is all very well. But a levelling voice might be found in the views of Bernard Van Dieren, who considered *Parsifal* 'the clumsy materialization of the dream of a combination of all the arts by a megalomaniac' using 'a mincing aestheticism'.[151] And Vaughan Williams, in his hallmark good humour, wondered whether Act I was a precedent for the ceremony at the end of the first Act of his *Pilgrim's Progress*: 'On the other hand my ceremony only takes about seven minutes whereas Wagner's takes over half an hour'![152]

Parsifal's pseudo-Christianity can also be explained by Marxist Rutland Boughton, who wrote in 1934 that 'artists have worked under difficulties during the whole period of Christian civilization; but not until now have they been so cut off from their sources of inspiration that they have nothing to express'.[153] This severing of inspiration creates a vacuum. Peter Hitchens has recently likened responses to both the two world wars to the devotion and myth that was once afforded to Christian observance. Thus, the passions and parables of the Second World War in particular (the 'Good War') become a sort of pseudo-Christianity, its theology, however, requiring 'a great deal of evasion, suppression and forgetfulness'.[154] In the Great War of 1914–18, the thousands of lives laid down were comparable to Christ's sacrifice, suggested one hymn of the time, *Valiant Hearts*, he writes. Looking from afar, the appropriation of Christian sacrifice in the service of a National Struggle now seems mere political expediency. The Second World War was fought in defence of Christian civilization, but we would rather forget or ignore the compromises that were made, particularly after Yalta. 'The reason for this forgetfulness and ignorance is obvious. If it was a 'Good War' against the powers of Evil, how can it have been won with the aid of such a wicked power, a power we spent much of the following 50 years claiming to despise?' asks Hitchens.[155]

A series of wartime theatre events staged by Basil Dean is 'but one demonstration of how the extremes of war produce unlikely bedfellows,' notes Clare Warden.[156] In February 1943, the Royal Albert Hall hosted *Salute to the Red Army*, a pageant involving massed bands, orchestras and poetry in celebration of the silver anniversary of the creation of the Red Army, in which William Walton and the BBC's Dallas Bauer, who had worked together on *Escape Me Never* in 1934, along with a host of other artists, collaborated. Basil Dean recalled in his autobiography that both troops and civilians marched and counter-marched until all the acting areas were 'jam-packed with participants in a tribute that had something of a religious quality'.[157] For the occasion, the Albert Hall was spectacularly decked out in massive Union flags and the red flag of the Soviet Union: raising the flag, raising the scarlet standard high.

Notes

1 'Musicians in Distress', *The Times*, 6 April 1934, p. 10.
2 *BBC Annual* 1935, p. 69.
3 'Concerts: London Philharmonic Orchestra', *The Times*, 4 December 1934, p. 12. As an indication of the wealth of music available in London that Saturday, in the afternoon Sir Hamilton Harty and a section of the LSO performed at the

Wigmore Hall in which Denise Lassimore played two Mozart piano concertos, 'the familiar one in D Minor and the last one that Mozart wrote, in B Flat (K.595).' A performance of the 'delightful' Symphony in C Major (K.200) was given between the two concertos. That very night saw the premiere of Walton's monumental First Symphony.

4 Levi, 2013: 88.
5 Ibid., 89.
6 'Unemployment among Musicians: BBC and Foreign Artists Blamed', *The Times*, 3 January 1935, p. 6.
7 'Blackshirt Band: Organising Professional Musicians', *The Blackshirt*, Issue 58, 1 June 1934. One advertisement ran: 'BLACKSHIRTS. Engage Fascist Professional Musicians for your dances – and so help employment. Blackshirt Bands for all occasions may be engaged on reasonable terms.
8 Macklin, 2013: 430–57.
9 Farndale, 2005: 73–4.
10 Studio Services Ltd. released a gramophone record of the occasion: 'Sir Oswald Mosley on fascism. Extracts from his memorable speech. April 22nd 1934 – the Royal Albert Hall': The opening trumpets and marches, the audience singing an English version of the Italian fascist hymn 'Giovinezza', Mosley's speech and the audience, led by Mosley, singing the National Anthem.
11 Mosley, 1998: 313.
12 Hilton, 2012: 64–5.
13 'Alien Musicians', *The Blackshirt*, Issue #61, 22 June 1934, p. 11.
14 'Unemployed Musicians: Contrast with Berlin, John F. Porte', *Fascist Week*, Issue 24, 13–19 April 1934, p. 7.
15 'Nationalism in German Music: Foreign Names Forbidden by Decree', *The Times*, 8 October 1934, p. 13.
16 *The Musical Times*, Volume 75, Issue 1095, May 1934, p. 448: Letters to the Editor, 'A British Ministry of Fine Arts.'
17 J. H. Elliott, *The Musical Times*, Volume 75, Issue 1096, June 1934, pp. 538–9,
18 *The Musical Times*, Volume 75, Issue 1098, August 1934, pp. 737–8.
19 Russell, 1942: 150.
20 Ibid.
21 Ibid., 153.
22 Brook, 1946: 76.
23 'Looking Ahead – III by "Feste"', *The Musical Times*, Volume 75, Issue 1093, March 1934, pp. 211–13.
24 'Opera in Britain: Need of a Centre. Sir T. Beecham on the Foreign Advantage', *The Times*, 5 January 1934.
25 God help the Minister who meddles with Art, said Lord Melbourne in 1834. And 100 years later, this remained the prevailing attitude of the British government.

26 Thomas Beecham to Geoffrey Toye, letter dated 15 May 1934, in Foreman, 1987: 174–6.
27 *Fascist Week*, 19–25 January 1934, p. 4.
28 'E. D. Randall, Fascism & Culture: True Place of Creative Genius', *The Blackshirt*, Issue 48, 23–30 March 1934, p. 14.
29 *The Blackshirt* (published on Fridays) and *Fascist Week* (published on Mondays) were different in tone. The former was more a call to action with the latter fulfilled a more intellectual role with an emphasis on the abstract, including policy.
30 J. G. Noire, 'Art & Nationality', *The Blackshirt* (Letters), Issue 62, 29 June 1934, p. 12.
31 John S. Porte, '"Merrie England" – A Lovable Opera of National Music', *Fascist Week*, Issue 29, 25–31 May, p. 7.
32 It must be admitted that both Vaughan Williams and Walton struggled with opera at Covent Garden; both had 'bad' experiences, the former with *The Pilgrim's Progress* in 1951, and the latter with *Troilus & Cressida* a few years later.
33 Alma D. Tolley, 'Hammersmith, "The Best Music"', *The Blackshirt* (Letters), Issue 64, 13 July 1934, p. 5.
34 German (1862–1936) was born in Whitchurch, Salop, and was a frequent visitor to Wales.
35 Foreman, 1987: 169.
36 Marshall, 2011: 267.
37 Elgar died just a fortnight after this article appeared.
38 'Rescue of British Music, John F. Porte', *Fascist Week*, Issue 14, 9–15 February 1934, p. 7.
39 'Blackshirt Music: Crystallises New Sentiment', *Fascist Week*, Issue 28, 18–24 May 1934, p. 7. 'The Greater Britain' is a reference to Mosley's book, the 2nd edition of which was being plugged at the time. The phrase appears regularly in many of the Movement's songs.
40 J. Graham, 'Songs of the Revolution: Inspired by a Common Bond', *Blackshirt*, Issue #52, 20–26 April 1934, p. 1.
41 'Music in the Branches, Mr J. Graham's Tour through the Country', *The Blackshirt*, Issue #71, 31 August 1934, p. 2.
42 'Blackshirt Songs to be sung at Albert Hall', *The Blackshirt*, Issue #50, 6–12 April 1934, p. 2.
43 William Walton to David Horner, 5 January 1933, in Hayes (ed.), 2002: 88.
44 Macklin, 2013: 431.
45 Ibid., 433.
46 Ibid., 432.
47 Spence, 2015: 280.
48 Seymour, 2014: 280.
49 Macklin, 2013: 442.

50 Ibid., 435.
51 Ibid., 442, Note 67.
52 Ibid., 439.
53 Ibid., 441.
54 'Music Section to be Self-Supporting', *The Blackshirt*, Issue #54, 4–10 May 1934, p. 2.
55 Mosley, 1998: 515.
56 Ibid., 518.
57 *The Blackshirt*, Issue 75, 28 September 1934, p. 7.
58 George Baker, 'The Tragedy of the Concert Hall', *The Blackshirt*, Issue 77, 12 October 1934, p. 6.
59 'BUF Symphony Orchestra, Lady Mosley's Appreciation', *The Blackshirt*, Issue 84, 30 November 1934, p. 11.
60 Edwin C. Cornforth, Seeking a Newer World - An Aristocracy of Talent: 'Fascism has Life Which Attracts Life', *The Blackshirt*, Issue 63, 6 July 1934, p. 4.
61 Edwin C. Cornforth, 'The Twilight of British Culture', *The Blackshirt*, Issue 80, 2 November 1934, p. 8.
62 Heffer, 2000: 84.
63 Frogley, 1996: 12–13.
64 Ibid., 18.
65 Vaughan Williams, 1964: 212.
66 Vaughan Williams, 1996: 5.
67 Ibid., 62.
68 Ibid., 72.
69 Ibid., 69.
70 Ibid., 72.
71 Ibid., 5.
72 Ibid., 41.
73 Ibid., 47.
74 Ibid., 20.
75 Lambert, 1966: 130.
76 Ibid., 49.
77 Ibid., 47.
78 Ibid., 51.
79 Ibid., 48.
80 Ibid., 75. I quote Lambert reservedly. Many views of the time are expressed in a language that is not necessarily appropriate, but his quote here should be seen in the context of using an analogy to describe a musical conundrum.
81 Scott, 1958: 22.
82 Ibid., 137.

83 Ibid., 142–4.
84 Lambert, 1966: 177.
85 Ibid., 183.
86 Ibid., 184–5.
87 Ibid., 194.
88 R. Saw, 'Fascism and our Cultural Heritage – Beauty must be preserved for Britain', *The Blackshirt*, Issue 64, 13 July 1934, p. 12.
89 Leonard Blanning, 'Idle Amusements are Undermining National Stability', *The Blackshirt*, Issue 69, 17 August 1934, p. 6.
90 George Arnold Baker, 'Art & Fascism', *The Blackshirt*, Issue 87, 21 December 1934, p. 9.
91 'Jazz goes with Jewry – Afflicted Modern Youth with a form of St. Vitus Dance', *The Blackshirt*, Issue 85, 7 December 1934, p. 9.
92 "Jazz Bands": Entertainment of a New Kind – Championship Contest at Crystal Palace, *The Times*, 23 April 1934, p. 11.
93 Macklin, 2013: 448.
94 Letter by Sir Hamilton Harty to Joseph Holbrooke dated 21 February 1934, in Foreman, 1987: 169. Holbrooke (1878–1958) was an English composer, conductor and pianist. By the 1930s Holbrooke had been passed by as a composer, so this performance of the work (which had been his first orchestral success) is of special note. Like his contemporary Vaughan Williams, Holbrooke was an advocate of British music, and vigorously denounced the lack of support given to it in favour of that to other countries, particularly Germany. He was also a critic of the BBC and, increasingly marginalized, became yet another neglected British composer.
95 Lambert, 1966: 29 (Preface to the First Edition).
96 Lambert, 1966: 131–2.
97 Linehan, 2014: 194.
98 See CP/CENT/CULT/16/02 (communistparttyarchive.org.uk/9781851171354.php#cult).
99 Linehan here refers to two issues of the *Daily Worker* from 1920.
100 Linehan, 2014: 172.
101 Watson, 2005: 137.
102 Ibid., 135.
103 Theatre Notes, by A. A., *Daily Worker*, 4 September 1934, p. 4.
104 Lambert, 1966: 90.
105 http://vaughanwilliams.uk/letter/vwl3742 (accessed online 31 May 2021).
106 Cobbe (ed.), 2008: 276.
107 Ibid., 314.
108 Ibid., 315.
109 Wallis, 1998: 54.

110 'Death of a Well-Known Soviet Composer', *Daily Worker*, 12 June 1934, p. 4.
111 'Music and the Struggle of the Classes throughout the Ages: Important Book by Rutland Boughton', *Daily Worker*, 2 May 1934, p. 4. The book is dedicated to Ursula Greville and Kenneth Curwen. The former, a singer and composer of songs, whose work *Illusion* was featured in a 1930 Prom, lived from 1894 to 1991. She was editor of *The Sackbut*, a musical journal published by Curwen in the twenties and thirties.
112 Boughton, 1934: ix.
113 Ibid., 183.
114 Ibid., 192.
115 Ibid., 159.
116 Ibid., 129.
117 Ibid., 161.
118 Ibid., 168.
119 Ibid.
120 Ibid., 194.
121 Ibid., 199.
122 Ibid., 206.
123 I consider *The Spirit of England* in a blog post: http://theibtaurisblog.com/2013/11/11/the-battle-for-music/.
124 Boughton, 1934: 206.
125 Ibid., 225.
126 An account of the British Council's activities regarding music before and during the war appears in *Culture and Propaganda in World War II*.
127 Boughton, 1934: 210.
128 Cobbe (ed.), 2008: 501–2.
129 Berger, 1988: 395–6.
130 Cobbe (ed.), 2008: 391–2. Winston Churchill had been returned to Parliament as prime minister in a Conservative election victory in October 1951, the prevailing view that Clement Atlee had failed the country.
131 http://vaughanwilliams.uk/letter/vwl2445 (accessed online 31 May 2021).
132 Cobbe (ed.), 2008: 503.
133 Vaughan Williams, 1964: 217–18.
134 Cobbe (ed.), 2008: 503.
135 Mosley, 1998: 565.
136 Ross, 2020: 50.
137 Ibid., 51.
138 Hollis, 1994: 77–8.
139 Ibid., 85.
140 Lawrence, 1981: 132.
141 Runciman, 1913: 414.

142　Macklin, 2013: 444.
143　Ross, 2020: 659.
144　Macklin, 2013: 436.
145　Ibid., 456.
146　Linehan, 2007: 287–301.
147　Ross, 2020: 537–8.
148　Mosley, 1977: 142.
149　Scruton, 2021: 123.
150　Ibid., 124.
151　Van Dieren, 1933: 189.
152　Cobbe (ed.), 2008: 431.
153　Boughton, 1934: 224.
154　Hitchens, 2018: 6.
155　Ibid., 5.
156　Warden Claire (2013), Saluting the Red Army: Basil Dean's Russian adventures. In Northern Modernism Seminar, 15 Mar 2013, University of Birmingham.
157　Dean, 1973: 285.

Conclusion

Throughout this book, we have seen that 1934 is, indeed, a special year for British music. Yes, it is a 'black' year, but there are so very many other stories to tell about music and musicians that it is wrong to see it as some sort of musical *annus horribilis*. At the beginning of the year, with the proceedings of the Peace Conference still fresh and, with hopes very high, British people were happy to support the idea of lasting peace. But as the year wore on, it became apparent that developments on the Continent did not bode well. At the year's end the government could confirm that rearmament had begun, and the hitherto secret preparations for war could be made public. 'British rearmament from 1934 coincided with recovery from the Slump,' writes David Reynolds in his volume on the legacy of the First World War.[1]

On New Year's Day, the year's musical offerings had begun with a celebration of British music, care of the BBC, including a symphony by one of Britain's many 'unsung' composers, R. O. Morris. Rutland Boughton's 'Choral Drama' *Bethlehem* also began the year's musical offerings. Although a broadcast of *Bethlehem* from the Bath Pavilion a couple of days before the New Year demonstrated to some degree the BBC's willingness to engage with Boughton, his relationship with the Corporation served as a warning as to what could happen if your political beliefs did not meet with its approval. A BBC internal document acknowledges the differences between the Corporation and the composer, whose reputation was affected by his communist leanings. During the year Boughton attempted the revival of earlier successes at the first Glastonbury Festivals, which had been set up to rival Bayreuth during the First World War and continued until the General Strike. He had suggested to the BBC that it could broadcast a relay of part of his opera *The Immortal Hour* or, preferably, one of his new operas *The Lily Maid* (the third opera in his Arthurian Cycle) from Stroud in September. The BBC Music Department decided it could only send a representative to report on the work, 'in view of the relations which have unfortunately existed between Mr Boughton and the BBC'.[2] Although the first Glastonbury Festivals had been an enormous success under his direction, he had since fallen out of favour. The Rutland Boughton Music Trust explains:

The downfall of the Glastonbury Festivals came about when Boughton, sympathising with the Miners' Lockout in 1926, insisted on staging his 'Bethlehem' at Church House, Westminster, London, with Jesus born in a miner's cottage and Herod portrayed as a top-hatted Capitalist, surrounded by soldiers and police. The event caused much embarrassment to the people of Glastonbury and they withdrew their support. The Festival Players went into liquidation and Boughton was forced to move out.

A letter to Herbert Thompson reveals that Boughton knew several professional musicians who believed that he was, indeed, being penalized for his political opinions, even though his political activities ceased in 1929. 'Is this a free country?' he asked. 'But I decline to grow into a man with a grievance – there are too many beautiful things to enjoy in any circumstances; and this Spring I've had an amazing attack of composition – a fever inducing a thoroughly optimistic tendency.'[3] Despite George Bernard Shaw's acquisition of 'a great taste' for Boughton's music, saying of him in 1934 after Elgar's death, that the composer had 'the only original personal English style on the market', Boughton's music was neglected for the next forty years, as the Rutland Boughton Music Trust recounts:

> From 1927, and until his death in 1960, Boughton lived in the tiny village of Kilcot, near Newent, in Gloucestershire where he went on to produce, arguably, some of his finest works, only a handful of which have been realised in the past 25 years. These include his second and third symphonies, short orchestral pieces, a number of concertos and chamber pieces – many of which took a further 50 years to be revived.[4]

Just seven works of Rutland Boughton have been performed at the Proms. His Oboe Concerto No.1 in C Minor was performed on 23 August 1939, with a few other compositions performed and excerpts from *The Immortal Hour* receiving the most significant number of performances (including at the Last Night in both 1943 and 1949), and then just once again in 1953, the year of a revival at Sadler's Wells. Given that *The Immortal Hour* was once considered an outstanding contribution to English opera, this is remarkable. Revived by Barry Jackson in 1932 at the Queen's Theatre with the legendary Gwen Ffrangcon-Davies (1891–1992) playing the character Etain in an opera which, in the 1920s, had captivated audiences, keeping them coming again and again. One of the most extraordinary successes in all opera history, 216 consecutive performances took place from October 1922, with another 160 consecutive performances beginning in November 1923 and a revival taking place in 1926. Sixty years have since elapsed since a Proms outing for Boughton, whose political leanings made would-be supporters wary. Boughton wrote seven 'choral dramas' for Glastonbury, which included *The Immortal Hour*, *Bethlehem*, *Alkestis*, and *The Queen of Cornwall*, and were highly regarded. His *Arthurian Cycle* was another mammoth undertaking possibly rivalling even *The Ring* cycle even if in sheer length. Beginning in 1908 with *The Birth of Arthur*, the cycle of Arthurian music dramas includes *The Round Table* (1915) and *The Lily Maid*, performed at Stroud in 1934. *Galahad* (1944) and *Avalon* (1945) have never been performed.

Though for one pundit on the Right, Edward German's comic opera *Merrie England* was suggested as the nearest thing we could get to *Meistersinger* (Wagner's only comedy), and an expression of the British national spirit, could the music dramas of Rutland Boughton or *Merrie England* have filled this lacuna? The answer is, unfortunately, a resounding 'No' if one towering figure of musical life (and left-leaning) Ralph Vaughan Williams can be relied upon to provide a belated answer. In a 1942 letter to the BBC's Stanford Robinson, Vaughan Williams complained about the dearth of good librettists. While he regarded the libretti of three of his own operas as 'good', he complained that contemporary playwrights will not write them:

> I recoil with horror from the hack librettist however much he may know about stage business. (Have you ever read in cold blood, the libretto of 'Merrie England'?).[5]

Once again Vaughan Williams helps to throw some light on why neither *Merrie England* nor *The Immortal Hour* will do. Initially rather opposed to Boughton's 'sham imitation' efforts at staging *The Immortal Hour* at Glastonbury in 1916 and incensed that Boughton 'had applied for exemption on the grounds that he was doing work of national importance at Glastonbury!',[6] a more mellow Vaughan Williams later complimented Boughton on some of its 'lovely things' and admired him for not being afraid of 'writing a tune',[7] that marker of the 'middlebrow' listener. However, Boughton's commitment to communism accounts for the neglect, and prevention, of his progress. Certainly, the later correspondence between him and Ralph Vaughan Williams reveals much emphatic disagreement on the subject. An exchange of letters in the summer of 1952, with Boughton defending Communism and Vaughan Williams preferring to term its present form as 'Kremlinist' indicates a highly nuanced debate, with Vaughan Williams declaring that 'All right-minded people are in theory communists insofar as they believe that everything ought to be done for the common good, but when Socialism in practice means the unholy mess which the late government made of things and when Communism in practice means tyranny, double dealing and insincerity by Russia, one cannot join with its present manifestation.'[8] A few days later he wrote to Boughton again, declaring that he had the courage to dissociate himself from what he called the 'present manifestations of what used to be a fine creed', and that he was not afraid to have the 'finger of scorn' pointed at him for refusing to be taken in 'by all these bogus "peace" moves', which be thought had duped Boughton. He ended his letter saying, 'I believe in freedom and that is why I will not be bullied by Nazis, Fascists and Russians.'[9]

Throughout the course of this book, we have also explored a variety of political viewpoints. The question of unemployment, despite the appearance of 'green shoots' in the economy, continued to be the concern of commentators on both the Right and Left. But for even those who had regular employment (or even housing, for that matter) in the 1930s, this did not mean a life of unfettered luxury and a carefree existence. The working lives of many, particularly in the coal mining industry, was highly dangerous. And in an industry that was lightly regulated, it was often up to individual mining magnates to decide just what safety measures were in place, and how far regulations would be implemented. Perhaps one of the most poignant moments of 1934 for ordinary workers, the Gresford pit explosion took the lives of hundreds of miners that September. *The Gresford Disaster*, a modern folk song published anonymously shortly after the disaster, was written in aid of 800 widows and orphans, and the haunting 'Miners Hymn' *Gresford* by Durham miner Robert Saint, from Hebburn, South Tyneside, was written in 1936 to commemorate the loss of the 266 miners who died. Shortly after the disaster, a relief fund was set up, and on 4 October the film *Jew Süss* was premiered at the Tivoli Theatre in aid of the Lord Mayor's Gresford Colliery Disaster Fund, in the presence of the Prince of Wales. *The Times* carried reports of the film's reception both in London and the United States (given just a few hours later). A 'large and melodramatic' story, its 'various spectacles are expensive, erudite, and designed with genuine taste, and the most opulent of them is at one point greatly enhanced by the music and an admirable song.'[10] In New York, the marvels of technology were once again apparent:

> At the close of last night's performance a radio photograph taken in London the same evening, and depicting Prince George attending the London premiere of the film, was shown. The reproduction was indistinct, but the picture was notable as the first attempt to use a radio photograph on the screen.[11]

There it is, an important film of the period, with notable music and screened in an early transatlantic technical experiment and all in aid of the Gresford disaster fund. Much of 1934 captured in a single event.

The inexorable rise of music broadcasting provided the perfect means for the dissemination of British music – that is, if you met with the BBC's approval – though not to everyone's pleasure, least of all those that were worried about the effect of the use of recorded music on unemployment. Major progress in broadcasting was made in 1934, with the Olympia exhibition in August showcasing all that was new and upcoming. Television took its first major leap forward. In music, there were many triumphs, as well as tragedies. One young composer worked frantically to finish his musical outburst, and although it did not appear in its final form until the following year, Walton's First Symphony provoked many a passionate response. And was Vaughan Williams's oddly anguished Fourth Symphony another disagreeable outburst which reflected the political state of Europe? No, but many thought it was. *The Times'* year-end review of music in 1934 inevitably began with the shocks of the earlier part of the year:

> While the general musical life of the country has shown signs of recovery from the effects of the economic crisis of 1931, it has been overshadowed by an unusually heavy death toll.

The deaths of pianist Fanny Davies and Sir George Henschel added to the 'heavy losses', as well as that of Norman O'Neill, the composer of light music. New symphonies by Walton and Bax (No.5) and cello concertos by Bax and Tovey were 'among the important novelties of the year'. The concert broadcast of *Wozzeck* in March 'attracted exceptional interest' and among the many opera performances (opera seeming to strike its roots deeper) was the Mozart festival at Glyndebourne in June – 'an acquisition of enormous artistic value' – and abroad, the Salzburg Festival 'was overshadowed but not much deranged by the murder of the Austrian Chancellor. Political events have in Germany had repercussions on music, culminating in the resignation of Dr Furtwängler from all his posts.'[12]

In the New Year, Beecham had urged the public not to worry about developments in Germany. But before the year was out, no such assurances were possible. By December, with Hitler now firmly in power and the Nazis beginning to show their true colours, there were only worrying developments from the Continent. Political turmoil throughout Europe did not bode well for the future. The mood on the domestic front had also changed. In January, the *Daily Mail* was printing Hail to the Blackshirts! But the ugly truth about the BUF toughs was known by June, and one of the most difficult aspects to recognize is that until June 1934 no one had a problem with calling themselves a fascist; or that the BUF was a tolerated, if not accepted, political party enjoying the patronage of the Rothermere press. The term 'fascist' did not necessarily have the pejorative meaning that is associated with it today. Certainly, many of the ideas presented quite openly by members of the BUF have been consigned to history. But the debate around nationalism continues. What this meant politically was one thing, but Vaughan Williams's *National Music* explained it in the musical sense. Boughton in his 1934 volume gave the Marxist viewpoint, and of the many fascinating works published that year, *The Reality of Music* was the most explicitly political. Lambert's sensational *Music, Ho!* was the young man's passionate view about music in general. Two other curious books of a more esoteric nature were also doing the rounds: John Foulds's *Music To-Day*, and Cyril Scott's *Music: Its Secret Influence Throughout the Ages*, competed with his Plato-like warnings about the effects of a change in music on society.

Foulds takes the reader on an obscure journey into the realms of esoteric thought. He was to take *his* journey the following year to India to further explore music of that continent, collecting folk music and composing for traditional Indian ensembles. Foulds worked in Delhi as Director of European Music at All India Radio, dreaming of a 'musical synthesis' between East and West. His journey took the rest of his life (he died of cholera there in 1939). Born in Manchester in 1880 and considered to be part of the British musical renaissance, he composed much light music and works for solo instrument, chamber music, choral works, 'serious' orchestral works, and music for piano, songs and many theatre scores, as well as *A World Requiem* (1919–21), composed in memory of the war dead of all nations. Henry Wood was an early supporter, featuring some of his early works at the Proms. *Music To-Day* begins with a conversation between a musician of former times and a musician of today, who discuss three fragments of music that are printed at the head of the chapter (all from Foulds's own compositions).

The Musician of Former Times, scratching his head over examples of polytonality, atonality and the use of microtones concludes, 'Well, although interesting, it is all rather confusing. And I still wish that composers would say what they have to say in terms which I can understand.' In response, the Musician of Today quotes Berlioz: 'Music nowadays, in her vigorous youth, is free, is emancipated and can do what she pleases.' New needs of the mind, of the heart and of the sense of hearing, make necessary new endeavours. Thereafter the book veers dizzyingly from modality to Eastern mysticism by way of abstruse theorizing about the ensouling of music and an art of the future that would be perceived by all the senses at once. Foulds concludes by quoting the Swiss philosopher Henri Frederic Amiel: 'Music is harmony, harmony is perfection, perfection is our dream, and our dream is heaven.'[13]

A *Radio Times* article of 21 April 1933 had set the tone for the continued debate on 'Symphony *versus* Cacophony' in an 'unhelpful' article of that name.[14] In Britain, dissonance was still the subject of much debate. And as the far Right continued to wage its ideological battle with the radical Left, apart from some of the vitriol that made its way into the various organs of propaganda, there was much sense to be heard on both sides of the argument, with some of their convictions shared by some very eminent people, indeed, though levelling voices were to be found everywhere. We have the benefit of hindsight. We have understood that varieties of totalitarianism at either end of the political spectrum have more in common with each other than they do with democratic ideals. For many, strong opinion forced people to take sides in that turbulent decade, and we might still be inclined to do the same. Or we can simply appreciate the best of the 1930s – and the extraordinary output of 1934 in particular – and conclude that it would be better to consign the worst to history.

I would argue that the BUF's views on music, and particularly its sense that the corrosive 'Jewish–Bolshevist' influence of jazz and its yearning for 'pure' British music was merely the negative aspect of a view that was held by many more eminent persons who shared some of the same concerns. But theirs was a positive contribution to the debate and was rooted in musicality of the utmost standard, their music transcending the debate entirely. Vaughan Williams, for one, appears not to have an opinion at all on jazz (there are no letters, for example). In comparison, Walton was clearly uncomfortable, Lord Berners shied away, and 'definitely stopped liking Wagner when he was taken up by the Nazis'[15]. With Vaughan Williams silence, all the evidence testifies that for them at least, the ravings of contributors to BUF newsletters were amateur, misguided and irrelevant. But it will be surprising to know that even Vaughan Williams (regarded by the BUF as 'the greatest living, English composer'[16]) shared some of their concerns, though certainly, Constant Lambert's views provide a more nuanced argument than the rabid outpourings on jazz that can be found in the *Blackshirt*. But for Vaughan Williams, a Socialist (and therefore 'suspect'), the 'tiny flower' of English music was forever in danger of being overwhelmed, and that was his only concern.

National Music and *Music, Ho!* are key texts, and the first overtly Marxist study of music, *The Reality of Music*, appeared in the same year. But why write about music, asks Bernard Van Dieren in *Down Among the Dead Men*? It is, he says, a way of holding together all those elusive musical forms: 'The crew of musical authors are all in one small boat with short rations.'[17]

On reflection, what we listen to today continues to be somewhat mediated by the politics of the 1930s. Rutland Boughton has been missing from Proms programmes since 1953 – an early victim, perhaps, of 'cancel culture'. And what of Edward German? Lambert's 1934 reckoning that German was a fine composer 'of symphonies and suites with a distinctly English flavour and original character' was an early attempt to revive his music, but he remains completely overlooked. Although Vaughan Williams referred to the 'hack libretto' of German's comic opera *Merrie England*, he made no comment on the music. And despite some of the 'lovely things' he found in Boughton's *The Immortal Hour* (of which there are, indeed, many), this work too remains regrettably unheard today. A hundred years after its initial triumph, perhaps it is time for a revival.

We have heard from Vaughan Williams, representing the moderate left, as well as Boughton and Alan Bush, whose views were more extreme. We have also met some of the fanatics on the right whose ramblings were (and are) irrelevant. But what emerged from this period was great music, great British music, from Vaughan Williams and William Walton in particular. Benjamin Britten's time was yet to come, his pre-eminence rising after the war. Like both *The Red Flag*, and *Die Fahne Hoch*, his song *Advance, Democracy* written in 1938 is, admittedly, in his publisher Boosey & Hawkes's words, a piece of unabashed political propaganda. Commissioned by the London Cooperative Society and set to a poem by Randall Swingler, the work paints a dark picture of the threat of dictatorship if democracy doesn't 'rise up and cry that what our fathers fought for we'll not allow to die'. With a 'forcefully emphatic' ending, its final section is written in 'Britten's brightly flag-waving C major',[18] a fitting reference to raising the standard high, and with which to end.

Notes

1. Reynolds, 2013: 233.
2. BBC WAC R27/221/1, BBC Music Department Minutes of 12 July 1934.
3. Rutland Boughton to Herbert Thompson, 16 April 1934, in Foreman, 1987: 171.
4. Ibid.
5. Ralph Vaughan Williams to Stanford Robinson at the BBC, 4 January 1942, in Cobbe (ed.), 2008: 333.

6 Ralph Vaughan Williams to Gustav Holst, June 1916, in Cobbe (ed.), 2008: 109–10.
7 Ralph Vaughan Williams to Rutland Boughton, 21 June 1953, in Cobbe (ed.), 2008: 525.
8 Ralph Vaughan Williams to Rutland Boughton, 25 June 1952, in Cobbe (ed.), 2008: 501–2.
9 Ralph Vaughan Williams to Rutland Boughton, 25 June and 9 July 1952, in Cobbe (ed.), 2008: 501–3.
10 'The Tivoli: "Jew Süss"', *The Times*, 5 October 1934, p. 12.
11 '"Jew Süss" Film: Reception in New York', *The Times*, 6 October 1934, p. 10.
12 'Music', *The Times*, 31 December 1934, p. 35.
13 From a 2011 reprint of the work, published by the Noverre Press.
14 Doctor, 1999: 259.
15 Macklin, 2013: 443.
16 Ibid.
17 Van Dieren, 1933: vii.
18 https://www.boosey.com/cr/music/Benjamin-Britten-Advance-Democracy/25940 (accessed online 21 July 2021).

Bibliography

Every effort has been made to trace copyright holders and to obtain their permission for the use of copyright material. The publisher apologizes for any errors or omissions in the list that follows and would be grateful if notified of any corrections that should be incorporated in future reprints or editions of this book.

The third party copyrighted material displayed in the pages of this book are done so on the basis of fair dealing for the purpose of criticism and review, or fair use for the purpose of teaching, criticism, scholarship or research only in accordance with international copyright laws, and is not intended to infringe upon the ownership rights of the original owners.

Aster, Misha, *The Reich's Orchestra*, London: Souvenir Press, 2010.
Balcon, Michael, *Michael Balcon Presents . . . A Lifetime in Films*, London: Hutchinson, 1969.
Barry, Keith, *Music for the Listener: A Guide to Musical Understanding*, Melbourne: Robertson & Mullens, 1934.
Benjamin, Walter, *The Work of Art in the Age of Its Technical Reproducibility, and Other Writings in Media*, Cambridge, MA: Harvard University Press, 2008.
Bennett, Alexis, 'Music Directors and Composers in British Cinema of the 1930s: The Creative Process and Working Musical Relationships', *Facta Universitatis: Visual Arts and Music*, Volume 1, Issue 1, 2015, pp. 13–19.
Berger, William, *Wagner Without Fear*, New York: Vintage, 1988.
Boughton, Rutland, *The Reality of Music*, London: Kegan Paul, Trench, Trubner & Co., 1934.
Boyd Neel, Louis, *The Story of an Orchestra*, London: Vox Mundi, 1950.
Brook, Donald, *Composers' Gallery*, Nottingham: Thornton Press, 1946.
Cardiff, David and Paddy Scannell, *A Social History of British Broadcasting, Volume One, 1922–1939: Serving the Nation*, Oxford: Basil Blackwell, 1991.
Chambers, Deborah, 'The Material Form of the Television Set', published online by Taylor & Francis, *Media History*, Volume 17, Issue 4, August 2011, pp. 359–75.
Cobbe, Hugh (ed.), *Letters of Ralph Vaughan Williams, 1895–1958*, Oxford: Oxford University Press, 2008.
Cooke, Alistair, *Alistair Cooke at the Movies*, Harmondsworth: Penguin, 2001.
Craggs, Stewart R., *William Walton: Music and Literature*, Aldershot: Ashgate, 1999.

Dean, Basil, *Mind's Eye: An Autobiography, 1927–1972*, London: Hutchinson, 1973.
Dobson, Jeremy, *Why do the People Hate Me So?* Leicester: Matador, 2009.
Doctor, Jennifer, *The BBC and Ultra-Modern Music, 1922–1936: Shaping a Nation's Tastes*, Cambridge: Cambridge University Press, 1999.
Edgerton, David, *The Rise and Fall of the British Nation: A Twentieth Century History*, Harmondsworth: Penguin, 2019.
Farndale, Nigel, *Haw-Haw: The Tragedy of Williams and Margaret Joyce*, London: Pan, 2005.
Foreman, Lewis, *From Parry to Britten: British Music in Letters, 1900–1945*, London: Batsford, 1987.
Foss, Hubert and Noël Goodwin, *London Symphony: Portrait of an Orchestra*, London: The Naldrett Press, 1954.
Frogley, Alain, 'Constructing Englishness in Music: National Character and the Reception of Ralph Vaughan Williams', in Alain Frogley (ed.), *Vaughan Williams Studies*, Cambridge: Cambridge University Press, 1996.
Gardiner, Juliet, *The Thirties: An Intimate History*, London: Harper Press, 2011.
Geddes, Keith and Gordon Bussey, *The Setmakers: A History of the Radio and Television Industry*, London: John Libbey & Co. Ltd., 1991.
Giliomee, Herman, *The Afrikaners*, Cape Town: Tafelberg, 2020.
Gottlieb, Julie V., 'Britain's New Fascist Men', in Julie V. Gottlieb and Thomas P. Linehan (eds), *The Culture of Fascism: Visions of the Far Right in Britain*, London: IB Tauris, 2004.
Griffin, Roger, 'This Fortress Built against Infection', in Julie V. Gottlieb and Thomas P. Linehan (eds), *The Culture of Fascism: Visions of the Far Right in Britain*, London: IB Tauris, 2004.
Harper-Scott, J. P. E., *The Quilting Points of Musical Modernism: Revolution, Reaction, and William Walton*, Cambridge: Cambridge University Press, 2012.
Harrison, Julius, 'The British Symphonists', in A. L. Bacharach (ed.), *The Musical Companion*, London: Victor Gollancz Ltd., 1934.
Hayes, Malcom (ed.), *The Selected Letters of William Walton*, London: Faber & Faber, 2002.
Heffer, Simon, *Vaughan Williams*, Boston: Northeastern University Press, 2001.
Hely-Hutchinson, John, *Music for the Millions: The Life and Times of Victor Hely-Hutchinson, His Role in the Explosion of Musical Entertainment in the First Half of the 20th Century*, Swellendam, 2002.
Hetherington, S. J. and Mark Brownrigg, *Muir Mathieson: A Life in Film Music*, Dalkeith: Scottish Cultural Press, 2006.
Hilton, Lisa, *The Horror of Love: Nancy Mitford and Gaston Palewski in Paris and London*, London: Phoenix, 2012.
Hitchens, Peter, *The Phoney Victory: The World War II Illusion*, London: Bloomsbury Academic, 2018.
Hobson, J. A., *The War in South Africa: Its Causes and Effects*, London: Macmillan, 1900, reprinted by Ostara Publications in 2013.

Hollis, James, *Under Saturn's Shadow*, Toronto: Inner City Books, 1994.
Hughes, Meirion and Robert Stradling, *The English Musical Renaissance, 1840–1940*, 3rd edition, Manchester: Manchester University Press, 2001.
Jameson, Michael, *Ralph Vaughan Williams: An Essential Guide to his Life & Works*, London: Pavilion Books, 1997.
Kennedy, Michael, *The Works of Ralph Vaughan Williams*, 2nd edition, Oxford: Clarendon Press, 1980.
Kennedy, Michael, *Glyndebourne: A Short History*, Oxford: Shire Publications, 2010.
Lamb, Richard, *The Drift to War, 1922–1939*, New York: St. Martin's Press, 1989.
Lambert, Constant, *Music, Ho! A Study of Music in Decline*, 3rd edition, London: Faber & Faber, 1966.
Lawrence, Dan H. (ed.), *Shaw's Music: The Complete Musical Criticism of Bernard Shaw, Vol. 3, 1893–1950*, 2nd revised edition, London: The Bodley Head, 1981.
Lebrecht, Norman, *The Companion to 20th Century Music*, London: Simon & Schuster, 1992.
LeCras, Luke, *A. K. Chesterton and The Evolution of Britain's Extreme Right, 1933–1973*, Abingdon: Routledge, 2020.
LeMahieu, D. L., 'The Gramophone: Recorded Music and the Cultivated Mind in Britain Between the Wars', *Technology and Culture*, Volume 23, Issue 3, July 1982, pp. 372–91.
LeMahieu, D. L., *A Culture for Democracy: Mass Communication and the Cultivated Mind in Britain Between the Wars*, Oxford: Clarendon Press, 1988.
Levi, Erik, *Mozart and the Nazis: How the Third Reich Abused a Cultural Icon*, London: Yale University Press, 2010.
Levi, Erik, 'Those Damn Foreigners', in Fairclough (ed.), *Twentieth Century Music and Politics*, Farnham: Ashgate, 2013.
Linehan, Thomas, '"On the Side of Christ": Fascist Clerics in 1930s Britain', *Totalitarian Movements and Political Religions*, Volume 8, Issue 2, 2007, pp. 287–301.
Linehan, Thomas, *Communism in Britain, 1920–39: From the Cradle to the Grave*, Manchester: Manchester University Press, 2014.
Lloyd, Stephen, *William Walton: Muse of Fire*, Woodbridge: The Boydell Press, 2001.
Lloyd, Stephen, *Constant Lambert: Beyond the Rio Grande*, Woodbridge: Boydell Press, 2014.
Macklin, Graham, '"Onward Blackshirts!" Music and the British Union of Fascists', *Patterns of Prejudice*, Volume 47, 2013, pp. 4–5, 430–57.
Marshall, Em, *Music in the Landscape*, London: Robert Hale, 2011.
Martin, Nicholas and Jasper Rees, *Florence Foster Jenkins: The Inspiring Story of the World's Worst Singer*, London: Pan, 2016.
Mellers, Wilfrid, *Vaughan Williams and the Vision of Albion*, London: Pimlico, 1991.
Mitchell, Jon Ceander, *Vaughan Williams' Wind Works*, Gatesville, MD: Meredith Music Publications, 2008.
Morrison, Richard, *Orchestra: The LSO: A Century of Triumph and Turbulence*, London: Faber & Faber, 2004.

Mosley, Diana, *A Life of Contrasts*, London: Hamish Hamilton, 1977.

Mosley, Nicholas, *Rules of the Game/Beyond the Pale: Memoirs of Sir Oswald Mosley and Family*, London: Pimlico, 1998.

Mouton, F. A., *The Opportunist: The Political Life of Oswald Pirow, 1915–1959*, Pretoria: Protea Book House, 2020.

Nettel, Ronald, *Havergal Brian and his Music*, London: Dobson Books, 1976.

Northrop-Moore, Jerrold, *Edward Elgar: A Creative Life*, Oxford: Clarendon Press, 1984.

Orwell, George and Michael Gardiner (eds), George Orwell: 'England Your England', in *Orwell and England: Selected Essays*, London: Macmillan Collectors Library, 2021.

Ottoway, Hugh, *Vaughan Williams' Symphonies (BBC Music Guides)*, London: BBC Books, 1972.

Potter, Simon J., *Wireless Internationalism and Distant Learning: Britain, Propaganda, and the Invention of Global Radio, 1920–1939*, Oxford: Oxford University Press, 2020.

Powell, Neil, *The Language of Jazz*, Manchester: Carcanet Press, 1997.

Reynolds, David, *The Long Shadow: The Great War and the Twentieth Century*, London, Simon & Schuster, 2013.

Richards, Jeffrey, *Imperialism in Music: Britain, 1876-1953*, Manchester: Manchester University Press, 2001a.

Richards, Jeffrey, Review published in *Albion: A Quarterly Journal Concerned with British Studies*, Volume 33, Issue 1, Spring 2001b, The North American Conference on British Studies.

Ross, Alex, *Wagnerism: Art and Politics in the Shadow of Music*, London: 4th Estate, 2020.

Runciman, John F., *Richard Wagner: Composer of Operas*, London: G. Bell & Sons Ltd., 1913.

Russell, Thomas, *Philharmonic, Thomas Russell*, London: Hutchinson, 1942.

Scott, Cyril, *Music: Its Secret Influence Throughout the Ages*, new and expanded edition, London: Rider & Co., 1958.

Scruton, Roger, *Wagner's Parsifal: The Music of Redemption*, Harmondsworth: Penguin, 2021.

Seymour, Miranda, *Noble Endeavours: The Life of Two Countries, England and Germany, in Many Stories*, London: Simon & Schuster, 2014.

Snowman, Daniel, *The Hitler Émigrés: The Cultural Impact on Britain of Refugees from Nazism*, London: Pimlico, 2003.

Spence, Lyndsey, *Mrs Guinness: The Rise and Fall of Diana Mitford, the Thirties Socialite*, Stroud: The History Press, 2015.

Steyn, Richard, *Seven Votes: How WWII Changed South Africa Forever*, Johannesburg: Jonathan Ball Publishers, 2020.

Stocker, Paul, *Lost Imperium: Far Right Visions of the British Empire, c.1920–1980*, Abingdon: Routledge, 2021.

Symons, Julian, *The Thirties: A Dream Revolved*, London: The Crescent Press, 1960.

Thompson, Laura, *Life in a Cold Climate*, London: Headline, 2003.
Tovey, Donald Francis, *The Main Stream of Music and Other Essays*, Oxford: Oxford University Press, 1947.
van Dieren, Bernard, *Down Among the Dead Men and Other Essays*, reprinted by Binstead, Hampshire: Noverre Press, 2013.
Vaughan Williams, Ursula, *R. V. W.: A Biography of Ralph Vaughan Williams*, Oxford: Clarendon Press, 1964.
Vaughan Williams, Ralph, *National Music and Other Essays*, 2nd edition, Oxford: Clarendon Press, 1996.
Volker, Reimar, 'Herbert Windt's Film Music to *Triumph of the Will*: Ersatz-Wagner or Incidental Music to the Ultimate Nazi-Gesamtkunstwerk?' in Robynn J. Stilwell and Phil Powrie (eds), *Composing for the Screen in Germany and the USSR: Cultural Politics and Propaganda*, Bloomington: Indiana University Press, 2008.
Wallis, Mick, 'Heirs to the Pageant', in Andy Croft (ed.), *A Weapon in the Struggle: The Cultural History of the Communist Party in Britain*. London: Pluto Press, 1998.
Walton, Susana, *William Walton: Behind the Facade*, Oxford: Oxford University Press, 1989.
Warden, Clare, '"We are here to Salute the Red Army": Basil Dean and His Russian Adventures', *Theatre Survey*, Volume 54, Issue 3, September 2013, pp. 347–66, published online by Cambridge University Press, 2013.
Watson, Derek, 'Alan Bush and Germany, 1920–1950', in Christa Bruestle and Guido Heldt (eds), *Music as a Bridge: Musikalische Beziehungen zwischen England und Deutschland, 1920–1950*, Hildesheim: Georg Olms, 2005.
Winder, Simon, *Germania*, London: Picador, 2011.
Wood, Henry, *My Life of Music*, London: Victor Gollancz, 1938.
Woolf, Virginia, 'Middlebrow' (1932), in *The Death of the Moth and Other Essays*, London: Hogarth Press, 1942.

Index

Anglo-German Fellowship   147
Arts Council   190–2
Auden, W. H.   4, 6

Bach, J. S.   7, 35, 49, 58, 65–6, 114–15,
    139, 156–7, 160, 162–7, 173,
    177, 214
Baird, John Logie   10, 40–1
Baldwin, Stanley   4, 5, 8
Bantock, Granville   33, 103, 111, 172
Bax, Arnold   80, 99–101, 106, 111,
    151–2, 184, 208, 239
BBC   41
    Afrikaans Service   58
    Arabic service   58
    Empire Service   48, 55, 56, 58
    and employment of British
        artists   62–3
    Festival of British Music   110, 147,
        197, 235
    and foreign artists   183–4, 203–4
    Foundations of Music series   2, 139
    and German music   2
    and jazz   32
    and license fee   39
    and modern music   31, 56, 115
    monopoly status of   41
    Music Advisory Committee   62
    and music policy   34, 52
    and new music   49
    and recorded music   44
    and religious broadcasting   156
    and tastes in music   1
BBC (Symphony) Orchestra   32, 36, 54,
    65, 81, 91, 104, 109, 151, 160,
    162, 166, 174
Beecham, Thomas   5, 22, 32, 43, 57, 100,
    104, 106, 124, 133, 141, 159–60,
    169, 192, 193, 238
Beethoven, Ludwig van   1, 2, 8, 22, 35,
    50, 58, 64, 80, 92, 105–7, 124,
    156, 165–9, 172, 205

Bell, W. H.   52–4
Benjamin, Walter   6, 46
Bennett, Alexis   76–8
Berg, Alban   13, 21, 116–19, 134
    Wozzeck   12, 18, 116–19, 239
Berlin Philharmonic Orchestra   5, 6,
    124–6, 130–4
Berlioz, Hector   103, 105, 240
Berners, Gerald   99, 200, 241
Bing, Rudolf   142
Bliss, Arthur   24–7, 54, 71, 77, 78, 88,
    89, 208
Bloch, Ernst   65
Blom, Eric   9, 141, 215
Borodin, Alexander   105
Boughton, Rutland   79, 97, 150, 217–22,
    226, 235–8, 240, 242
    and the BBC   236
    The Immortal Hour   79, 99, 240
    The Reality of Music   240
    and Vaughan Williams   221–2, 237
Boult, Adrian   2, 6, 32, 44, 47, 62–4,
    71, 80–3, 87, 97, 99, 104, 110,
    116–18, 163
Boyd Neel, Louis   65–7
Brahms, Johannes   8, 18, 58, 105, 124,
    156, 166, 172, 197
Brian, Havergal   165–6
Bridge, Frank   66, 102, 106
British Council   8, 26, 55, 59
    Music Advisory Committee   3, 23, 71,
        101, 137, 178, 220
British Empire Union   33
British Union of Fascists (BUF)   1, 4,
    12, 21, 62, 119, 123, 148, 177,
    185–8, 192, 194, 198–201,
    204–7, 213, 217, 224–5, 239–41
    and jazz   12, 211–12, 241
    and opera   194–7
    songs of   198–9
Britten, Benjamin   6, 11, 66, 87, 91, 139,
    173, 242

reaction to Walton's first
    symphony 87
Burrows, Grace 111
Busch, Adolf 142
Busch, Fritz 131, 133, 142
Bush, Alan 176, 215–17, 222, 242
Busoni, Ferruccio 46, 151
Butterworth, George 23, 89, 97, 111

Calvocoressi, M-D. 13, 36, 136–7
Cardus, Neville 16, 56–7
Cawood, Henry 14–15
Chesterton, A. K. 60
Chopin, Frederic 80, 162, 205
Christie, John 141
Churchill, Winston 5
Church music 49, 51, 114, 153–6
Clark, Kenneth 11
Coates, Albert 7, 108, 151, 201
Colles, Henry (H. C.) 9, 23, 24, 90, 99, 109, 153, 193
Collingwood, Lawrance 151
Communist Party of Great Britain 214, 216
Cripps, Stafford 39
Cultural propaganda 8, 54, 55, 58–9, 137

Dale, Benjamin 99, 151
Dean, Basil 79, 227
Debussy, Claude 25, 26, 107, 109, 170, 209
Delius, Frederick 10, 23, 25, 26, 33, 58, 63, 89, 101, 105, 106, 111, 151–2, 158–62, 166, 172
    death of 158–9, 161–2
    A Mass of Life 11, 63, 159–61
Dent, Edward J. 127–8, 172, 215
Doernberg, Imma van 72, 79, 87

Eames, Frank 149
Ebert, Carl 117, 141–2
Eisler, Hans 138–40, 215
Elgar, Edward 2, 3, 10, 23, 25, 50, 58, 66, 71, 87, 89, 91–2, 97, 99–101, 150–1, 156–60, 172, 195, 197, 206, 208, 218, 222
    death of 71, 158
    memorial concert 183
    Mina 67
    Third Symphony 10, 67, 71

Ellington, Duke 14, 16, 211
Entartete Musik 17, 118, 136–7, 206

film music 74–6
Foulds, John 9, 240–1
Furtwängler, Wilhelm 5, 50, 91, 124–5, 130–3, 138, 192, 239

German, Edward 237, 241
    Merrie England 194, 196–7, 237, 242
Germany, broadcasting in 45–6
Germany, policy towards Jews 45
Germany, rearmament 5
Gershwin, George 13
Giovinezza 7, 21, 22, 186, 198, 201, 202
Glastonbury Festivals 235–7
Glyndebourne Festival 12, 19, 74, 140–2, 239
Goebbels, Josef 37, 45, 126, 130–3, 135, 136, 138, 225
Goodall, Reginald 224
Grainger, Percy 104
Gramophone magazine 16, 35
Gray, Cecil 13, 18, 85
Gresford colliery disaster 238–9
Grieg, Edvard 17, 66, 105
Guinness, Diana. *See* Mosley, Diana

Hadamovsky, Eugen 45, 129
Handel, G. F. 66, 92, 105–6, 114–15, 157–8, 162, 173, 210, 213
Harrison, Julius 101–2, 184, 215
Harty, Hamilton 71–2, 82, 84, 147, 213
Haw-Haw, Lord. *See* Joyce, William
Hely-Hutchinson, Victor 9, 10, 54, 191
Henschel, George 11, 239
Hertzog, J. M. 60–1
Hess, Myra 168, 190
Hindemith, Paul 13, 17, 20, 50, 74–5, 79, 104, 128, 130–3, 137–8, 170, 204
Hindenburg, President von 5, 134
Hitchens, Peter 227
Hitler, Adolf 5, 6, 13, 17, 21, 36, 77, 123, 125–7, 130, 132, 134, 136, 165–6, 192, 212, 220, 225–6, 239
Holbrooke, Joseph 213
Holst, Gustav 10, 53, 58, 63, 66, 71, 88–9, 101–2, 105, 111, 151, 156–8, 160, 172–5, 206–8
    death of 158, 174

Index

Honegger, Artur 18
Horst Wessel song 1, 3, 7, 21, 123, 186, 198, 201–2, 240
Howells, Herbert 56, 57, 106, 222

Imperial Fascist League 59
Incorporated Society of Musicians 112, 149, 173, 184, 186–7, 192–4, 222
International Broadcasting Union 6
International Society for Contemporary Music 90, 119, 127–8

Jazz 13, 15–17, 210–13
Joyce, William 186

Kleiber, Erich 132, 137
Klemperer, Otto 131
Klenovsky, Paul 12, 162–5, 177
Knappertsbusch, Hans 132

Lambert, Constant 17, 85, 103, 104, 123, 125, 151, 169
  and folk song 208–9
  on jazz 12, 210–11
  Music, Ho! 9, 17, 19–21, 35
Langenhoven, C. J. 61
Leese, Arnold 59–60
Liszt, Franz 23, 164
Londonderry, Lord 147
London Labour Choral Union 215
London Music Festival 44, 71, 83, 104
London Philharmonic Orchestra 32, 42, 44, 92, 190
London Symphony Orchestra 11, 42, 63, 81, 83, 140, 201

Mackenzie, Alexander 23, 97, 103
Mackenzie, Compton 16, 18
Mathieson, Muir 76–8
Mendelssohn, Felix 124, 126, 132, 135, 140, 156, 157
Menuhin, Yehudi 12, 220
Meyer, Ernst 139–40, 215
Middlebrow tastes 1, 16–19, 55–8, 237
Mitford, Diana. *See* Mosley, Diana
Mitford, Nancy 148, 200
Mitford, Unity 123
Moeran, E. J. 102, 167, 197
Morris, R. O. 93, 97, 98, 150, 235
Mosley, Cynthia 22, 199–200

Mosley, Diana 22, 200, 201, 226
Mosley, Oswald 4, 22, 33–4, 148, 165, 186, 188, 200
  on Wagner 222–3
Mozart, W. A. 2, 65, 66, 105, 141, 142, 156, 162, 172
Musicians' Benevolent Fund 183
Music of the Tudor era 113–14
Mussolini, Benito 19, 27, 89, 127, 165, 193, 202
Muzak 18, 37, 42, 65, 74

National Association of Broadcasters (U.S.) 38
Newman, Ernest 47–8, 82, 167

Orwell, George 3

patronage in music 50
Performing Right Society 39, 52
Pirow, Oswald 61
Plunket Green, Henry 184
Priestley, J. B. 56
programme music 107–8
Prokoviev, Sergei 64, 105, 109–10
Promenade Concerts 12, 64, 83, 104, 105, 166–8
Puccini, Giacomo 150
Purcell, Henry 26, 55, 154–5, 173–4

Rachmaninov, Sergei 19
Red Flag, The 1, 214, 227, 242
Refugees, German 136, 140–2
Reith, John 2, 32–3, 59, 77, 140, 158
  in Cape Town 32, 52, 59
Riefenstahl, Leni 5, 127
Royal College of Music 76, 77, 98, 139, 158, 160
Royal Philharmonic Society 147, 160

Salute to the Red Army (1943) 227
Sargent, Malcom 44, 92, 175
Schoen, Ernst 45–8
Schoenberg, Arnold 2, 20, 25, 56, 115–16, 134, 139, 162, 170, 210
Schreiner, Olive 60
Schubert, Franz 18, 72–3, 80–1, 116, 156, 172, 205
Schumann, Robert 9, 124, 156, 172
Scott, Cyril 115, 153, 166, 184, 209, 240

Scriabin, Alexander   103, 161
Scruton, Roger   224, 226
Shaw, George Bernard   1, 172, 221, 223, 236
Sibelius, Jean   18, 20, 25, 87, 106, 111, 162, 172, 177
Simon, John   5
Smuts, Jan   60–1
Smyth, Ethel   22, 23, 103–5
South Africa   52–3, 59–62, 148
Spanish Civil War   6, 7
Stalin, Josef   35, 165
Stokowski, Leopold   19
Stone, Christopher   16, 44
Strauss, Richard   25, 103, 124, 132–5, 150, 187–8
Stravinsky, Igor   1, 10, 13, 17, 20, 25, 35, 218
Swingler, Randall   6, 215, 242

Tchaikovsky, Pyotr   17, 80, 100, 103–5, 109, 172, 214
television   10, 40–2
Tertis, Lionel   11, 72, 92, 99, 174–5
Three Choirs Festival   15–17, 19
Tippett, Michael   98, 216–17
Toscanini, Arturo   47, 64
Tovey, Donald   66, 107, 109, 239
Toye, Geoffrey   97, 117–18, 193

van Dieren, Bernard   152–3, 226, 242
Varése, Edgard   46
Vaughan Williams, Ralph   2, 3, 7, 8, 10, 17, 20, 22, 24, 26–7, 53, 58, 67, 78, 87–93, 97–102, 113–14, 154, 156–7, 163, 166, 172–7, 191, 206–8, 216, 221–2, 226, 237, 241–2
  defence of Alan Bush   216, 217
  and Elizabethan music   206
  and the English folksong movement   208–9
  Fantasia on Greensleeves   11, 106, 166
  Fourth Symphony
    gestation   87–90
    interpretation   89–91
  on German music   17
  as guarantor to WMA   222
  National Music   9, 19, 20, 24, 206–8, 240
  and Rutland Boughton   221–2, 237
Vaughan Williams, Ursula   7, 89, 91, 98, 157, 207

Wagner, Richard   5, 25, 105, 114, 129, 135, 141, 149, 152, 166, 193, 195–6, 202–4, 207, 221–6, 237, 241
  Parsifal   47, 141, 222–6
Walford Davies, Henry   34, 43, 55, 150
Wallace, William   103
Walter, Bruno   44, 104, 109, 124, 131
Walton, William   2, 3, 8, 17, 56, 103, 104
  Belshazzar's Feast   71, 102, 220
  connection to BUF   199–200
  Escape me Never   75–6, 79
  film music   8, 18, 72
  First Symphony, gestation   71–2, 79, 81–7
Webern, Anton von   90, 115, 116
Weingartner, Felix   44
Wells, H. G.   5, 77–8
Wessex Orchestra   170
Whittaker, W. Gillies   113, 140, 173
Wimborne, Alice   85
Windt, Herbert   5, 126–7
Wood, Henry   12, 106, 116, 151, 162–5, 183, 240
Woolf, Virginia   17
Workers Music Association   214, 216, 222

Zweig, Stephan   133

www.ingramcontent.com/pod-product-compliance
Lightning Source LLC
Chambersburg PA
CBHW062131300426
44115CB00012BA/1880